FIREFLY

GUIDE TO
MOUNTAINS

DOUG SCOTT, GENERAL EDITOR

FIREFLY BOOKS

A FIREFLY BOOK

Published by Firefly Books Ltd. 2006

First printing

Publisher Cataloging-in-Publication Data (U.S.)

Guide to mountains / Doug Scott, general editor.
[272] p. : col. photos., maps ; cm.
Includes index.
Summary: An illustrated guide to mountains
including an atlas of the world's mountain regions.
ISBN 1-55407-052-X (pbk.)
1. Mountains – Guidebooks.
I. Scott, Doug. II. Title.
551.43 dc22   GB501.2G85 2006

Library and Archives Canada Cataloguing in
Publication

Guide to mountains / Doug Scott, general editor.
Includes index.
ISBN 1-55407-052-X
1. Mountains–Guidebooks. I. Scott, Doug, 1941–
GB501.2.G84 2006   551.43'2   C2005-902201-9

Published in the United States by
Firefly Books (U.S.) Inc.
P.O. Box 1338, Ellicott Station
Buffalo, New York 14205

Published in Canada by
Firefly Books Ltd.
66 Leek Crescent
Richmond Hill, Ontario L4B 1H1

TEXT *Andrew Cleave, Julie Cribb, Dr. Stephen J.
Cribb, David Henderson, Dr. Tim Stott*
COMMISSIONING EDITOR *Frances Button*
EDITOR *Ingalo Thomson*
EXECUTIVE ART EDITOR *Mike Brown*
DESIGNER *Caroline Ohara*
PRODUCTION *Åsa Sonden*

FRONT COVER : *tl* Volcano, Philip's; *tr* Karakoram Highway,
Galen Rowell/CORBIS; *c* Andean condor, Philip's;
bl climber, Paul A. Souders/CORBIS; *bc* Map of the Andes,
Philip's; *br* Calymene
BACK COVER : Wolverine, Philip's; King Protea, Philip's

ISBN 13: 978-1-55407-052-7

Printed in China

Contents

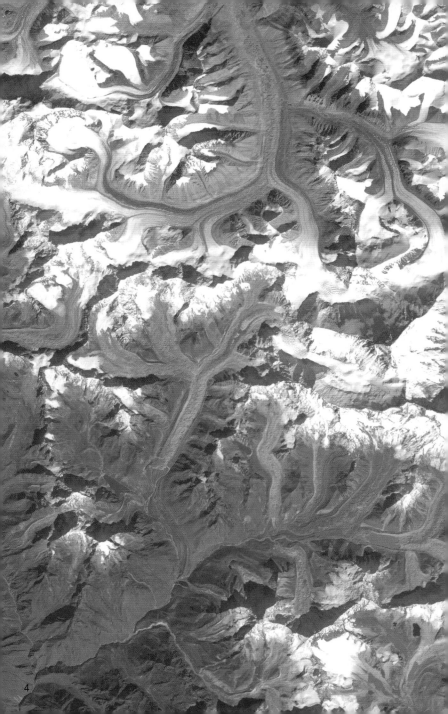

4

Introduction

This is the most comprehensive "Guide to Mountains" available in a single volume. I'm sure it will appeal not only to those who need to know more about the mountains for their professions but also to those who wish to inform themselves before or after visiting mountain regions. The book is distinguished by the high-quality reproduction of the photographs, superb artworks and excellent mapping.

As a former geography teacher, I find the early chapters on the formation and geology of the mountains, mountain erosion and weathering, and climate and weather of particular interest. They are surprisingly deep in content given the limited space available, and they'll be a useful reference for those embarking on mountain studies for the first time. There is also up-to-date information on the effect of global warming on the mountains themselves.

The authors comment perceptively on the decline of mountain communities – so many of which are heading down to the towns – and provide sensible suggestions and practical steps to rectify this appalling situation. The history of mountaineering is brief yet impressively comprehensive, as is the atlas of mountains, even if space does not permit the inclusion of everyone's favorite haunts.

The "Guide to Mountains" provides a solid grounding in mountain studies, and may inspire readers to embark upon studies of a more esoteric nature, such as mountains in art or poetry, or mountains as sacred to the many people who live among them.

Doug Scott, CBE

Mount Everest – the highest mountain in the world, at 8,848 m (29,028 ft) – lies just north of center in this image. The two arms of the Rongbuk Glacier flow away from the triangular shaded north wall, with the Kangshung Glacier due east. The international boundary between China and Nepal bisects the peak.

Mountain Formation

Genesis of the Earth
Composition

Soon after the molten, hot, liquid round mass we now call Earth was formed, around 4.5 billion years ago, it began to cool. During this cooling process lighter materials floated above a heavier liquid mass. This separation of materials caused layers to form in concentric spheres. The cooling lighter layers formed a skin or crust around the outside of the Earth, and this lighter, more buoyant crust floated on top of a denser layer called the mantle.

The Earth's crust extends down about 6 km (4 mi) under the ocean and possibly up to 65 km (40 mi) under some mountain ranges. The thickness of the ocean crust is more or less constant throughout the ocean basins, whereas the thickness of the continental crust varies considerably. Directly under the Earth's crust lies the layer of rock called the mantle. The mantle extends to a depth of about 2,900 km (1,800 mi) and is thought to consist of ferromagnesian silicate minerals such as olivene and pyroxene. Heat and pressure at this

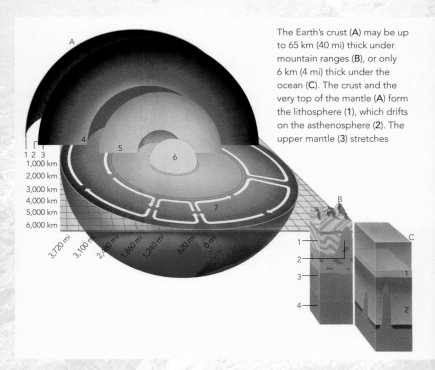

The Earth's crust (A) may be up to 65 km (40 mi) thick under mountain ranges (B), or only 6 km (4 mi) thick under the ocean (C). The crust and the very top of the mantle (A) form the lithosphere (1), which drifts on the asthenosphere (2). The upper mantle (3) stretches

great depth keep the material in a very thick liquid state. The division between the upper section and lower, denser section of the mantle occurs at a depth of about 700 km (435 mi). The upper mantle is in turn divided into the upper lithosphere, which extends down for between 50 and 250 km (30 and 155 mi). Below this lies the asthenosphere, a partially molten zone some 200 km (125 mi) thick. The asthenosphere defines the lower boundary of the relatively rigid outer lithosphere, which includes the crust. The plates of the lithosphere move over the semimolten asthenosphere, giving rise to the phenomenon of continental drift.

Below the asthenosphere lies the mesosphere, which is separated, at a depth of around 400 km (250 mi) by a transition zone, from the lower mantle, which lies between 1,000 and 2,000 km (600 and 1,200 mi) in depth. The lower boundary of the mantle is marked by the Gutenberg discontinuity, which separates the lower mantle from the underlying dense core. The core itself is divided into an inner and outer layer at a depth of between 4,980 and 5,120 km (3,090 and 3,170 mi). The core most probably consists of an iron-nickel alloy, with a

down to overlie the lower mantle (4) at 700 km (430 mi) depth. From the surface the temperature inside the Earth increases by 30°C/km (85°F/mi) so that the asthenosphere is close to melting point. After 100 km (60 mi) depth the rate of temperature increase slows dramatically. Because we know so little about what happens deep within the Earth, there is a uncertainty about the temperature of the core—estimates put it to be about 3,700°C (6,700°F). Pressure also increases with depth: already in the asthenosphere the pressure is equal to 250,000 atmospheres. At the Earth's core it may go as high as four million atmospheres. The density near the surface of the Earth is only about 4 g/cm^3, and this does not vary by much more than 30% right down through the lower mantle. The increase in density that does occur is due to closer atomic packing under pressure. There is a leap in density to

10 g/cm^3 in passing to the outer core (5) and a further leap to between 13 and 16 g/cm^3 in the inner core (6). The heat at the core fuels vast convection currents (7) in the material of the mantle. Continental crust is made by many different processes and is therefore difficult to generalize.

A typical cross section (B) might well consist of deformed and metamorphosed sedimentary rocks at the surface (1), underlain by a granite intrusion (2). The remaining crust would consist of metamorphosed sedimentary rock and igneous rock (3) reaching to the mantle (4). In oceanic crust (C), ocean sediments (1) overlie basalt which is pillowed and also chemically altered by seawater. Below this layer (2) the basalt is made up of dikes—small vertical intrusions that are packed so close together they intrude each other. Gabbros are coarse-grained igneous rocks with a similar composition to basalt.

liquid outer core and an inner solid core with a radius of about 1,300 km (800 mi). Intense pressure at such great depth keeps the inner core from turning liquid, despite a temperature of 3,700°C (6,700°F).

Plate tectonics

As cooling of the Earth continued, the crustal materials of the lithosphere began to move on the sluggish currents within the asthenosphere. This movement eventually caused the crust to break apart along lines of natural weakness, forming tectonic plates. These plates form a jigsawlike layer at the Earth's surface. Tectonic plates are about 100 km (60 mi) thick and are constantly moving, at rates of between 1 cm (0.4 in) and 16 cm (6.3 in) per year. Currents of heat rising from deep in the Earth's core and up through the mantle are believed to cause the plates to move.

By about 500 million years ago, the crust had cooled and separated into distinct plates, which drifted around the globe, colliding with their neighbors, coming together then separating. Around 300 million years ago, the plate movements brought all the pieces together into one single landmass called Pangaea (Greek for "all lands"). About 200 million years ago Pangaea broke into two continents, Gondwanaland and Laurasia. Around 100 million years ago all the landmasses we now know as continents separated from Laurasia and drifted in different directions. Eventually these plates began to collide into one another and began the process of creating the landmasses we recognize today.

Plate boundaries, or junctions, map out the surface of the Earth. Some pass very close to the boundaries between continents and oceans, but the great majority of them bear

▼ *Map of the Earth* *depicting the position,* *the direction of* *movement, and type* *of plate boundaries.*

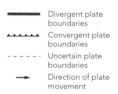

——— Divergent plate boundaries
▲▲▲▲▲ Convergent plate boundaries
– – – – Uncertain plate boundaries
——➤ Direction of plate movement

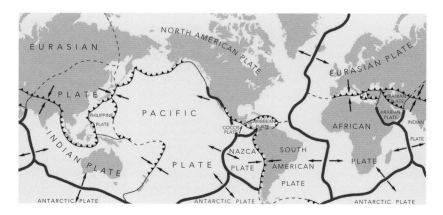

no relationship to the edges of continents. For example, the Australian plate contains Australia but also a large part of the Indian Ocean, as well as other surrounding oceans.

Plate margins

The regions where tectonic plates come together are referred to as active margins. It is at these boundaries that plates collide and scrape against one another or, indeed, pull away from each other, leaving a trench to be filled with magma, which then solidifies and forms new crust. Volcanoes and earthquakes are much more frequent around the boundaries of tectonic plates. Geologically active mountain belts, such as the Himalayas, Andes, Hindu Kush, Southern Alps and Tien Shan, are particularly recognized as zones at high risk of earthquakes.

▲ **The size of the plates** *is not constant. The African plate is bounded on three sides by midocean ridges that indicate the presence of constructive margins. The plate is constantly enlarging from these ridges, and there is no intervening destructive margin, therefore the ridges are moving apart as the plate enlarges.*

Orogenesis

Some mountains are isolated masses—Kilimanjaro, in Tanzania, for example, rises from the surrounding flat plains to an elevation of approximately 6,000 m (20,000 ft) above sea level. Other mountains are part of extensive mountain belts such as the Himalayas and the Andes. The reasons behind the differences lie in the process of orogenesis—that is, mountain building.

Plate collision

When plates collide head-on (plate-to-plate collision), tremendous force is generated. When a moving plate meets a plate that is stationary or is moving toward it, energy is transferred inland and the pressure generated causes the crustal material at the plate boundary to rise up in a process known as uplift. When one plate rides over another, most often at the meeting of lighter continental plates with more dense oceanic plates, the lighter plate rises over the denser one in a process known as subduction. The top plate may buckle and crack where it bends upward, and the uplift causes materials from deep within the Earth to push upward, generating mountains.

There are three types of plate collision: oceanic to oceanic, oceanic to continental, and continental to continental. Each of these gives rise to mountains, which are formed from the folding of the Earth's crust or the thrusting of layers of rocks over other layers along fault lines. The resulting mountains are known as folded or thrust-faulted mountains.

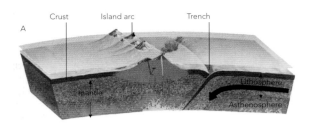

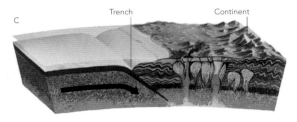

The Tonga Trench is a destructive plate margin, involving two oceanic plates. The margin is characterized by a deep trench and an arc of volcanic islands formed by melting within and above descending plates.

◄ *The Peru-Chile Trench* is a destructive margin, where one oceanic and one continental plate meet. The oceanic plate forms a trench as it is carried down. The lighter continental material rises into a mountain range.

Folded and thrust-faulted mountains

When two oceanic plates converge, one will be subducted beneath the other. The extremely high temperatures at the junction where they meet lead to partial melting of the crust; the upward migration of the resulting magma produces Island Arcs, which often develop mountainous terrains as they are eroded. An example of this is the Tonga Trench in the Pacific Ocean, which stretches north-northeast from the North Island of New Zealand giving rise to an arc of volcanic islands.

When oceanic crust meets continental crust, coastal mountain ranges are often the product. The first stage in the development of such ranges, of which the Andes is an example, often occurs at a type of plate boundary known as a passive margin. Thick wedges of shallow-water sediments, up to depths of 15km (9mi), accumulate adjacent to the continental mass. Eventually, plate movement increases the pressure at the boundary, the passive margin becomes an active margin, and the oceanic plate begins to be subducted beneath the continental plate. Sediment derived from the land and from the subducting plate is plastered against the continental side of the boundary to form an acretionary wedge which can be uplifted many km as new mountains are formed.

There are many signs of continuing uplift and other tectonic activity in the Andes. Many of the world's largest earthquakes originate here, and a large number of active

► *Tectonic forces* warp the Earth's surface and are powerful enough to bend strata of rock. An anticline (1) is created when the rock is pushed upward. When the rock is forced down, a syncline is formed. If the force continues an overfold (2) forms. If the strata are warped too much, they can in effect snap (3) making an overthrust fold or nappe, which is both a fold and a fault. At the top of an anticline, the rocks are "stretched" (4), while at the base of a syncline they are compressed (5). The extra joints and small cracks at the top of the anticline (6) make it more prone to weathering and volcanoes form some of the highest Andean peaks. The elevated plateau of the altiplano is made up of great quantities of ash produced by these volcanoes.

Continental collisions occur when both plates carry continental crust. This crust is too buoyant to be subducted; instead, rocks at the active margin are folded or thrust over each other, bringing material from deep within the Earth's crust to the surface, where weathering then takes place to carve out the mountain ranges. The Himalayas formed as the result of a continental collision about 55 million years ago, when India collided with the Eurasian plate. India continues to migrate north at the rate of a few centimeters per year, causing the Himalayas to be the fastest-growing chain of mountains at the present time. Should a subduction zone develop south of India, however, the growth of the Himalayas would cease, as the pressure on the continental plate would be reduced by the oceanic plate subducting beneath the continental crust, rather than continuing to push the continent of India northward.

Another effect of continental plate movement is the shortening of mountain ranges. This occurs when large-scale near-horizontal movement of upper crustal layers sees rock strata pushed over each other in a process known as thrusting. The structures in the Rocky Mountains involve multiple thrusting, and the upper layer of rocks that is pushed in the process is called a nappe.

erosion. If this process continues, over many thousands of years, an anticline can be eroded to form what appears to be a valley (7).

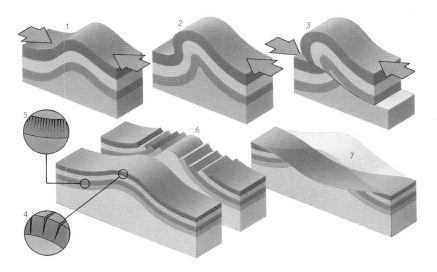

11

Rifts, block mountains and plateaus

When continental crust splits apart along a fault line, creating a new plate boundary, a rift valley is formed which will often have active volcanoes and earthquake zones within it. One of the clearest examples is the Great Rift Valley of East Africa, which runs from Mozambique to the Red Sea. When a rift valley forms within a landmass, the new crust on the valley floor will be oceanic crust, even though it is dry land. If the surface of the rift valley is below sea level and the rift reaches the edges of the landmass, the valley will fill with seawater. The land on either side of a rift valley often has extensive plateau areas covered in basalt lava where magma has risen and flowed as the rift formed. As the plates on either side of the rift continue to move apart, the fault may eventually reach the end of the continental plate allowing seawater to fill the valley.

Plateaus also form when pressure builds up within the continental crust as a result of the surrounding plates pushing against it; block mountains or horsts are created. If the continental crust is geologically faulted, then great slabs of the Earth's crust can be squeezed vertically, rising to great heights above the surrounding area. Table Mountain in South Africa, for example, was formed when its granite base resisted pressure from surrounding plate movement and began to rise above sea level around 280 million years ago; the process continues today.

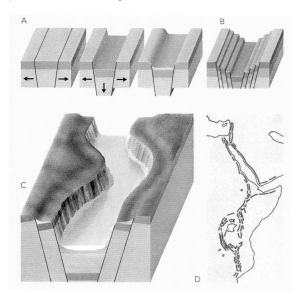

◄ *Rift valleys* form through tension between two roughly parallel faults (*A*), causing downward earth movement resulting in the formation of a graben (trough of land between two faults). Sometimes a number of parallel faults result in land sinking in steps (*B*). A typical example of a step-faulted rift valley is shown (*C*). A series of block faults can occur on either side of a graben, sometimes tilting in the process of creating the block-faulted rift valley. The East African Rift Valley (*D*) is perhaps the world's best example of this type of geological formation.

The highest level plateau in the world (with an average height of 4,500 m or 14,800 ft) is the Tibetan plateau, formed by the compression and uplifting of the Earth's crust that occurred when the Indo-Australian and Eurasian tectonic plates collided approximately 55 million years ago, creating the Himalayas. The process is ongoing, with young mountain formation occurring around the edge of the plateau.

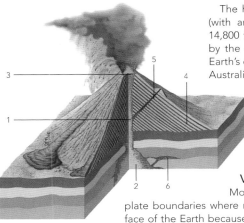

▲ **Volcanoes** are formed when molten lava (1) from a magma chamber (2) in the Earth's crust forces its way to the surface (3). The classic, cone-shaped volcano is formed of alternating layers of cooled lava and cinders (4) thrown out during an eruption. Side vents (5) can occur and when offshoots of lava are trapped below the surface, laccoliths (6) are formed.

Volcanic mountains

Most volcanoes occur in chains along plate boundaries where molten magma can reach the surface of the Earth because of the continual plate movement weakening the crust. The main volcanic ranges occur around the shores of the Pacific Ocean and in a belt through the Mediterranean to Indonesia along subduction zones and at spreading ridges.

Hot-spot volcanoes arise at weak points within plates, rather than at plate boundaries, and generate isolated mountains as a result. The Big Island of Hawaii was created when lava poured from the volcano Kilauea for 10 years during the 1980s and 1990s. The southern slopes of the island became covered with new lava and the island grew as lava flowing into the sea solidified to make new land. Above sea level the island makes up only a small fraction of the volcano, the rest being hidden below the sea. The entire volcano is over 10,000 m (33,000 ft) high, making it—from sea floor to summit—the tallest mountain on earth.

Dome mountains

Dome mountains take their name from the characteristic dome shape created when molten magma presses up under the Earth's crust but is not able to break through and form a volcano. The Earth's surface is instead pushed up to form a dome, often much higher than the surrounding land The Black Hills of South Dakota in the USA and the Lake District in England are fine examples of dome mountains.

13

Mountain Erosion

The various features of mountain landscapes as we recognize them are not the product of mountain formation, but rather of erosion. Many of the minerals that make up the rocks are stable at the high temperatures and pressures deep within the Earth's crust, but are chemically unstable in the Earth's oxygen-rich atmosphere. Rocks react chemically with the Earth's damp atmosphere in a process called weathering, which takes place right at the Earth's surface and, together with a range of other factors, changes the appearance and condition of the land. Some weathering is purely chemical in nature, such as the effects of acid rain on limestone, but factors such as temperature, wind, glaciation, water, slope and biological activity, as well as combinations of these reacting with the various rock types, all contribute to constant changes in mountain features.

Agents of change
Chemical weathering

Many of the rocks from which mountains are formed, limestone in particular, are susceptible to chemical reactions which change the mineral structure of the rocks in one of three ways: through carbonation, hydrolysis or oxidation.

Carbonation is the reaction of a weak solution of carbonic acid, formed from water and carbon dioxide in the atmosphere, with different minerals in the rock. Though significant in the process of mountain erosion, the destructive powers of this acid rain are more easily seen on natural stone buildings and monuments in urban settings. Other forms of acid rain are mild solutions of sulfuric or nitric acid formed when moisture and oxygen in the atmosphere react with sulfur dioxide or nitrogen oxide (both of them by-products of burning fossil fuels).

Hydrolysis is the moistening and subsequent transformation of minerals into other less stable mineral compounds, for example silicate minerals, such as feldspar, break down into clays, such as kaolin, better known as china clay. The process often involves the expansion of the mineral crystals, which also contributes to the breakdown of the rock surface. It is more prevalent in damp environments such as gorges and waterfalls.

The chemical combination of oxygen with certain minerals can create oxides which are insoluble and consequently left behind when other minerals are broken down. The distinctive red color of Ayers Rock in central Australia, for example, is due to iron oxide, while the distinctive blue-green coloration

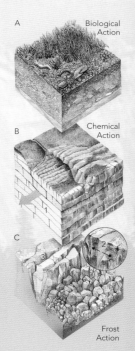

▼ *Weathering of rock occurs in two main ways: physical (A and C) and chemical (B). At the surface, plant roots and animals break down rock, turning it into soil (A). In chemical weathering (B), soluble rocks (1) are dissolved by groundwater. Cold can cause physical weathering (C). Water that settles in cracks and joints during the day expands as it freezes at night (2). The expansion cleaves the rock along the naturally occurring joints (3).*

A — Biological Action

B — Chemical Action

C — Frost Action

▲ *In many*
mountainous regions,
*as here on Mount
Katadhin in Baxter State
Park, USA, rock surfaces
can be severely affected
by the action of ice.
During the day snow
and ice melt and the
subsequent water fills
cracks in the rocks. As
temperatures drop
during the night the
water freezes and
expands as it turns into
ice. It is the expansion
that forces the rock face
to fracture and crack
over time in a process
known as freeze-thaw
weathering.*

at copper mining operations throughout the world, for example, comes from copper oxide (the process of oxidation having occurred at the mine surface).

In extreme cases water may simply dissolve the minerals in the rocks, creating pathways through rock layers. Many cave systems around the world are formed by limestone dissolved by the action of water.

Frost action

Water is unique. As it freezes, it expands in volume. In the mountains at high altitudes, snow melts during the day, and the resulting water flows into cracks in the surface rocks. Overnight, as temperatures drop, the water freezes and expands. This expansion provides an incredible wedging force and slowly chips away at the rock face. Most of the loose rock slopes or scree seen on mountainsides were formed by the slow action of ice wedging, shattering the surface.

A particular form of frost action is frost heaving. This occurs when a body of water lying between layers of rock freezes, expands and then lifts a whole section of rock clear of the surrounding layers, re-depositing it as the ice melts. This contributes to the creation of interesting rock shapes in remote settings but is more closely observed in the lifting and movement of roads, pavements and even buildings in towns and cities; it can be a particular danger in settlements at high altitudes.

Glaciation

Glaciers are enormous bodies of ice that persist all year round. If they are on a slope, they flow downhill. They act as an erosive agent that can scour, grind, scrape and plow mountain landscapes into the rugged form we see today. The tremendous weight of rock and ice in the glacier grinding together makes deep gouges in the rocky slopes and carves many features unique to glaciated areas. Hanging valleys, sharp peaks and ridges are the most notable evidence of past glacial activity.

Over long periods of time, glaciers can carve valleys, create lakes, and literally "move mountains!" When the front of the moving mass of ice is constricted, the glacier can act like a snowplow and force its way through a valley, pushing tons of material to the sides. When the ice melts, the material that remains in the valley is called moraine. This name also refers to all the material that was carried in the ice and deposited in disorganized heaps on the valley floors.

▼ *The Grand Canyon* in northwest Arizona, USA, is one of the great natural wonders of the world. Formed over six million years by the erosive action of the Colorado River on the region's soft sedimentary rock, the Canyon runs for almost 450 km (280 mi).

Avalanches

As snow accumulates high in the mountains, unstable layers are released in the form of avalanches. Since these releases will follow the most efficient route, they normally follow the same path year after year. In some years the path may widen if snowfalls are large, in others tree growth may slowly try to reclaim the path. The most obvious sign of an avalanche path is a treeless swathe running down a forested mountainside, ending in a fan-shaped clearing where the slope flattens out. There may be tree stumps and broken trees within the path and perhaps young tree growth coming through. Successive avalanches may have extended the path downward through several clearings.

The clearing of the tree canopy and hence the increased access to sunlight helps the snow and ice along the avalanche path to melt earlier; a wider range of ground plants can become established and have a longer growing season. Growth in these cleared areas is often more lush than on the surrounding mountainside and it offers good grazing for both wild animals and farm stock brought up from winter pastures.

Running water

Water is an extremely important factor in the weathering process, whether as falling rain and surface water that dissolves out certain minerals from the rock, or as running water carrying with it debris which has an abrasive action on the river bed, carving river channels and creating potholes or in extreme cases waterfalls. The extent of weathering depends upon the water's speed of flow, the underlying rock types and the length of time that weathering has taken place.

Canyons and gorges are the most recognized landforms created by the action of running water. The Grand Canyon in Arizona, USA is possibly the most famous, extending nearly 446 km (277 mi), up to 29 km (18 mi) wide in places and almost 1,600 m (5,250 ft) deep at its maximum point. This canyon has been carved out of the sedimentary rock layers for over six million years, a process that continues, with up to a half a million tons of sediment being carried away each day.

The weathering action of running water can also create underground rivers. Small fissures in limestone or sandstone surfaces can become widened into bigger cracks or slots, eventually becoming large enough to allow the whole body of water to drop through the rock, flow within it and then resurface, often many miles downstream.

Rock and soil movement

When a slope is steep and is affected by the action of water or another agent of erosion, some or all of the material will move down the slope under gravity. This may take the form of a rockfall or slide, where solid rocks are involved, or as slumping or a landslide if the material forming the slope is finer grained and uncompacted.

Wind

In mountainous areas, strong winds can increase the dramatic effects of other erosive agents by removing the broken-down rock material and transporting it away from the immediate area. This has the effect of exposing new material to weathering processes. In desert areas the action of the wind blowing granular material against rock faces weathers out the softer, less-dense surfaces more quickly, creating odd-shaped "monuments" and sculpted landforms.

Biological action

Rocks weather at the surface of the earth where they come into contact with moist air. This same moisture encourages plant growth whatever the altitude or climate. Once plant growth, however simple, is encouraged, so the process of making soil begins by breaking down the rock into its mineral constituents. On a larger scale, trees are able to seed and germinate on the steepest of slopes and continue to grow by jamming their roots down any available crack. This creates a classic wedging effect, which may eventually break off large pieces of rock.

Human impact

Finally, commercial activity and human intervention in mountain areas can also accelerate or be the cause of erosion. Mining, deforestation, dam-building and the developmental aspects of tourism will over time significantly affect the appearance of the landscape.

In certain regions routes may well be cut into mountains to allow construction traffic to reach mining and hydroelectric sites; to allow for the removal of forestry and other products; and to enable tourist facilities to be built to attract more visitors and their much-needed currency. The increased pollution levels as a result of these activities will affect the fragile ecozystems of the high mountain areas, in turn damaging the range and extent of flora and fauna that exist in the area. Roads and settlements on mountainsides affect the natural flow of water after rainfall and can increase the potential for landslides.

Rocks

The Earth, the Moon and the inner planets of the Solar System are built of the material we call rock. All matter comprises a combination of one or more chemical elements naturally bonded in different formations to make compounds. Most of the compounds formed in the Earth's crust are composed of only eight chemical elements—oxygen, silicon, aluminum, iron, calcium, magnesium, sodium and potassium—and are known as minerals. These minerals combine to make up rocks.

Rocks fall conveniently into three groups: igneous rocks, sedimentary rocks and metamorphic rocks.

Igneous rocks

Igneous rocks are the primary, original material that constitutes the Earth's surface, and they form when molten material from far down inside the Earth cools, either at the surface or deep underground. The first rocks on the Earth were the igneous rocks that formed the Earth's crust as the planet started to cool.

This molten material, or magma, continues to reach the Earth's surface today, through volcanic vents or at active plate margins in earthquake zones or in rift valleys, where the magma wells up as convection currents pull the plates apart. All oceanic crust is made up of igneous rock, and the ocean floor constantly renews itself along rift valleys, notably the Mid-Atlantic Ridge (tectonic activity can be observed in parts of Iceland where the Ridge breaks through the continental crust).

It is the crumpling of the rocks of the Earth's crust, its outer skin, which creates mountains. We can only see parts of the crust, which can be up to 65 km (40 mi) thick under the continents and extends down to about 6 km (4 mi) beneath the oceans. It is formed mainly of rocks of relatively low density. Beneath the crust is a layer of denser rock called the mantle, which extends down to a depth of nearly 3,000 km (1,900 mi). Much of the rock material in igneous rocks is generated by the melting of the upper parts of the mantle and the lower crust. This molten material migrates upward through the Earth's crust and when it cools it forms rock masses known as igneous intrusions. When magma reaches the Earth's surface and flows out over it, it is called lava. The type of rock that

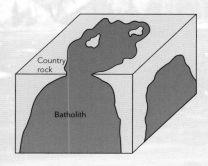

▼ **Igneous intrusions** are bodies of rock that are formed as molten magma is forced up through the Earth's crust, solidifying as it cools.

Country rock

Batholith

Obsidian

Vesicular basalt

emerges depends upon the composition of the magma, and the size of its crystals varies with the rate of cooling. Slow cooling at great depths within the crust gives large crystals, resulting in light-colored granites and dark-colored gabbros. Rapid cooling at or near the surface results in rocks with very fine crystals, as in basalt, or even no crystals at all, as in the glassy rock called obsidian. Most of the ocean floor is made up of basalts and on top of these basalts lie the continents which are made mainly of granitic materials.

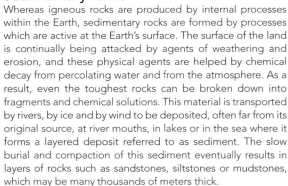

Muscovite granite

Sedimentary rocks

Whereas igneous rocks are produced by internal processes within the Earth, sedimentary rocks are formed by processes which are active at the Earth's surface. The surface of the land is continually being attacked by agents of weathering and erosion, and these physical agents are helped by chemical decay from percolating water and from the atmosphere. As a result, even the toughest rocks can be broken down into fragments and chemical solutions. This material is transported by rivers, by ice and by wind to be deposited, often far from its original source, at river mouths, in lakes or in the sea where it forms a layered deposit referred to as sediment. The slow burial and compaction of this sediment eventually results in layers of rocks such as sandstones, siltstones or mudstones, which may be many thousands of meters thick.

Oolitic limestone

Oolitic ironstone

Phosphate rock

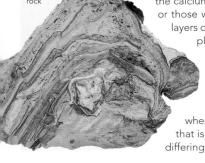

Limestones are another type of sedimentary rock, the majority of which are produced by the gradual accumulation of the calcium carbonate skeletons of animals such as corals or those with shells. In addition to the remains of shells, layers of sediment may contain organic material such as plants and the remains of dead creatures. Groundwater percolates through the sediment, leaving behind minerals that bind the sediment together around these remains, preserving them as fossils.

Limestones and ironstones can also form where fresh water carrying sediment meets seawater that is already saturated with carbonates. Waters with differing chemical contents can hold different amounts of mineral in solution. When these waters are mixed, the excess chemical compounds or minerals can no longer be held in solution and they appear as solid particles that sink. This process is known as precipitation.

Another type of sedimentary rock results from the evaporation of river, lake or seawater to form layers of salt or gypsum. These limestones are known as evaporites.

Marble

Metamorphic rocks

Metamorphism is the name given to the transformation of minerals within rocks as a result of temperature and pressure, or of temperature alone. The processes are extremely slow and occur over hundreds of millions of years. The original rock, whether igneous or sedimentary, first needs to be buried to a depth where metamorphism can begin and solid recrystallization take place. Eventually metamorphic rocks are carried to the Earth's surface when a mountain chain is formed and rock layers are pushed high above sea level through tectonic plate movement. With erosion of the rocks the metamorphic rocks are exposed. These processes are called regional metamorphism.

Folded granite gneiss

Folded biotite schist

Contact metamorphism is restricted to rocks in the immediate vicinity of igneous intrusions. Here it is the surrounding rocks that are changed, mainly by the heat of the molten material.

Metamorphic rocks display a wide range of textures and mineralogy because the rock type resulting

GEOLOGICAL TIMESCALE

Precambrian	Lower	Palaeozoic (Primary)			Upper		Mesozoic (Secondary)			Cenozoic (Tertiary, Quaternary)					Era
Precambrian	Cambrian	Ordovician	Silurian	Devonian	Carboniferous	Permian	Triassic	Jurassic	Cretaceous	Palaeocene	Eocene	Oligocene	Miocene / Pliocene	Pleistocene / Quaternary	System
			CALEDONIAN FOLDING		HERCYNIAN FOLDING								LARAMIDE FOLDING	ALPINE FOLDING	Orogeny
600 550 500	450	400	350	300	250	200	150	100	50						

Millions of years before present

▲ **The geological timescale** is a way of categorizing periods of time since the formation of the Earth 4,600 million years ago. The longest divisions of time are known as the four great eras, each of which is broken down into periods, and in the case of the most recent era, the Cenozoic, into epochs. The table was devised by studying the correlation of rock formations and fossils.

◀ **As fossils** are broken down, the organic part decays first, leaving a gap which is filled with sediment (**1**). The shell slowly dissolves (**2**), leaving a rock cast of the inside (**3**). The shell may be replaced by another material, giving a cast of the exterior (**4**). Sometimes no sediment fills the shell (**5**). Solutions may permeate (**6**), causing the shell to dissolve leaving a mold in the rock (**7**). A replica may later be cast (**8**).

from metamorphism depends upon the wide range of temperatures and pressures to which the original rock has been subjected and also upon the rock's original chemical composition. A featureless mudstone can be transformed into a sparkling mica-rich schist, or a pure limestone changed into a white marble.

Fossils

Fossils are the solid remains of plants or animals that lived millions of years ago (or evidence of animal life such as footprints or droppings) that have been preserved within layers of sedimentary rock.

Most fossils are found in sedimentary rocks that are laid down in water. This environment is protective of shells and skeletal material and so provides a better chance of preservation than to those creatures that have fallen on the land. Early visitors to mountain summits were intrigued to find that the sedimentary rocks at these great heights, once they had been weathered away, contained fossils of a variety of sea creatures. This is explained by our understanding today of the processes of mountain building—in particular the subduction of oceanic crust beneath continental crust, thereby depositing onto the land mud, silt and sediment from the ocean floor built up over millions of years.

Fossil records are frequently used to date rocks and geological events.

▶ **Trilobites,** such as Calymene, are any of an extinct group of arthropods fossilized in marine deposits. They grew in length from 6 mm (0.25 in) up to 75 cm (30 in) and first appeared some 600 million years ago. Covered in an outer skeleton, the body is divided into the head, thorax and tail.

Calymene

Water and Rivers

▼ *The water (or
hydrological) cycle is
the process of water
exchange between
oceans, atmosphere
and land. Water in the
oceans evaporates,
creating water vapor in
the atmosphere that
may condense and fall
back to the ocean.
Winds carry water vapor
over the land, and
evapotranspiration from
rivers, lakes, the land
and plants adds to
atmospheric moisture.
Precipitation is
absorbed by the
vegetation or flows on
the surface in rivers and
streams. Some infiltrates
the ground via porous
rock and may drain into
lakes or rivers; in other
areas lake water drains
into the groundwater.*

The water cycle

Almost all—some 97.5 percent—of the water on the planet is salty, and found in the oceans. Most of the remaining fresh water is stored as ice at high altitude, and some as groundwater. Only a tiny percentage is held in rivers, lakes and in the atmosphere as clouds and vapor.

Precipitation (rain, snow, sleet, hail, drizzle) is significantly higher in mountain environments than in the lowlands. Solar energy drives the water cycle by allowing water molecules to escape or evaporate from water bodies such as the oceans. Moist air moving toward mountains is forced to rise. While doing so it cools, and as it passes the condensation level, moisture vapor within it condenses to form clouds.

Once clouds develop, the minute water droplets within them move around and eventually collide with each other and coalesce to form larger droplets. When droplets reach 2–3 mm (0.07–0.11 in) in size they are heavy enough to fall through the atmosphere as rain (or as hail and snow when the temperature in the cloud is below 0°C/32°F).

Precipitation falling on mountainous drainage basins (or catchment areas) can take several pathways before it eventually ends up as river flow. Some precipitation may be caught on vegetation surfaces or intercepted by vegetation like forests which may impede its progress toward the river. Some moisture held on vegetation (especially leaf surfaces) or on the ground surface may be evaporated back into the atmosphere. Any moisture that enters the soil may get drawn into

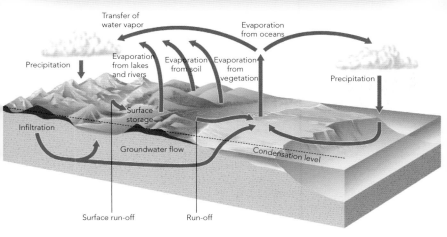

SOLAR RADIATION

Transfer of water vapor

Evaporation from oceans

Precipitation

Evaporation from lakes and rivers

Evaporation from soil

Evaporation from vegetation

Precipitation

Surface storage

Infiltration

Groundwater flow

Condensation level

Surface run-off

Run-off

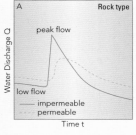

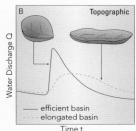

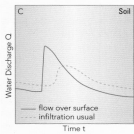

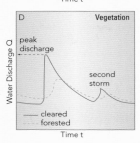

less flooding downstream. (B) Here the shape of the basin affects the graph. The rounded drainage basin gives a steep hydrograph, whereas the elongated basin shows a gradual rise in discharge as the water needs more time to flow along the length of the basin. (C) The effect of soil character on infiltration capacity is illustrated. Where infiltration capacity is low, as is typical of mountain soil, the hydrograph is more rapid and the flow higher than in a basin where infiltration into the soil occurs. (D) The hydrographs here are for storm events in a forested basin. The hydrograph rise is gradual and the peak flow is low because some of the rain is intercepted or evaporated back into the atmosphere by the trees. When the trees are harvested, however, the hydrograph rises steeply.

The hydrograph for two different drainage basins, but with each having the same rainfall event. The basins are identical in all but one respect. The hydrographs show (A) how an impermeable rock type does not allow water to enter easily, causing the hydrograph to be steep and the flow high. The hydrograph for permeable rock, which allows water to pass into it, starts later, is less steep and has a lower peak. A drainage basin, therefore, that has soil and rock allowing water to soak into the ground, will cause

plant root systems from where it will pass upward through the plant stem or trunk to be transpired back into the atmosphere. When precipitation does reach the ground, the nature of the ground surface determines whether it will infiltrate or run over the surface (called surface runoff). The rate at which water enters the ground surface, called the infiltration capacity, may determine whether the water enters the soil and possibly the rock below, or whether it runs quickly over the surface as surface runoff, into the nearby streams and rivers giving a rapid rise in the size and speed of the flow (together known as the river's discharge). This is a very important point in the water cycle, since it determines the extent to which a river will cause flooding downstream.

Runoff

Surface runoff is more likely in mountains, giving rise to rapid responses to rainfall in mountain streams and rivers. The way in which streams and rivers respond to precipitation can be understood by examining their hydrographs. A hydrograph is a means of showing the discharge of a stream or river at a given point over a short period of time.

Rock type, topography, infiltration capacity and vegetation exert important controls on the shape and size of hydrographs which in turn determine both the size of the flood downstream and the time between peak rainfall and peak discharge. Heavy storms in mountainous catchments often result in rapid rises in discharge in a matter of minutes. These events are called flash floods, and they can cause severe damage.

Energy

With precipitation totals in mountains being greater than average, this results in large volumes of water which typically give mountain rivers large amounts of energy. Most of this energy is used to overcome the forces of friction as the river moves over the rough river bed to flow down slope. Friction can be high in mountain areas where there may be uneven ground and complicated topography caused by deposits of boulders and glacial moraine. Any surplus energy (in times of rainfall) is used to erode the sediments of the bed and banks and to transport the eroded products.

The physical and chemical weathering of rock supplies material that water moving under gravity can easily erode and transportat downstream. Mountain rivers transport eroded products in three forms, depending on the grain size and shape. The first is the dissolved or solution load, in which eroded products break down chemically into ions which cannot be seen but which can be measured by electrical

*▼ **Rivers transport eroded materials** in three distinct forms. The finest is the dissolved, or solution load. In this load the eroded materials are broken down chemically forming ions in solution. The next finest form is mud or silt in suspension, and if there is sufficient energy, sands. Finally the largest form is the bed load. This comprises pebbles, gravel and boulders which are forced to roll, slide or get carried short distances by fast-moving water. In most rivers the suspended load accounts for the greatest percentage of the total load.*

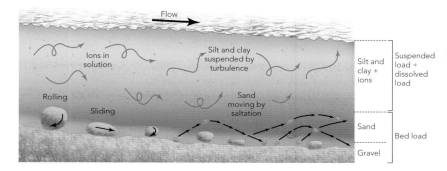

conductivity. Typically the solution load may be 20–50 percent of the stream's total load according to the geology and soil of the basin. The suspended load comprises fine particles of clays, silts and, when the river is in flood, sands. Usually consisting of material finer than 2 mm (0.07 in), the suspended load can account for 50–80 percent of the total load. The part of the load called the bed load tends to move only when the river has surplus energy during floods. It consists of all sizes of material larger than 2 mm (0.07 in) and includes pebbles, gravel, cobbles and boulders. It rarely contributes more than about ten percent of a river's load, though in some rivers it can contribute up to 50 percent of the total load.

▲ *Langden Brook* in *the Trough of Bowland, Lancashire, England. Floods frequently erode the banks and move sediments to create mid-channel bars. This is known as a braided river channel form.*

Landscape changes

Due to the large quantities of water dropped by clouds onto mountains, running water is the dominant agent producing landscape changes in mountain areas. Langden Brook in the Trough of Bowland, north England, is a good example of an upland river with its high energy, steep grade and frequent flash floods. Past glaciers in the valley, which melted around 10,000 years ago, have left thick boulder clay deposits that the river has reworked in a warmer climate. The bed material today is both large and mobile as it gets moved around most years by flooding. These mobile sediments give rise to an active channel with relatively unstable banks.

Snow and Ice

Introduction

The publication of *Études sur les Glaciers* by Louis Agassiz in 1840 marked the beginning of a widespread realization that a large part of the Earth's surface had once been covered by ice. Evidence from ocean floor deposits and polar icecaps suggests that in the last two million years there have been around 20 fluctuations in global temperature of between five and six degrees, which have led to cold phases (glacials) and warm phases (interglacials). When ice reached its maximum extent it is estimated that it covered 30 percent of the Earth's land surface, compared with ten percent today. There is no single agreed explanation for the onset of major ice ages, or for the warming during so-called interglacials. The Earth's position in space, its tilt and its orbit around the Sun may change, triggering the onset of ice ages. Variations in sunspot activity or injections of volcanic dust into the atmosphere can increase or decrease the radiation we receive. Currently, dramatic rises in atmospheric carbon dioxide largely produced by industry and transport appear to be responsible for the global warming the Earth is now experiencing, though the precise way in which Earth is responding to this proven increase is fiercely debated. What is becoming clear is that global warming is causing dramatic changes to the mountain environment, causing glaciers to retreat and snow

▼ *About 20,000 years ago* (A) *permanent ice sheets covered 42 million sq km (16 million sq miles) compared with the present* (B) *15 million sq km (6 million sq miles). They locked up vast amounts of water, causing world sea levels to fall by 120 meters (400 ft), revealing many new landmasses.*

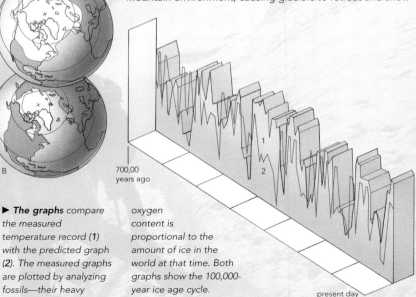

700,00
years ago

1

2

present day

► *The graphs* compare the measured temperature record (1) with the predicted graph (2). The measured graphs are plotted by analyzing fossils—their heavy oxygen content is proportional to the amount of ice in the world at that time. Both graphs show the 100,000-year ice age cycle.

seasons to change. These climate changes have implications for people visiting and living in and around mountains. The mountaineering and skiing industries are having to adapt to milder winters and warmer summers; water resources are being affected, as are flora and fauna, transport, farming and land use. In short, some scientists predict that climate change in the mountains may happen faster than the people, plants and animals that live there are able to adapt to.

Snow

When in the past the Earth's climate got colder (moving into a glacial period), more precipitation fell as snow in winter, and shorter summers meant that there was less time for that snow to melt. As the climate continued to get cooler, then snow would lie throughout the year forming a permanent snow line, and eventually glaciers began to form. The height of the snow line seen on mountains today depends on latitude. Near the equator the permanent snow line is around 6,000 m (20,000 ft); it is around 3,000 m (10,000 ft) in the Swiss Alps and at sea level at the poles. You would need to climb to near the top of Kilimanjaro in Africa to reach the permanent snow line, whereas Mount Vincent in Antarctica is permanently above the snow line.

The size and shape of a snow crystal are largely determined by the conditions of temperature and humidity that it experiences, both at its point of formation and during its journey to the ground. The different forms are all constructed on a hexagonal plan, but include a wide variety of shapes such as needles, stellar crystals, columns and plates. These forms are typical of crystals at their point of formation in a cloud, and in fairly calm conditions they can fall to the ground more or less intact, either individually, or in clusters of several crystals called snowflakes. When snowflakes accumulate on the ground, they have an open feathery appearance; if you collected a jar of new snow as much as 90 percent of it might be air. Where snow gathers in hollows it becomes compressed by the weight of new snow falling on top, and when the proportion of air drops to around 45 percent it becomes firn (a German word; névé in French)—a compacted snow that has survived a summer's melting. In temperate mountains such as the European Alps, summer meltwater percolates into the firn and freezes at night or during the following winter to form an increasingly dense mass. As air is progressively squeezed out over 25–40 years, the firn slowly turns into ice, its air content now less than 20 percent. This same process may take 200 years or more in Antarctica or Greenland

▼ **Different forms**
of snow crystal exist because the frozen water from which they are made can be subjected to both a variety of temperatures and varying degrees of humidity.

Plates

Columns

Stellar crystals

Needles

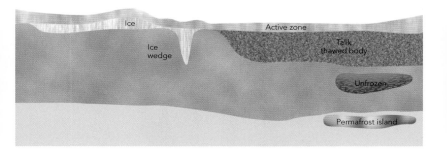

Ice

Active zone

Ice
wedge

Talik
thawed body

Unfrozen

Permafrost island

▲ *Schematic* diagram
through permafrost
ground showing the
features that are
typically found.

where there is little or no summer melting, but in warmer climates such as Alaska's, snow can transform to ice in as little as three to five years where meltwater is abundant.

Ice

When atmospheric temperatures fall below 0°C (32°F), any water at atmospheric pressure on or near the surface will freeze to form ice. Ice is an important agent for shaping mountain landscapes. It exists in two major forms: (1) as finely segregated aggregations in soils or rock, and massive pure bodies of ice called ground ice; (2) as large tabular or elongated masses of polycrystalline ice variously mixed with rock debris resting on the land surface and extending locally, known as glaciers.

Ground and soil ice includes a wide range of types. These include needle ice (pipkrake) formed as a result of strong radiative cooling of bare earth surfaces; pore ice caused by rapid freezing of saturated soils and segregated ice resulting from slow freezing of partly saturated soils where ice clusters form in some voids but not others.

Needle ice can lift soil grains several centimeters from the surface and can loosen soil in mountain areas prior to erosion by water or wind. Very low year-round temperatures experienced in high-latitude mountains in areas where snow cover is absent or thin can result in ground temperatures remaining below freezing down to depths of 100 m (330 ft) or more. Such perennially frozen ground is called permafrost. The upper surface of permafrost is called the permafrost table, the zone of seasonal thaw being called the active layer. Unfrozen zones (talik) may occur within the permafrost. In subarctic regions such as Alaska, permafrost can create many problems for buildings and roads due to the subsidence occurring in summer when the active layer begins to thaw.

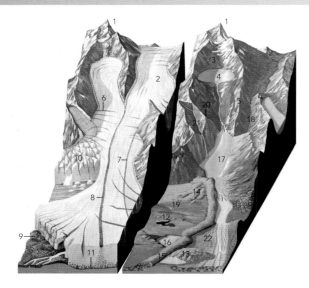

1 Pyramidal peak
2 Firn (granular snow)
3 Cirque
4 Tarn (corrie lake)
5 Arête
6 Marginal crevasse
7 Lateral moraine
8 Medial moraine
9 Terminal moraine
10 Sérac
11 Subglacial moraine
12 Glacial table
13 Roche moutonnée
14 Drumlin
15 Esker
16 Glacial lake
17 Finger lake
18 U-shaped valley
19 Erratics
20 Truncated spur
21 Hanging valley
22 Outwash fan

Glaciers

A glacier will form whenever a body of snow accumulates, compacts, and turns to ice. Glaciers are usually classified according to their size and shape. Niche glaciers are very small and occupy hollows and gullies on north-facing slopes in the northern hemisphere. Corrie or cirque glaciers (Cwm in Wales), although larger than niche glaciers, are small masses of ice occupying armchair-shaped hollows in mountains. Valley glaciers are larger bodies of ice that flow down from mountain ice sources. These glaciers usually follow former river valleys and are bounded by steep valley sides. Corrie or cirque glaciers may overspill to feed valley glaciers. Away from mountain areas piedmont glaciers are formed when valley glaciers extend on to lowland areas, spread out and merge.

Glaciers can form in any climatic zone where the snowfall exceeds the rate at which it melts. If the rate of snow accumulation is high, and the melt or ablation rate is low, then a glacier will form quickly. Once formed, a glacier's survival depends on the balance between accumulation and ablation. Ablation can occur by ice melt, iceberg calving (where the glacier flows into a lake or the sea, and blocks of ice will break from the snout or terminus) or by sublimation (the direct evaporation of ice). Most ablation occurs at the snout of the glacier, which is usually its point of lowest elevation and where air temperatures are usually highest. Most accumulation will occur at higher elevations where snowfall is greater

◄ *In spite of* *a return to warmer conditions, ice still covers many regions of the world, namely those nearer the poles. The movement of ice greatly alters the landscape of these areas. Erosion and deposition are the main processes in glaciated regions. Erosion takes place mainly in highland areas, leaving features such as pyramidal peaks, cirques, roches moutonnées, truncated spurs and hanging valleys. Most deposition occurs on lowlands, where, after the retreat of the ice, moraines, drumlins, eskers, erratic boulders, and alluvial fans remain.*

and temperatures lower. A glacier can therefore be divided into two areas: an accumulation zone where accumulation exceeds ablation, and an ablation zone where ablation exceeds accumulation. The line between these zones, where accumulation is balanced by ablation, is called the equilibrium line (sometimes also the snow line). A glacier experiencing a large snowfall in its accumulation zone will have a steep gradient and rapid flow to transfer quickly the accumulating snow and ice down slope to the ablation zone. The opposite applies when there is little snowfall in the accumulation zone. If the total amount of accumulation is equal to the total amount of melt at the end of the balance year, the glacier will occupy the same position as the previous year. If not, the glacier will advance or retreat. Many European glaciers showed evidence of major advances during the 18th century, the "Little Ice Age," with local records showing the maximum extent to have been around 1750–60, since which time glaciers have shown a steady retreat of their ice margins.

Glacier movement

A glacier moves because the ice within it deforms in response to gravity. The force that causes it to deform is known as the shear stress. While the overlying weight of ice and the surface slope of the glacier determine the shear

▼ *The Glacier Blanc,* *Ecrins National Park,* *France: (A) area of* *extending flow which is* *heavily crevassed; (B)* *area of compressing* *flow; (C) glacier snout or* *terminus; (D) frost-* *shattered material from* *valley sides; (E)* *meltwater stream.*

stress, glacier movement is largely controlled by temperature, and glaciers may be classified as temperate or cold (polar) glaciers. Movement is much faster in temperate glaciers and takes place by basal sliding where pressure and friction with the bedrock at the base of the glacier cause the basal ice to melt. The resulting melt water acts as a lubricant, enabling the glacier to move (slide) at around 2–3 m (6–10 ft) per day. Cold glaciers move less quickly, 1–2 cm (less than an inch) per day, by a process called internal flow in which the ice crystals slide past each other. All glaciers move more quickly on the surface and away from their valley sides where friction is greatest. Where the slope of the topography over which the glacier is flowing reduces, the ice gets thicker and speed decelerates. Where the gradient increases, the ice gets thinner and the surface may break and crack to form crevasses. Temperate glaciers are more likely to erode their bed and valley sides and to carry and deposit most rock debris. A single glacier may exhibit, at different points along its profile, the characteristics of both cold and temperate glaciers.

Glacial erosion

Ice that is stationary or contains little debris has limited erosive power, whereas ice carrying rock debris within and on its surface can drastically alter the mountain landscape. The rock debris called moraine which becomes incorporated into glaciers is derived from the process of frost shattering where melt water percolating into cracks high on the mountain side freezes, expands and prises the rock away from the mountain. Gravity delivers the loosened rock to the valley floor where it may build up to form talus cones or lateral moraines—or it resides on the glacier surface (called supraglacial moraine). Moraine that gets covered by snowfall and incorporated into the glacier ice—or which falls into crevasses—becomes englacial moraine, and that near the base of the glacier is called subglacial moraine.

▲ *View of the Glacier Noir,* Ecrins Massif, Dauphine Alps, southeast France. *(A)* Talus cone; *(B)* lateral moraine; *(C)* glacier snout; *(D)* meltwater stream; *(E)* debris-covered glacier; *(F)* vegetation colonization as glacier retreats; *(G)* arête; *(H)* pyramidal peak or horn. The rock walls on the left of the glacier were formed by glacial erosion.

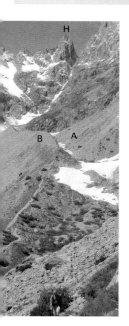

Glacier ice has great rigidity and the ability to melt and refreeze as it moves around obstacles in its path. Ice with moraine within it can act like sandpaper, causing abrasion to the landscape over which it flows. This process can produce smoothened, gently sloping landforms, on which it is often possible to see scratches or striations. The huge weight of a glacier creates enormous forces, especially when the ice meets with an obstruction. The increased pressure causes basal ice to melt and the glacier flows around the obstruction. However, the release of pressure then causes the ice to refreeze. This freeze-thaw activity means that melt water is continually entering cracks in the bedrock, freezing, then adhering to the glacier again so that when the glacier moves the process of "plucking" pulls away masses of rock.

Shaping landscapes

When corrie or cirque glaciers melt they leave an armchair-shaped hollow in the side of the mountain which, if overdeepened, can become occupied by a small lake or tarn. Where two of these form near each other on the sides of a mountain the sharp ridge between them is known as an arête. Where three or more of these form on the sides of a mountain a horn or pyramidal peak (such as that of the Matterhorn) may be shaped. When valley glaciers accumulate sufficient ice from their feeder corrie glaciers they have the ability to carve huge valleys into the landscape. A glacially scoured valley is called a trough or U-shaped valley. Corrie glaciers feeding valley glaciers can melt to leave side valleys called hanging valleys high above the main valley floors; streams flowing from these hanging valleys end in waterfalls. Sometimes, where the U-shaped valley has been over-deepened by the glacier, and/or the valley becomes dammed by moraine left at the glacier's snout, an elongated ribbon lake may form. In areas where glaciers have not been for 10,000 years or more (such as when the last ice retreated from Britain, for example), the moraines still mantle the landscape, though they are more difficult to recognize than more recent moraines because they are usually covered by soil and vegetation.

Glaciers have altered the appearance of a large proportion of the Earth's surface and continue to shape the mountain landscape in many parts of the world today. Where glaciers have retreated from their former maxima, we can still see plenty of evidence of the work they performed in the past.

Climate and Weather

Mountains and high plateau areas account for 20 percent of the Earth's land surface. They give rise to a wide range of meteorological phenomena and conditions which have great consequences for the ecology, hydrology, glaciology and land use of mountain areas, as well as for people wishing to visit to walk, ski, climb or use the mountain environment in any other way.

The distinction between climate and weather is one of scale. Weather refers to the state of the atmosphere at a local level, usually on a time scale of minutes to months, and it emphasizes aspects that affect us—such as sunshine, rain, snow, cloud, wind and temperature. Climate, on the other hand, is concerned with the long-term behavior of the atmosphere in a specific area. Data on temperature, rainfall, pressure, wind and humidity for example, are used to calculate daily, monthly and yearly averages to build up global patterns over periods of at least 30 years.

Intensive scientific study of mountain weather conditions did not begin until the mid-19th century. The effect of altitude on pressure was proved in 1684 when the French scientist Florin Perier operated a simple Torricelian mercury tube at the summit and base of the Puy de Dôme in France. In 1787, the Swiss physicist Horace-Bénédict de Saussure made observations of relative humidity during an ascent of Mont Blanc; in the next year, he and his son made two-hourly observations on the Col du Géant (3,360 m/11,020 ft) near Mont Blanc while comparative observations were made at nearby Chamonix (1,050 m/3,440 ft) and Geneva (375 m/1,230 ft). From these data, de Saussure—regarded as the first mountain meteorologist—was able to study temperature lapse rate and its diurnal variation. Since the 1850s meteorological observations have been systematically made on high mountains such as the Peak of Tenerife (Canary Islands), Mount Washington (New Hampshire, USA), Pike's Peak (Colorado, USA), Ben Nevis (Scotland), the Zugspitze observatory (Germany) and Mauna Loa (Hawaii). However, the expense and difficulty in maintaining high-altitude observatories meant that many were closed due to lack of

▼ *In 1787 the Swiss scientist and accomplished mountaineer H. B. de Saussure made a successful ascent of Mont Blanc, the third time the mountain had been climbed. During the climb Saussure recorded the relative humidity at regular intervals.*

▲ *Modern high-altitude weather stations,* such as this one on the top of Mount Washington, New Hampshire, USA, provide meteorological data, including temperature and wind speed. Data from such weather stations are often transmitted to manned weather stations via satellite links.

funding and/or support. Technological developments in the past half-century have meant that automatic weather stations can now be operated on mountains (such as that set up in the 1980s on the summit of Cairngorm, Scotland) which, via the internet, make their real-time and archive data available to skiers and climbers. In terms of meteorological data, the mountain ranges about which most is known are the European Alps; the least meteorological information exists regarding the mountain systems of central Asia and the Andes.

The study of mountain weather and climate is a challenge for three reasons: first, many mountain areas are remote from human habitation, their inaccessibility making it costly to install and maintain weather stations; second, the nature of mountain terrain sets up such a variety of local weather conditions at summits, on slopes and in valleys that any station is likely to be representative of only a limited range of sites; third, there are serious difficulties to be faced when making standard weather observations at mountain stations. For example, local topography may cause observations to be unrepresentative. This said, there are nevertheless a number of general differences in the weather and climate of mountains compared with their surrounding lowland areas, which we can investigate further.

THE ATMOSPHERE

The Earth's atmosphere is a thin envelope of transparent, odorless gases (78 percent nitrogen, 21 percent oxygen, with smaller and variable amounts of carbon dioxide, water vapor, ozone plus other trace gases and pollutants) held to the Earth by gravitational attraction. Half its mass lies below an altitude of 6 km (3.7 mi) and since the major mountain ranges project up to and beyond this level, they have a major impact on the weather systems that move around the globe and on the paths they follow. A vertical structure of the atmosphere would show that Mount Everest protrudes significantly into the lowest 12 km/7.5 mi) known as the "zone of weather" or troposphere which contains most of the mass of the atmosphere. Atmospheric pressure decreases with distance from the Earth's surface, the air pressure at the summit of Everest being about one-third of that at sea level. Temperature also falls, the rate at which it decreases with height being the environmental or temperature lapse rate. The average temperature falls rapidly from around 15°C (60°F) at the Earth's surface to around –30°C (–22°F) at the top of Everest, to –50°C (–58°F) at the top of the troposphere. So, despite moving away from the Earth's surface, and closer to the Sun, the temperature gets cooler. Why is this?

▶ *The vertical structure of the atmosphere, with Mount Everest for scale. Atmospheric pressure changes with altitude. The air thins as the pressure decreases, which is why climbers need oxygen masks to climb the Earth's highest peaks such as Mount Everest.*

SOLAR RADIATION: WHY ARE MOUNTAINS COLDER?

The Sun is the Earth's prime source of energy. It causes differences in temperature on Earth, which in turn drive the atmospheric circulation (winds) and ocean currents. Since the Sun is so hot, the energy it radiates is in the form of short wave radiation. The Earth intercepts a very small amount of this, and the quantity of incoming radiation that any point on the Earth's surface receives is affected by the solar constant, the Earth's distance from the Sun, the altitude of the Sun in the sky, and the length of day and night. However, when the effect of the atmosphere is taken into account, some 55 percent of the solar radiation is lost through absorption, scattering and reflection before it reaches the Earth's surface. The greater depth of atmosphere that the radiation has to penetrate at the poles (due to the angle of the Sun's rays) helps to explain why the polar regions are cooler than the equatorial regions. When the remaining 45 percent of incoming radiation does reach the Earth's surface it is absorbed and converted to heat energy. As the ground warms it radiates energy back into the atmosphere called terrestrial radiation (which consists of long or infra-red

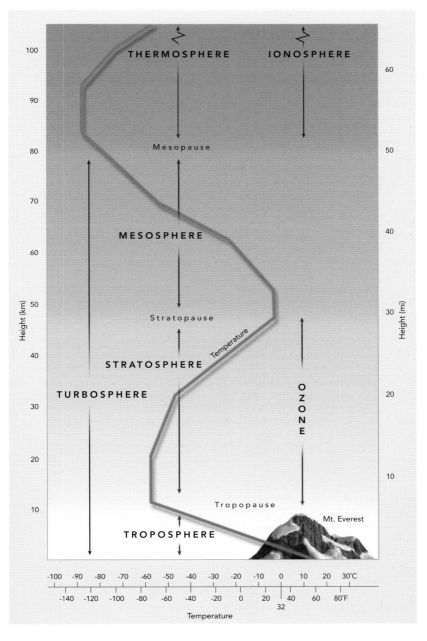

wavelengths because the Earth is much cooler than the Sun). Some 94 percent of this outgoing radiation is absorbed (only six percent is lost to space) and this natural "greenhouse effect" is what keeps the Earth warm enough to support life. The atmosphere, therefore, is not warmed directly by the Sun, but by heat radiated from the Earth's surface, which is distributed by convection and conduction. Consequently, as the altitude of a mountain increases, it presents a decreasing area of land surface from which to heat the surrounding air. Also, as the density or pressure of the air decreases, so too does its ability to hold heat because there are fewer air molecules, and those that are present are increasingly further apart. Mountaineers climbing Everest are not only subjecting themselves to a rarer atmosphere containing less oxygen; they also find it cooler because there is less land at higher altitudes to radiate heat into the air and the air is less able to hold what heat there is.

As you climb a mountain, the rate at which the temperature falls is called the lapse rate. On average the temperature falls by 6.5°C (11.7°F) per km (0.615 mi), or 0.65°C (1.17°F) per 100 m (330 ft), although this can vary with season, slope aspect, type of air mass, humidity and other factors. At night and in winter, the temperature gradient may be temporarily reversed over limited vertical distances, to form a layer or

▼ *The solar energy cascade. Incoming radiation from the Sun arriving at the top of the Earth's atmosphere is absorbed, reflected and scattered by the components of the atmosphere resulting in only 45 percent of the radiation reaching the Earth's surface.*

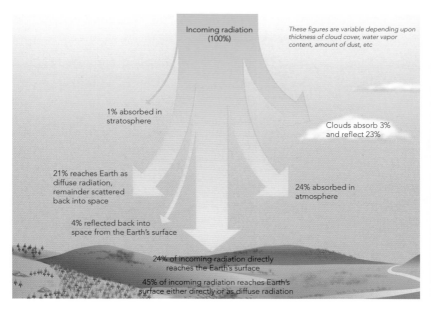

Incoming radiation
(100%)

These figures are variable depending upon thickness of cloud cover, water vapor content, amount of dust, etc

1% absorbed in stratosphere

Clouds absorb 3% and reflect 23%

21% reaches Earth as diffuse radiation, remainder scattered back into space

24% absorbed in atmosphere

4% reflected back into space from the Earth's surface

24% of incoming radiation directly reaches the Earth's surface

45% of incoming radiation reaches Earth's surface either directly or as diffuse radiation

temperature inversion when cold surface air is trapped by overlying warmer, less dense air. If you are fortunate enough to be high on a mountain and above such an inversion, you may get a spectacular view over a flat cloak of clouds. If you are even luckier, and happen to have the Sun behind you and the cloud below, your shadow may get projected onto the clouds and you may see your broken specter, a ghostly shadow with a halo around it.

▲ *Temperature* *inversion* *in Skeldal* *Valley, East Greenland.* *This often picturesque* *phenomenon occurs* *when dense cold air is* *trapped in low-lying* *regions by a layer of* *warm air.*

PRECIPITATION: WHY ARE MOUNTAINS WETTER?

Mountains, as we have seen, force moist air to rise over them. In so doing, the air cools and condenses to form droplets as it passes the condensation level. Research has generally shown that precipitation totals increase with altitude. However, the conversion of these droplets into clouds, and the subsequent deposition of rainfall, is uneven across mountain ranges. As relatively warm moist air driven off the oceans encounters a mountain range it is forced to rise over it. As it does so the air cools, causing vapor to condense into droplets and form clouds. As the droplets coalesce and enlarge, they become too heavy to remain in the atmosphere and they fall as precipitation (rain or snow) on the

39

windward and summit mountain slopes. As the clouds pass over the mountain summit and descend over the leeward slopes, most of the precipitation has fallen and the area in the lee of the mountain range is known as a rain shadow. Warm dry air descending on the leeward slopes in the Rockies is known as the "Chinook" or "snow eater."

As temperatures decrease with higher altitudes, a greater proportion of the precipitation in mountains falls as snow. North-facing aspects (in the northern hemisphere) will hold snow for longer than southerly aspects.

The concentration of carbon dioxide and other trace gases in the atmosphere has increased substantially over the last century, and a doubling of the concentration of carbon dioxide is expected by 2050 if no control measures are adopted. This steady increase in the concentration of greenhouse gases has resulted in global warming. The Intergovernmental Panel on Climate Change has indicated that the average global surface air temperature has increased by 0.6±0.2°C (1±0.4°F) since the late 19th century and it is projected to increase by 1.4–5.8°C (2.5–10.4 °F) over the period 1990–2100. These predictions clearly have important implications for the amounts and duration of snow cover in the mountain areas across the world.

WIND: WHY ARE WIND SPEEDS GREATER IN MOUNTAINS?

Wind is caused by differences in pressure that result from differential heating of the Earth's surface. In warmer parts the air rises causing lower pressure than that in surrounding cooler areas. Air moves to equalize these pressure differences, and the resulting movement of air we call wind. Wind speeds are categorized using the Beaufort scale, a scale from 0 (calm) to 12 (hurricane force, >117 km/h/73 mph). A range of mountains constitutes a barrier to the flow of air, particularly if it is orientated at right angles to the air stream. The air has only two options: to rise up and over the top of the range, or to flow round the obstacle. Both have the same effect: an increase in wind speed because of "overcrowding" of the air. Data from the Cairngorm summit weather station suggest that as a general rule, you can expect average wind speeds to be two to three times greater up high than in the nearby valleys. However, for the mountain user, it is not the average wind speed, but the maximum gust speed that may be more relevant, especially if venturing near to cliffs and ridges. The maximum wind speed at Cairngorm summit is over 274 km/h (170 mph), recorded on 20 March 1986. The

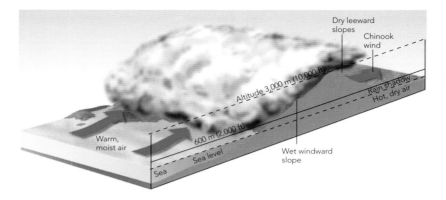

Dry leeward slopes

Chinook wind

Altitude 3,000 m (10,000 ft)

Rain shadow
Hot, dry air

600 m (2,000 ft)

Sea level

Sea

Warm, moist air

Wet windward slope

▲ **The rain shadow effect** in the Rocky Mountains. Warm moist air blowing in from the ocean rises when it meets the mountains. As the moist air rises, it cools and vapor condenses into droplets, forming clouds. Droplets within the clouds merge and when they get too heavy they fall as rain on the mountain slopes and summit. Warm dry air then descends on the leeward slopes. The lee side of the mountain range is known as a rain shadow.

world record highest wind speed measured on a mountain—at the summit of Mount Washington, in New Hampshire, USA—is 372 km/h (231 mph).

In recent times it has become fashionable among walkers, climbers and skiers to talk about wind chill or the wind chill factor. Wind chill relates to exposed flesh and the concept comes from some early experiments performed in Antarctica designed to estimate the risks of frostbite. Tables presenting wind chill equivalent temperatures provide a measure of the loss of heat from exposed skin, but do not take into account modern clothing which has high wind-blocking and insulating properties. Where temperatures are above freezing such tables can be misleading. For example, an air temperature of 4°C (39°F) and wind speed of 40 km/h (25 mph) would produce a wind chill of –11°C (12°F) on exposed skin. However, snow around you would be thawing as the air temperature is above freezing. Wind chill is therefore a feeling we have on our exposed skin, and not an actual meteorological measurement.

Differential heating of mountains and valleys in calm, clear settled weather can cause mountain and valley winds to blow. During the morning, valley sides are heated by the Sun, especially if they are steep and south facing (in the northern hemisphere) and lack vegetation cover. The air in contact with these slopes will heat, expand and rise—creating a pressure gradient. By early afternoon at the time of maximum heating, a strong uphill or anabatic wind will blow up the valley and up the valley sides. These are the ideal conditions for paragliders who are a common sight in steep Alpine valleys in summer. Sometimes, rapid rising can cause the unstable air to cool and clouds to form, in which case

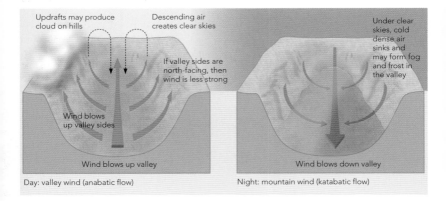

Updrafts may produce cloud on hills

Descending air creates clear skies

If valley sides are north-facing, then wind is less strong

Under clear skies, cold dense air sinks and may form fog and frost in the valley

Wind blows up valley sides

Wind blows up valley

Wind blows down valley

Day: valley wind (anabatic flow)

Night: mountain wind (katabatic flow)

thunderstorms are a possibility. During the clear evening, the valley loses heat through radiation. The surrounding air then cools and becomes more dense so, under gravity, the air begins to drain down the slope in what is called a mountain or katabatic wind. This gives rise to a temperature inversion and if the air is moist enough it may create a dense fog.

In summary, mountains modify the regional weather pattern by modifying winds, usually increasing average and maximum wind speeds; they increase precipitation totals; they attract and hold snow for longer, particularly on north-facing slopes (in the northern hemisphere); and the temperature lapse rate means that temperatures on mountains are cooler. The combination of higher winds and lower temperatures can—through the wind chill factor—be a significant hazard to anyone who frequents the mountains without adequate windproof and insulating clothing.

▲ *Mountain and valley winds* *can change direction during a 24-hour period. During the day, as the valley sides heat up, the air around them rises, creating updrafts and drawing air in along the valley. As the land cools during the night the reverse can occur. The air becomes increasingly dense and sinks creating a wind that blows back down the valley.*

The Flora of Mountain Zones

PLANT ADAPTATIONS TO ALTITUDE

Overall, the high mountain or montane zone is characterized by its severe, arctic-type environment, with low temperatures, short growing seasons and prevalence of strong winds. At high altitudes, broadleaf deciduous trees usually give way to conifers, which persist on the upper slopes until conditions become so unfavorable that trees cannot grow. The highest altitude at which trees can survive is called the tree line. Coniferous trees or evergreens have needles and are well adapted to cold winters and short growing seasons. Needle-shaped leaves are better adapted than broadleaves because less area is exposed to wind damage and loss of moisture through evaporation. The shape of conifers is also better suited to shedding snow quickly, and they are in a better position to be ready to photosynthesize as soon as conditions become suitable in spring. Furthermore conifers require fewer nutrients than broadleaf trees to survive. However, in extremely cold conditions such as are found in northern Siberia, conifers cannot maintain their live needles through the winter, and trees such as larch (*Larix* spp.) which lose their needles in winter, or broadleaf trees such as birch (*Betula* spp.) or aspen (*Populus* spp.), may take over.

▼ *Conditions in high mountain regions are not well suited to flowering plants and deciduous, broadleaved trees. The only trees that can survive at altitude are certain species of coniferous tree. These species have adapted to the high winds, nutrient-deficient soil and frequent coverings of snow.*

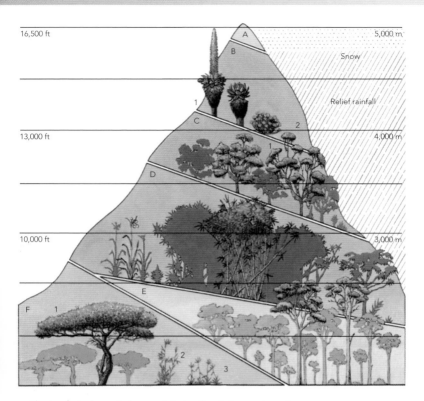

Plants of windswept places minimize the drying and cooling effects caused by exposure by adopting low growth forms which are also more likely to retain an insulating layer of snow, wind speeds at ground level being only a fraction of those even at knee height. Herbs with taproots tend to form cushions (such as moss campion) or rosettes (such as Alpine saxifrage); others may be prostrate, growing horizontally over the ground surface (purple saxifrage) or creeping (three-leaved rush). Woody plants form prostrate mats (dwarf willow, mountain avens). These adaptations restrict montane plants to Arctic-Alpine environments—they cannot grow tall enough to compete elsewhere, and many can also be killed by high summer temperatures. Soil instability from frost heaving and downhill movements is another hazard.

Cold, wet, windy and unstable conditions make the process of pollination and seed formation difficult. For these reasons, true mountain plants are perennials. This means that they do not have to produce viable seeds every year in order

◄ *An equatorial mountain* has several vegetation zones. At its summit (*A*), it is too cold for anything to grow, while lower down lies the Afro-Alpine region (*B*), where plants such as giant lobelia [1] and senecio [2] can survive the cold. Beneath this layer is the sub-Alpine moorland region (*C*), where larger plants such as shrublike tree heaths [1] can take root. The bamboo belt (*D*), as it approaches its lower reaches at about 2,500m (8,500 ft), gives way to montane forest (*E*). Beneath the montane belt, savanna (*F*), usually characterized by acacia trees [1], red oat [2] and Bermuda grasses [3], begins.

to survive. Many have developed vegetative reproduction methods to supplement reproduction by seed. Some plants such as the Alpine meadow grass (*Poa alpina*) produce small plantlets in their flower heads, so that flowers are rarely formed. The climatic conditions that make pollination and seed production difficult become progressively more severe with increasing altitude—the climatic gradient is from lowland conditions at the foot of mountains to severe montane conditions at the top.

The montane zone, nonetheless, offers plants a wide range of possible habitats, ranging from stable rock faces to constantly-moving gravel screes. The latter, surprisingly, supports quite a few plant species, such as the parsley fern and wavy hair grass. Dry cliffs harbor only a few plants, but moist, north-facing cliffs and the numerous, inaccessible ledges safely out of the reach of grazing animals are homes for a high proportion of the montane flora. The highest altitudes reached by vascular plants (advanced plants having strands of conducting tissue) are located not in the tropics, as one might expect, but at latitudes of 20–30° in the Himalayas and Andes where they exist at a height of 5,800–6,100 m (19,000–20,000 ft).

PLANTS OF WET AND BOGGY AREAS

Where drainage is poor and water frequently collects, peat tends to accumulate and bogs form. Most trees do not grow well, though some species such as alder (*Alnus* spp.) can thrive. Most species present in wet areas are confined to such places, for while a few of the common upland heath and grassland species are found living in these bogs, many cannot tolerate the waterlogged and usually acid soils.

Perhaps the most familiar plants of bogs are the hummock-forming Sphagnum moss species, cotton grasses (*Eriophorim* spp.) and the yellow-flowered bog asphodel (*Narthecium ossifragum*). Also present are a few more widespread moorland plants: heather (*Vaccinium* spp., *Erica* spp.), purple moor-grass (*Molinia caerulea*) and deer-grass.

A fascinating group of plants often found growing on bogs are those that trap insects. Bog soils are extremely low in plant-available nitrogen and so some groups of plants, including the sundew (*Drosera rotundifolia*), have become insectivorous. They attract flies and invertebrates to the sticky surface of their leaves, which then snap shut, trapping the insect. Hairs on the leaves then secrete digestive enzymes, digestion of an insect normally requiring three to five days.

TREES AND FORESTS

The coldest of the biotic regions (those that relate to living organisms) is the tundra. Found in the regions below the Arctic ice caps, stretching from North America across to Siberia, tundra is desert-like on account of the low precipitation levels. Alpine tundra is located above the tree line of high mountain areas. It is as a result generally treeless, with only low-lying vegetation, although small trees growing to a mere 2 cm (0.8 in) include dwarf willow and birch. Such prostrate growth is an adaptation to the high winds and cold found at higher altitudes.

South of the Arctic tundra, boreal coniferous forest extends almost without a break across countries from northern Europe to North America that possess cold winters and moist climates. Ninety percent of the coniferous trees dominating the mountains of the northern hemisphere belong to only three genera: pine (*Pinus* spp.), spruce (*Picea* spp.) and fir (*Abies* spp.).

In the broadleaf deciduous forest of the northern hemisphere—mainly found in western Europe, eastern Asia and eastern USA—the major genera are oak (*Quercus* spp.), maple (*Acer* spp.), beech (*Fagus* spp.), elm (*Ulmus* spp.),

▲ *High-altitude regions of tundra, such as can be found in certain areas of Siberia, are characterized by low-lying vegetation. A complete absence of trees is due primarily to the frequent high winds, severe cold and lack of rainfall.*

hickory (*Carya* spp.), chestnut (*Castanea* spp.) and birch (*Betula* spp.). Conifers dominate the wet Cascade mountains in the USA and the Atlas mountains in north Africa, and are found at the upper timber line of many other northern-hemisphere mountains.

Deciduous broad evergreen forest, which dominates much of the Himalaya region, has Rhododendron forest (*Rhododendron* spp.) as its dominant tree.

Tropical mountain forests are very different from those of more northerly regions. They consist of broadleaf evergreen and coniferous trees with rounded, umbrella-shaped crowns and relatively luxuriant foliage. Many species occur, flowering almost continuously throughout the year. In some areas with both a wet and a dry season, broadleaf trees will lose their leaves. A study on Mount Maquiling in the Philippines showed that the height of the tallest trees decreased from 36 m (118 ft) at an altitude of 45 m (150 ft) to only 13 m (43 ft) at 1,020 m (3,350 ft) in the cloud forest. In addition, the number of species decreased from 92 to 21, while the leaf size also decreased.

Bamboo forests are a distinctive plant community on the mountains of East Africa. Where conditions are dry, such as on the isolated peaks of Kilimanjaro, Kenya and Ruwenzori, in the mountains of the Sahara in Africa, or on the western side of the Andes, they do not support a forest but instead have scattered xerophytic (adapted to drought) trees and shrubs. The lack of cloud and prolonged periods of sunshine, however, ensure that pine forests can grow up to 4,000 m (13,000 ft) in central Mexico; in western Bolivia, a stunted Polylepis forest (*Polylepis tomentella*) exists at 4,800 m (15,700 ft), thought to be the highest forest in the world. In Australia, the Snow gim (*Eucalyptus niphophila*) can regenerate from underground organs after its crown has been destroyed by fire.

The cool temperate rain forest of New Zealand is dominated by the mighty Kauri tree (*Agathis australis*).

THE COMMON TREES OF THE MOUNTAINS

Trees that grow in the mountains are often the same species that can be seen lower in the valleys, though they will have adapted to mountain life by growing small, by having needles instead of leaves, and thick waxy layers on their leaves to help to conserve water, and by having extensive spreading root systems to give them better support and moisture-gathering ability in thin dry soils.

Common alder (*Alnus glutinosa*) A small spreading and sometimes multitrunked tree with a broad crown, ascending branches which spread in older trees and a gray-brown bark fissured into squarish plates. Young twigs feel sticky, older twigs have raised orange lenticels. Leaves are rounded with a notched apex. Purple male catkins appear in winter, with separate reddish cone-like female catkins on the same tree. They form hard green, later woody, cones with papery winged seeds. Frequently found growing by water throughout Europe.

Alder

Aspen (*Populus tremula*) Medium tree to 20 m (65 ft), suckering and forming dense stands. Smooth gray-green bark has diamond-shaped hollows. Leaves diamond-shaped and thin on flattened stalks, fluttering freely in light breeze, but leaves on suckers are deeply lobed. Male and female catkins, up to 8 cm (3 in) long, borne on separate trees. Common and widespread in damp areas.

Aspen

Common ash (*Fraxinus excelsior*) Deciduous tree up to 40 m (130 ft) high with an open, domed crown. Pale gray bark, smooth on young trees, becoming ridged and fissured when old. Buds large and sooty-black. Pinnate leaves have 7–13 toothed leaflets. Flowers can be male, female or both, appearing before leaves, stamens purplish. Clusters of green-brown "keys" develop in late summer. A common species throughout Europe, and frequently cultivated, especially on damp base-rich soils.

Common hawthorn or **Quickthorn** (*Crataegus monogyna*) Spiny, multistemmed shrub or small tree up to 10 m (35 ft) with deeply lobed leaves and flat-topped clusters of fragrant white flowers. Bunches of red berries form in fall. Common and widespread, often planted in upland areas where it may appear wind-blown.

Common hazel (*Corylus avellana*) Multistemmed shrub with straggling stems, gray-brown bark and pores on twigs. Leaves broad, toothed and pointed at tip. Male catkins long and yellow, appearing early in spring, female flowers small and red, followed by clusters

Common hawthorn

of woody nuts in papery toothed cups. Common as coppice in hedgerows and as undershrub in woods throughout Europe, and frequently planted in gardens.

Common Larch (*Larix decidua*) Deciduous cone-shaped tree up to 50 m (160 ft) with whorled branches and fissured, brownish barks shed in small plates. Light green pointed needles up to 3 cm (1 in), ridged and borne in tufts. Small yellow male cones sit on twigs, small red female cones ripen to brown woody cones persisting on old twigs. Common and widespread, introduced into many areas.

Dwarf or **least willow** (*Salix herbacea*) Creeping shrub growing no higher than 2 cm (0.8 in). Most of its branching is underground or rhizomatous. Round and shiny leaves have prominent veins and rounded teeth. Found only at high altitudes 1,700–3,000 m (5,500–10,000 ft), in short grass, bare or stony ground. Its distribution covers the European Alps, central Apennines, Pyrenees, Carpathians, Balkans, Scotland, Greenland and North America.

Lodgepole Pine (*Pinus contorta*) A variable tree, 3–30 m (10–100 ft) tall, with short contorted branches; young trees have broad bushy base and vigorous central shoot; old trees usually tall and narrow. Shoots are smooth, green in the first year, orange-brown and striped white in the second year. Needles are sharply pointed, dense on young shoots, spreading on older shoots, paired and twisted. Male cones in dense whorls, female cones in clusters of 2–4, near tip of the shoot. Widely planted for timber on peatlands and moors throughout much of central and northwestern Europe.

Monkey puzzle/Chile pine (*Araucaria arauecana*) Very tall evergreen tree, up to 29 m (95 ft) high, with a cylindrical trunk and tough gray wrinkled bark, and a domed outline. The branches are horizontal or slightly drooping and the scale-like leaves are arranged spirally. Separate male and female cones are produced. Found in the high mountains of Chile and Argentina.

Common hazel

Common larch

Monkey puzzle

49

Mountain ash (*Eucalyptus regnans*) One of the tallest trees in the world, up to 90 m (295 ft) high with the first branches up to 30 m (100 ft) up the pale gray trunk. The bark peels in ribbons on the branches. Small pear-shaped fruits are borne among the long, stalked leaves. Prefers well-drained mountain slopes in the wetter parts of Australia.

Norway spruce (*Picea abies*) Pyramidal evergreen up to 60 m (200 ft) with whorls of branches on slender unbranching trunk and rough, reddish-brown bark. Needles stiff and short, angled and arising from a woody peg which gives twigs a rough texture. Small yellowish male cones clustered at tips of twigs, oval female cones up to 18 cm (7 in) and pendulous. Common and widespread, often planted outside of range.

Oak

Oak (*Quercus* spp.) Large deciduous trees or sometimes shrubs. Leaves usually toothed or lobed, though sometimes entire. Bright yellow-green male and female wind-pollinated catkins appear in spring. The familiar acorns form in late summer, the fertile seed sitting in a woody cup which may be stalked or sessile. Common and widespread across Europe.

Norway spruce

Rhododendron (*Rhodendron* spp.) Shrub that adapts its environment to preclude competition from other species by blocking out light and altering the soil; over 900 species. Dominant on acid sandy or dry peaty soils. Has large sticky buds, dark-green leaves and large brightly colored flowers in spring and summer. In the Himalayas Rhododendron trees are favored as fuelwood. Large stands are found at 600–2,400 m (2,000–8,000 ft), at the same altitudes as the summer grazing grounds for sheep and goats.

Rowan

Rowan or **Mountain ash** (*Sorbus aucuparia*) A medium-sized tree up to 20 m (65 ft) high with a domed crown. The smooth bark is silvery-gray and the ascending branches bear twigs which are grayish or purplish, hairy at first, becoming smooth later, with purple, downy buds The pinnate leaves have leaflets in 5–8 pairs; heads of small creamy-white flowers open in summer followed by clusters of bright red fleshy fruits. It occurs in much of Europe and is commonly planted as a street tree or garden ornamental.

Scots pine (*Pinus sylvestris*) Evergreen tree up to 40 m (130 ft) with a domed crown, fissured, reddish or gray-brown bark and whorls of branches. Resinous buds give rise to long, paired blue-green twisted needles. Male cones are yellow, clustered on first-year old twigs, female cones grow on tips of twigs, becoming woody in third year. Very widespread and common, especially on poor soils and in upland areas.

Scots pine

Silver birch (*Betula pendula*) A slender fast-growing deciduous tree with a tapering crown and trailing branches when mature. Twigs are thin and smooth with white resin glands and pointed buds. Mature trees have a thick, fissured bark near the base, but smooth, peeling white bark higher up. The pointed leaves have toothed margins and hairless petioles. In early spring male catkins grow at the tips of twigs and female catkins appear in leaf axils; papery, winged seeds form in them in the summer. Widespread and common, except in the far north and far south.

Silver birch

Sitka spruce

Sitka spruce (*Picea sitchensis*) Slender conical tree up to 60 m (200 ft) with stout buttressed trunk and grayish-brown scaly bark when mature. Ascending branches bear hairless side shoots; needles are 3 cm (1 in) long, bright blue-green with a ridge above and two pale bands below. Female cones are yellowish at first becoming woody, growing to 9 cm (3.5 in) and covered with shiny scales. Native of western North America, commonly planted as a timber tree or for ornament in northwestern Europe and parts of central Europe.

THE COMMONER MOUNTAIN SHRUBS AND PLANTS

Bell heather

Bell heather (*Erica cinerea*) Generally confined to the driest parts of heathland, and widespread throughout northern Europe up to about 700 m (2,300 ft). Does not form the dense uniform stands characteristic of common or ling heather, but occurs as neat compact plants, the stems more slender and less woody. Red-purple flowers appear in May and can last until the end of September.

Bilberry or blueberry, whortleberry, huckleberry (*Vaccinium myrtillus*) Perennial broad-leafed shrub belonging to the heath family; closely related to the North American blueberry. Grows abundantly in heathy, mountainous districts up to 1,500 m (5,000 ft) throughout Europe. Plants commonly reach 0.5 m (1.5 ft), but can extend to 1 m (3 ft). Prefers woodland, peat bogs or fens. Blue or black edible berries produced in late summer and fall.

Bilberry

Bridal heath (*Erica bauera*) Large heather species with tall spikes of white or pink-tipped white flowers, found on poor sandy soils in drier areas. Several similar species occur. Its tubular, slightly curved flowers ensure that visiting insects, usually small bees, collect the pollen. Mountain slopes in South Africa.

Chilean firebush (*Embothrium coccineum*) Shrub or small tree with spear-shaped leaves up to 20 cm (8 in) long and purple-gray flaking bark. The striking red flowers, pollinated by hummingbirds, are 10 cm (4 in) long and divided at the tip. Found on mountain slopes in South America and introduced elsewhere for its colorful flowers.

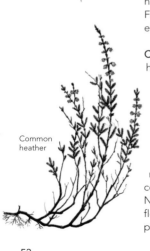

Common heather

Common or **ling heather** (*Calluna vulgaris*) Most common heather species in the UK. Carpet-forming shrub with small leaves on a shrubby stem, growing to 0.6 m (2 ft) high. Bears pale pink-purple or white flowers. Dominates extensive tracts of land on hills, moors, bogs, open woods, even fixed dunes. Widespread throughout northern Europe up to about 700 m (2,300 ft), and introduced to North America.

Crowberry (*Empetrum nigrum*) Prostrate mat-forming or more erect evergreen shrub with needlelike oval leaves, common in moors and bogs throughout northern Europe, North America and into the Arctic. Pink six-petalled small flowers appear April–June; berries produced are green then pink, turning purple then black in the fall. The tasteless raw berries are used in cooking combined with other berries such as the blueberry.

Helichrysum meyeri-johannis Low-growing perennial with everlasting, composite flowers, heads of about five being held erect on a tough stem up to 15 cm (6 in) tall. Red petallike bracts of a papery texture surround tiny yellow florets; grayish-green leaves form a basal rosette. Large colonies may form in some dry African mountain slopes. Many similar Helichrysum species occur in other mountain ranges.

Juniper

Hesperantha schelpeana Attractive small crocus-like, bulbous plant, up to 15 cm (6 in) tall, usually found growing in small clusters on open stony ground on high mountain slopes. Several species occur and they show a range of colors from pink to white. Leaflike bracts clasp the stems.

Juniper (*Juniperus communis*) Perennial shrub or small tree growing to 3 m (10 ft), though on high mountains adopts a prostrate growth form. Prefers stony pastures and woods. Common throughout Europe, Algeria, northern and western Asia to the Himalayas and in North America, growing at altitudes of up to 2,400 m (7,870 ft). Produces yellow flowers, and green berrylike fruits become blue-black in their second year. An important spice, also used in the production of gin and as a medical remedy.

King protea (*Protea cynaroides*) Woody shrub up to 2 m (6.5 ft) high with large glossy dark green leaves and many flower heads up to 30 cm (12 in) in diameter. The colorful bracts can vary from white to deep crimson and remain open for weeks. Common in mountains of South Africa.

Puya (*Puya alpestris*) A dense crown of silvery green 50 cm–(20 in–) long leaves is topped by a flower spike 1–2 m (3–6.5 ft) tall bearing large clusters of triangular blossoms up to 5 cm (2 in) across; the blue-green flowers have striking orange anthers. The whole plant may branch many times to form large striking clusters. Mountains of South America.

Small-leaved boronia (*Boronia microphylla*) Low shrub, up to 50 cm (20 in) tall, with small oval, aromatic leaves; oil-glands release perfume when crushed. Showy pink flowers are borne in early summer and many similar species occur in the mountain regions of Australia where there are poor, well-drained rocky soils.

King protea

53

Waratah (*Telopea speciosissima*) Stout shrub up to 4 m (13 ft) tall, with 25 cm–(10 in–) long green leathery leaves, which bears striking red flowers; they are actually made up of clusters of smaller flowers surrounded by bright red petallike bracts. Pollinated by birds and resistant to fires, which are are a fairly regular occurrence on its habitat on the mountain slopes of New South Wales, Australia.

Waratah

HERBACEOUS FLOWERING PLANTS

Alpine aster (*Aster alpinus*) Perennial member of the composite family growing 5–20 cm (2–8 in) in mountain grassland, stony pastures and on scree; prefers alkaline conditions, and is usually found at 1,400–3,200 m (4,600–10,500 ft). The flowers, ranging in color from violet through blue to pink and white, are produced July–August. Common throughout the northern hemisphere.

Alpine aster

Alpine avens (*Geum montanum*) Perennial member of the rose family. Grows 5–30 cm (2–12 in) high in mountain grassland, preferring moist acid humus-rich soils. Its yellow flowers are produced in June–August. It is common throughout the European Alps, Pyrenees and Corsica; usually found at an altitude of 600–2,700 m (2,000–9,000 ft).

Alpine clover (*Trifolium alpinum*) Member of the pea family growing 5–15 cm (2–6 in) high in mountain grassland. It prefers acid-rich soils and is usually found at 1,200–3,200 m (3,900–10,500 ft); common throughout the European Alps, Apennines and Pyrenees. Purple, reddish purple and pink flowers are borne between June–August.

Alpine forget-me-not

Alpine forget-me-not (*Myosotis alpestris*) Small delicate plant that grows at altitudes of 1,400–2,600 m (4,600–8,500 ft), in mountain grassland, on stony pasture, rocky ground and scree; 5–20 cm (2–8 in) in height. Produces blue, azure and dark azure flowers from April–August. Common throughout the European Alps, Apennines, Pyrenees and Balkans; in the UK it is local to northern England and the Scottish Highlands.

Alpine lady's mantle (*Alchemilla alpina*) Perennial member of the rose family grows 15–25 cm (6–10 in) high in mountain grassland; prefers neutral to acid soils and is usually found at 1,300–2,500 m (4,300–8,200 ft). Its yellow flowers are produced in June–August. It is common in northern Europe, but within the UK is mainly confined to the highland regions of Scotland.

Alpine pasqueflower (*Pulsatilla alpine*) Perennial member of the buttercup family growing 15–30 cm (6–12 in) in height in mountain grassland, usually at altitudes of 1,400–3,000 m (4,600–10,000 ft). It prefers alkaline soils. White flowers are produced from June–August. It is common throughout the European Alps.

▼ *During the summer months, many lower-lying areas of Alpine regions are home to an abundant variety of flowering plants.*

Arnica

Arnica (*Arnica montana*) Member of the composite family found in mountain grassland, meadows, woods, even wet peaty areas and fens; prefers acid soils. Growing 20–60 cm (8–25 in) tall, it is usually found at 200–2,900 m (660– 9,500 ft). Its yellow and orangey-yellow flowers are produced in June–August. Common throughout the European Alps, the UK, the Carpathians and Apennines.

Biting stonecrop or **Wallpepper** (*Sedum acre*) Small but striking plant which grows to a height of 5–10 cm (2–4 in) on stony ground and rocks; usually found up to 2,400 m (8,000 ft). Between June–August it produces yellow five-petalled flowers. Common throughout the European Alps, northern Asia, North America and north Africa.

Bog asphodel (*Narthecium ossifragum*) As its name suggests, this perennial is limited to bogs and wet heaths. Its leaves are sword-shaped, and its starlike six-petalled flowers are orange-yellow, growing on leafless stems in July–August. Grows to 20 cm (8 in), and found throughout much of the UK up to altitudes of 1,000 m (3,300 ft), as well as in north and western Europe, extending east to southeastern Sweden and south to northern Portugal.

Bracken

Bracken (*Pteridium aquilinum*) Plant favoring well-drained hillsides, shaded forests, grasslands and open sunny areas. Can grow at any altitude up to 3,300 m (10,800 ft), spreading vigorously by deep rhizomes. Its triangular fronds grow to 30–100 cm (12–40 in), and die back in winter (unlike other lacy ferns). Bracken is carcinogenic, avoided by grazing animals; to improve upland pastures effort is put into its eradication.

Chamois ragwort (*Senecio doronicum*) Member of the composite family found in mountain grassland, meadows, stony pastures, even on scree. Prefers alkaline or neutral soils, growing 20–50 cm (8–20 in) tall, usually at altitudes of 1,500–3,200 m (4,900–10,500 ft). Yellow and orangey-yellow flowers appear from July–September. Common throughout the European Alps, southern Europe, Balkans, Carpathians and northern and central Apennines.

Common bird's foot

Common bird's foot trefoil (*Lotus corniculatus*) Small and very common plant growing 10–40 cm (4–16 in) high on stony ground and in meadows; usually found up to 2,500 m (8,200 ft). Yellow flowers are borne between April–September. It is very common throughout Europe, northern Asia, north Africa, Japan and Australia.

Common cotton grass (*Eriophorum angustifolium*) Plant varying in height from between 20–60 cm (8–24 in), with distinctive white cotton-like flower heads appearing from April–August. Characteristic of wet areas at altitudes of 200–2,600 m (660–8,500 ft). Its distribution includes European mountains, Siberia, Caucasus, North America, Greenland and South Africa.

Common sundew (*Drosera rotundifolia*) Insectivorous plant that is only found in acid wet heaths, moors and sphagnum bogs. It produces small white five-petalled flowers on long stems (up to 10 cm/4 in high) in June–August. The sticky leaves trap insects, which the plant uses to supplement its nitrogen intake.

Sundew

Creeping azalea (*Loiseleuria procumbens*) Member of the heather family growing 5–20 cm (2–8 in) tall on scree, gravelly areas and mountain pastures; usually found at 1,500–3,100 m (5,000–10,200 ft). Pink, red and pale pink flowers are produced in June–August. It is common throughout the European Alps, Pyrenees, the UK, Lapland, Iceland, Carpathians, Asia, Arctic America and Greenland.

Early purple orchid (*Orchis mascula*) Member of the orchid family, which grows 15–50 cm (6–20 in) high in meadows or woodland; usually found up to 2,100 m (7,000 ft). Flowers appearing June–August are a range of colors from purple to red. Common throughout central and southern European, Sardinia, central Russia, western Asia, Caucasus, Iran, Urals and north Africa.

Early purple orchid

Fairy's thimble (*Campanula cochlearifolia*) Delicate plant, 5–15 cm (2–6 in) in height, growing on scree, gravelly areas, moraines and stony pastures; usually found at 1,300–3,500 m (4,300–11,000 ft). Violet, azure, lilac and white flowers are produced from June–August. It is common throughout the European Alps, Pyrenees, northern and central Apennines, Carpathians and Balkans.

Fragrant orchid (*Gymnadenia conopsea*) Member of the orchid family; grows 25–60 cm (10–24 in) tall in mountain grassland, meadows, woods, even wet peaty areas. Usually found at 200–2,500 m (660–8,200 ft). Flowers produced May–August range in color from pink through to violet. Common throughout Europe, Apennines, the UK, Caucasus, western Asia, northern Iran, Asia, Siberia, northern China, Korea, Japan and Manchuria.

Fairy's thimble

Glacier crowfoot (*Ranunculus glacialis*) Perennial member of the buttercup family, growing 5–15 cm (2–6 in) high on moraines and scree; usually found at 2,300–4,500 m (7,500–15,000 ft). Its white, pink, purple and reddish-brown flowers are produced in July–August. It is common throughout the European Alps, Scandinavia, Iceland, Svalbard and Alaska.

Globeflower (*Trollius europaeus*) Member of the buttercup family which grows 10–60 cm (4–24 in) tall; found in meadows and mountain pasture at altitudes of 900–2,000 m (3,000–6,500 ft). Its yellow flowers appear from May–August. Common throughout the Alps, northern and central Apennines, the UK, Europe, Carpathians, Caucasus, even the arctic coasts of Russia.

Great yellow gentian (*Gentiana lutea*) Member of the gentian family which grows in mountain grassland, meadows and stony pastures. Preferring acid humus soils, it is up to

▼ **An Alpine meadow**
in the Grand Paradiso National Park, Italy, covered with mountain buttercups. Even at high altitude the summer months can be so dry that artificial watering is necessary.

1.5 m (5 ft) in height and usually found at 300–2,600 m (1,000–8,500 ft). Produces yellow flowers between June–August. It is common throughout the European Alps, Sardinia, Spain, the Balkans, Carpathians and Apennines.

Hepatica (*Hepatica nobilis*) Member of the buttercup family growing 5–15 cm (2–6 in) high, in woods up to 2,000 m (6,500 ft) in altitude. Violet, blue, pink and white flowers are borne in March–May. It is common throughout Europe, Siberia, Japan and North America.

Great yellow gentian

Moss campion (*Silene acaulis*) Small plant growing in carpets less than 5 cm (2 in) tall which is found in mountain pastures, at 1,900–3,200 m (6,200–10,500 ft). It produces small pink and purplish-red flowers from June–August. Common throughout the European Alps, Arctic Europe (Svalbard, Lapland), Iceland, Pyrenees, Carpathians, Asia, Greenland and North America.

Mountain avens (*Dryas octopetala*) Low creeping perennial which grows in carpets, with composite flowers that are 10–15 cm (4–6 in) high. Found up to 1,500 m (5,000 ft), in tundra, rocky pastures and on scree. Its white flowers are produced from May–July. It is common throughout Europe and the Arctic (Greenland, Svalbard).

Hepatica

Mountain buttercup (*Ranunculus montanus*) Member of the buttercup family growing 15–30 cm (6–12 in) in height, in mountain grassland and on scree; usually found at 1,800–3,000 m. It produces yellow flowers between June–August. Common throughout the European Alps.

Mountain cornflower (*Centaurea triumfetti*) Member of the composite family that grows in meadows, woods, mountain grassland and rocky ground. Its height is 20–60 cm; usually found at 800–2,100 m (6,000–6,900 ft). It produces azure, blue, violet and purplish-red flowers in June–July. Common throughout the European Alps, Apennines, Pyrenees, Carpathians, Balkans, western Asia, Caucasus and north Africa.

Mountain avens

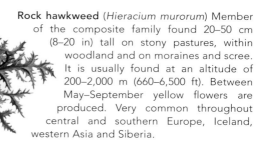

Stemless
carline

Rock hawkweed (*Hieracium murorum*) Member of the composite family found 20–50 cm (8–20 in) tall on stony pastures, within woodland and on moraines and scree. It is usually found at an altitude of 200–2,000 m (660–6,500 ft). Between May–September yellow flowers are produced. Very common throughout central and southern Europe, Iceland, western Asia and Siberia.

Stemless carline thistle (*Carlina acaulis*) Perennial member of the composite family growing 10–30 cm (4–12 in) high on mountain grassland and woodland; usually found at 800–2,100 m (2,600–6,900 ft). It bears white, purple and brownish-purple rosettes from July–September. Common throughout European Alps and Russia.

Trumpet gentian (*Gentiana acaulis*) Low-growing member of the gentian family which reaches 5–10 cm (2–4 in) in height. Found on mountain grassland and stony pasture, usually at 800–3,100 m (2,600–10,200 ft). Dark blue, dark azure and blue trumpet-shaped flowers are produced in May–August. It is common throughout the European Alps, Apennines, Pyrenees, Balkans and Carpathians.

Viper's-bugloss (*Echium vulgare*) Striking purple, upright plant which is 30–90 cm (12–36 in) tall. Widespread on stony pastures and rocky ground, and usually found at an altitude of up to 2,200 m (7,200 ft). Blue, violet blue, violet and pink flowers are produced between June–September. It is common throughout Europe, western Asia, western Siberia, north Africa and North America.

GRASSES, SEDGES AND RUSHES

Viper's-
bugloss

Grasses form the largest group of plants likely to be encountered in the mountains. They have long, narrow, parallel-veined leaves, hollow, rounded stems and small flowers. Sedges are grasslike, but their stems are solid, often triangular; leaves wrap around the stem. Rushes are very similar, but with stems that are solid or pithy, not triangular.

Heath rush (*Juncus squarrosus*) Grows in dense tufts, 15–50 cm (6–20 in) high; easily recognized by the rosette of leaves strongly bent back against the ground and the straight, tough flowering stem in the center. It flowers between May–July.

Common on acid soils on moorland heaths and bogs, especially where sheep grazing is heavy.

Mat grass (*Nardus stricta*) Grass 10–40 cm (4–16 in) tall that is common on heaths, moors and hill grassland. Sheep prefer not to eat the grass since it becomes hard and fibrous through the season; it therefore dominates hill pasture. The small, hard tufts may be found uprooted and discarded on such areas. Flowers appear from June–August.

Mountain sedge (*Carex montana*) Perennial with thick mat-forming rhizomes, growing in rough grassland usually on limestone. Its height is 10–40 cm (4–16 in); its leaves are pale green. Flowers are produced in May, and fruits from May–June.

Purple moor-grass (*Molinia caerulea*) Perennial that forms tufts or tussocks; has a height range of 15–120 cm (6–50 in). Common, and often dominant, on damp moors, heaths and fens. It flowers July–September, the flower head usually dark purple, but may be pinkish, yellowish or green.

Sheep's fescue (*Festuca ovina*) Grows in thick tufts, to a height of 5–60 cm (2–24 in); flowers from May–July. Common on the poor soils of hills and moorland, it grows abundantly on pastures where it is a valuable part of the diet of sheep.

MOSSES
Mosses have stems and leaves but no roots, only modified stems forming rootlike structures known as rhizoids. Mosses reproduce by producing spores in capsules, which may, once on the ground, develop into new plants.

Alpine clubmoss (*Diphasiastrum alpinum*) Stems are four-sided and branched, some producing small yellow cones, which contain spores. Found on moors and grassland in the mountains of Scotland, north England, Wales and Ireland. Spores are ripe between June–August.

Gray woolly hair moss

Gray woolly hair moss (*Racomitrium lanuginosum*) Plants are up to about 15 cm (6 in) high, with branching stems and hair-pointed leaves often curved in one direction. The moss forms a distinctive mountain-top community known as "racomitrium heath" where it grows in extensive grayish mats. Common in hill and mountain districts on acid rock and peat.

Sphagnim auriculatum

Polytrichum commune Common moss forming dark green tufts in wet heaths, bogs and moorland and by streams in woodland. Its height is 2–40 cm (0.8–16 in). Capsules are often found in summer and are four-sided with yellowish hairy caps when young.

Sphagnum auriculatum Grows in large masses, with shoots up to about 20 cm (8 in), generally green but often tinged orange or reddish-brown. Stems are dark brown or black. Long, pointed branches may be curved. Fruit capsules are occasionally produced in summer. Several variations on this species, and other Sphagnum species, exist, but *Sphagnum auriculatum* is the most prevalent, seen in moors, bogs, damp woods, around pools and in acid flushes.

LICHENS

Lichens are pioneer plants that have the ability to survive in some of the harshest conditions. They do not even need soil but obtain nutrients from rain and from the bare rock surfaces. These they colonize by secreting chemicals called enzymes, which help to break up and weather the rock, which in turn speeds up the release of vital nutrients. The body of the lichen is a fungus, but it also harbors an algae that can photosynthesize and make carbohydrates. Careful observation will allow lichens to be discovered on most apparently bare rock surfaces. There are thousands of species.

Cladonia floerkeana

Cladonia floerkeana The basal scales form scattered patches which are small and greenish-gray. Stalks are gray and simple or sparsely branched. They bear larger attractive scarlet spore-producing bodies at the tips, resembling matchsticks. Height range is 2–5 cm (0.8–2 in). Common on the peaty soil of moors and heaths.

Rhizocarpon geographicum Yellowish-green species that obtains its name "geographicum" because colonies close together are separated by black margins, giving the impression of countries on a map. Common on hard acid rocks and walls in mountain areas.

The Fauna of Mountain Zones

▼ *The mountain lion (puma or cougar to give it its other names) is a solitary animal that preys on other mountain mammals and birds, and, unusually for a big cat, is often active during the day. Found in wide-ranging habitats, including mountain regions up to a height of around 3,000 m (10,000 ft), male adults can grow up to almost 2.5 m (8 ft).*

Birds and insects are relatively easy to see during a walk in the mountains, but mammals are not. This is mainly because, unlike birds, mammals cannot easily escape danger, so the strategy most mammals adopt is one of danger avoidance. Many rely on the protection of the dark, being nocturnal or crepuscular (active only at dawn or dusk), resting or sleeping in the safety of their dens, nests or other cover by day. Others are protected by their camouflage fur patterns which resemble their environment. The stoat and mountain hare, for example, live in areas that regularly have snowy winters, and so change for protection into a white coat each fall. Other mammals stand absolutely still, or lie motionless on the ground, in order to make their camouflage most effective. They jump from danger only at the last moment. Other species such as deer and musk ox live in herds, working on the principle of safety in numbers, hoping to confuse an attacking predator such as a wolf.

The following is a simple guide to the most common and widespread mammals, birds, reptiles and insects likely to be encountered in the mountain environment.

▲ *The Himalayan Alpine zone* extends near to the summit of Mount Everest. Animals are limited in numbers and range by availability of food. At 5,000 m (16,500 ft), Alpine choughs (*1*) eat insects and worms. The golden eagle (*2*) flies far in search of carrion or small animals. The Tibetan pika (*3*) feeds on small green plants, storing some for winter. The snow leopard (*4*) preys on the bharal sheep (*5*).

MAMMALS

Alpine ibex (*Capra ibex*) A brownish-gray goatlike mammal, up to 90 cm (35 in) high and 150 cm (60 in) long with a pale belly; males weigh up to 120 kg (265 lb). Both sexes have horns: long, curved and ridged in males, smaller in females. Males have small beards. Confined to high mountains over 2,000 m (6,600 ft), feeding on grasses, herbs and lichens. Lives in small herds.

Alpine marmot (*Marmota marmota*) A large ground squirrel, up to 50 cm (20 in) long, with a stout body, short tail and short legs; weighs up to 4.5 kg (10 lb) in fall. Dense fur is golden-brown above, paler below. Lives in high alpine meadows, digging burrows for hibernation. Feeds on grasses and herbs. Gives shrill whistle when alarmed. Feeds during the day, but retreats from hot sun.

Alpine shrew (*Sorex alpinus*) A dark gray shrew, 75 mm (3 in) long with a similar length tail and weighing up to 11 g (0.4 oz). The underside and feet are pale. Found in alpine meadows and rocky slopes, and often on streamsides, up to 3,300 m (11,000 ft), feeding on snails, earthworms and insects. A good climber, it uses its tail for support.

Brown bear (*Ursus arctos*) A very large bear with a stocky build, up to 2.5 m (8 ft) long and weighs up to 600 kg (1,300 lb). It has small rounded ears, no visible tail and variable brown fur. Leaves broad footprints with long clawmarks. Lives in high mountain woods and pastures above tree line, but is very rare. Hibernates in caves. Feeds on wide range of plant and animal food.

Brown bear

Chamois (*Rupicapra rupicapra*) Sheeplike mammal up to 130 cm (50 in) long and weighing up to 60 kg (130 lb). It has short horns in both sexes and dark stripes on side of head. Summer coat pale brown with dark legs and stripe on back, winter coat is dark. Lives in small herds in high, rocky mountains, feeding on grasses and herbs. Very agile and sure-footed.

Common pipistrelle bat (*Pipistrellus pipistrellus*) The smallest and commonest bat with dark brown fur, paler below. Wing span up to 24 cm (9 in), but body length only 3.5–5 cm (1.4–2 in). Emerges from cave or tree roots at dusk to feed on insects, especially moths. May form colonies of thousands in areas with good caves and plentiful food.

Elk (*Alces alces*) The largest deer, up to around 2 m (6 ft) tall and 3 m (10 ft) long, with broad palmate antlers; males weigh up to 800 kg (1,800 lb). Broad hairy muzzle has pendulous upper lip. Coat is grayish-brown, legs are paler. Feeds on shoots and twigs, herbs and pond plants, often wading in deep water. Lives in forests and lake margins.

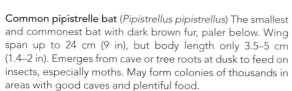

Mink

European and **American mink** (*Mustela lutreola, Mustela vison*) Resembles otter, but smaller with shorter, bushy tail. Up to 40 cm (16 in) long, plus 20-cm (8-in) tail, weighs up to 800 g (28 oz). Fur dark, but may be paler in escaped American mink. European mink has white chin and lips. Prefers wooded riverbanks, living in dens. Feeds on fish, birds, small mammals and insects.

Fox

Red Fox (*Vulpes vulpes*) Reddish-brown coat and bushy white-tipped tail, dark, pointed ears, dark paws and white throat are usual color pattern, may be more uniform in winter. Up to 90 cm long, plus 65-cm (25-in) tail, and weighs up to 10 kg (20 lb). Very widespread and sometimes common, even at high altitudes, making dens in rocky slopes. Wide range of food, but mostly small mammals, invertebrates, some fruits and seeds.

Llama

Llama (*Lama glama*) Largest of the camel family in the Andes, about 1.2 m (4 ft) tall with a thick, rough coat, often reddish-brown with white patches. The two-toed feet have thick pads for good grip. Lives in small herds over a wide range of altitudes, up to 4,000 m, feeding on low-growing shrubs. Introduced to many other countries.

Mountain hare (*Lepus timidus*) Small hare, up to 60 cm (25 in) long and weighing up to 6 kg with white coat in winter and gray-brown coat in summer; blue-gray underfur showing through on flanks. Ears and legs shorter than in brown hare. Lives in high moorlands and mountain pastures up to 1,300 m (4,300 ft), feeding on grasses, herbs, shoots of shrubs, often active at night.

Musk ox (*Ovibos moschatus*) A rare species found in arctic tundra (Greenland, Norway, Sweden) with a thick heavy coat, almost enveloping body in winter. Up to 2.5 m (8 ft) long and 1.6 m (5 ft) tall, weighing up to 400 kg (900 lb). Both sexes have large down-turned horns, males larger. Feeds on grasses, lichens, twigs. Forms small herds and makes defensive group when threatened.

Norway
lemming

Norway lemming (*Lemmus lemmus*) A small rodent with a variable fur pattern of black, yellow and brown, with no two alike. Tail short, body up to 15 cm (6 in). Lives in tundra and high alpine meadows feeding on grasses, herbs and lichens. Makes small grassy nests in burrows. In some years large numbers move over open ground. Prey to owls and hawks.

Pine martin (*Martes martes*) A dark-brown weasel-like mammal up to 55 cm (22 in) long, plus 30 cm (12 in) tail, and may weigh up to 1 kg (2 lb). It has a yellow throat patch, long legs, furry feet, bushy tail and broad ears. Lives in pine forests and upland areas, up to 2,000 m (6,500 ft), feeding on small birds and mammals, bee nests and berries. Good climber.

Red deer (*Cervus elephus*) A large deer; males up to 1.2 m (4 ft) high, females shorter, weighs up to 255 kg (560 lb). Plain reddish coat in summer and brown coat in winter. Males have large pointed, branched antlers. Both sexes have creamy rump patch. Lives in forests and upland grassland, eating grasses, shoots and bark. Form huge herds in fall.

Reindeer (*Rangifer tarandus*) Up to 1.2 m (4 ft) tall and weighs up to 150 kg (330 lb). Both sexes have branched, irregular antlers, larger in males. Dark gray-brown coat in summer molts to lighter brown in winter. Lives in high mountain and tundra areas, sometimes forests, feeding on lichens, grasses, shoots and fungi. Feet make clicking sound when walking.

Spectacled bear

Snow vole (*Microtus nivalis*) A small plump rodent up to 14 cm (5.5 in) long, plus 7-cm (2.5-in) tail, weighs up to 50 g (2 oz). A dense gray-brown coat, long whiskers and a pale medium-length tail. Lives on high mountain slopes, mainly in Alps, above tree-line, feeding on grasses shoots and fruits, hiding in small burrows.

Spectacled bear (*Tremarctos ornatus*) Large bear with a dark brown or black coat, and individually variable white face markings giving the spectacled appearance. May be up to 1.8 m (6 ft) long and weigh 140 kg (300 lb). Feeds mostly on roots, fruits and seeds, but takes small animals at times. Is found on the high slopes of the Andes, descending to sheltered areas in winter.

Spiny-tailed skink (*Egernia cunninghami*) Well-built lizard, up to 35 cm (14 in) long, with a thick spiny tail. Its mottled markings help it blend with the rocky terrain it favors in the granite highlands of southern Australia. It feeds on low-growing vegetation but will also take insects. Basks on open rocks in the early morning, but scuttles for cover when disturbed.

Elk

Red deer

Reindeer

Vicuña

Stoat (*Mustela erminea*) Long, sleek body with short black-tipped tail. Males larger than females, up to 30 cm (12 in), plus 10-cm (4-in) tail. Coat is chestnut brown above, pale below, but may turn white in winter but with black tail tip. Feeds on small rodents, rabbits, birds. Widespread, including mountain slopes and forests.

Vicuna (*Vicugna vicugna*) Small long-necked member of the camel family, about 1 m (3 ft) tall, with a beautiful cinnamon-colored coat and longer white hair on the chest. Its padded, cloven feet give a good grip on the high mountain slopes of the Andes. Very hardy, despite its delicate gentle appearance. Can run very fast to escape danger.

Weasel (*Mustela nivalis*) Small cylindrical shape up to 35 cm (14 in) long with 15-cm (16-in) tail, weighs up to 55 g (2 oz). Chestnut brown coat and white underside, furry feet and short tail. Lives in many habitats, including mountain slopes and high forests, feeding on small rodents and birds. Usually very secretive, hiding in small dens when not hunting.

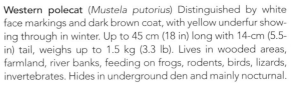

Wildcat

Western polecat (*Mustela putorius*) Distinguished by white face markings and dark brown coat, with yellow underfur showing through in winter. Up to 45 cm (18 in) long with 14-cm (5.5-in) tail, weighs up to 1.5 kg (3.3 lb). Lives in wooded areas, farmland, river banks, feeding on frogs, rodents, birds, lizards, invertebrates. Hides in underground den and mainly nocturnal.

Wildcat (*Felis sylvestris*) Resembles domestic cat but is stockier with bushy, round-tipped banded tail. Males up to 70 cm (25 in) long with tail up to 35 cm (15 in), weighs up to 8 kg (18 lb). Coat grayish-brown and striped, never mottled. Yellowish eyes and pink nose seen at close range. Lives in dense forests, moorland edges, feeding on small mammals, rabbits, birds.

Wild goat (*Capra aegagrus*) Resembles Ibex, but horns have sharper edge, females horns much smaller than males. Males up to 75 cm (30 in) tall, weighing up to 80 kg (180 lb). Males have distinct beard, both sexes have dark coat and pale underside. Lives in shrubby mountainous areas in Greek islands and mainland feeding on grasses, herbs and shrubs. Interbreeds with domestic goats.

Wolf (*Canis lupus*) Resembles large Alsatian dog but with broader head, thick neck and shallow chest. Males up to

1.5 m (5 ft) long with 50-cm (20-in) tail, weighing up to 60 kg (130 lb). Coat grayish brown with red-brown back and ruff of thicker hair on cheeks. Mainly nocturnal living in high forests, mountains and tundra, preying on mammals, birds and carrion, hunting in packs.

Wolverine (*Gulo gulo*) Dark-brown badger-like mammal, may be up to 70 cm (25 in) long with 25-cm (10-in) tail and weighing up to 30 kg (65 lb). Yellowish band along flanks and tail and light cheek patches. Thick set with short legs, powerful feet and long claws, and bushy tail. Lives in mountainous areas, forests and lakesides, feeding on mammals, birds, berries, carrion. Reputation for ferocity.

Wolverine

BIRDS

African white-necked raven (*Corvus albicollis*) Large glossy black raven, 55 cm (20 in) long, with a white collar and white-tipped bill. Sometimes solitary, and very agile in the air, but many may collect at good feeding sites on ground where they move clumsily. Deep croaking call. Inhabits high mountains, cliffs and gorges, but also scavenges human habitations.

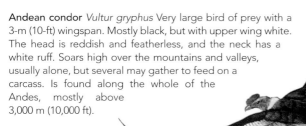

Alpine chough

Alpine chough or **Alpine (Rock) crow** (*Pyrrhocorax graculus*) Bird with coal-black plumage with greenish gloss on wings and tail. Distinctive features are the bright yellow bill, feet and legs, their color ranging from pink-orange to deep red. Lives high in the Pyrenees, Atlas, Alps, Apennines and Caucasus, but descends in winter. Feeds on insects, berries and small fruits; also scavenges about human dwellings and campsites.

Andean condor *Vultur gryphus* Very large bird of prey with a 3-m (10-ft) wingspan. Mostly black, but with upper wing white. The head is reddish and featherless, and the neck has a white ruff. Soars high over the mountains and valleys, usually alone, but several may gather to feed on a carcass. Is found along the whole of the Andes, mostly above 3,000 m (10,000 ft).

Andean condor

Andean hillstar hummingbird

Capercaillie

Chough

Common buzzard

Andean hillstar hummingbird (*Oreotrichilus estella*) Relatively large hummingbird, 13 cm (5 in) long, found up to 4,200 m (14,000 ft) high in the Andes. Mainly olive-gray above and pale below, with a brilliant green throat patch. The curved bill is used to feed in flowers of Puya plants which it pollinates. It is common and widespread, descending lower in winter.

Blue mountain duck (*Hymenolaimus malacorynchus*) Stocky, dark-gray duck with a contrasting pale bill and iris. The bill looks square-ended because of strange flaps at the tip. Inhabits rapid, stony mountain rivers in regions of New Zealand, where it dives and swims easily, and can often be seen standing on boulders.

Capercaillie (*Tetrao urogallus*) This very large black bird is easily distinguished by its big black fanned tail. The male, 85 cm (35 in) long, is 15 cm (6 in) longer than the female. Flight has typical game-bird alternation of quick whirring and gliding on downturned wings; great clatter made when leaving trees, where it perches and feeds. Widespread and common throughout Scandinavia and east to Russia; also in Alps, Pyrenees and Apennines.

Chilean flamingo (*Phoenicopterus ruber*) Tall, pale flamingo, 120 cm (50 in) long, its wingspan 150 cm (60 in); has a black-tipped pink bill and grayish legs with contrasting pink joints. Breeds on shallow saline lakes high in the Andes, usually in very large colonies building raised mud nests on the margins. The similar Andean flamingo, with yellow legs, is more restricted in range.

Chough (*Pyrrhocorax pyrrhocorax*) Glossy black bird 40 cm (15 in) long with a long, curved and distinctive red bill. Wings have six clearly-spread "fingers." Superb aerial acrobat, diving headlong at breakneck speed with closed wings. Breeds in mountain districts and along rocky coastlines in south and west Europe. Found in west Britain and Ireland, Spain, north Africa, the Alps and southeastern Europe.

Common buzzard (*Buteo buteo*) Bird with a wingspan of 1–1.25 m (3–4 ft). Plumage very variable, from pale to dark. Has a majestic soaring flight, often circling and rising on thermals. Mainly inhabits forest and woodland on the edge of mountainous country, nesting in tall deciduous trees. Feeds on hares, small rodents, birds and carrion. Widespread in Europe, north Africa, and Turkey.

Dotterel (*Eudromias morinellus*) Bird with coloring that blends well with the shades and patterns on the mountaintop; eye stripes and band on the breast, however, are conspicuous from a distance. Breeds on dry mountain heaths. Feeds mainly on insects and their larvae. Found in Norway and Arctic Scandinavia, with local populations in Scotland, the Alps and Caucasus.

Dotterel (breeding plumage)

Golden eagle (*Aquila chrysaetos*) Large bird of prey living in mountainous, often treeless, habitats, but needing large trees or rock faces for nesting. Ranges across Europe, North America, Asia and north Africa. It does not migrate. Has a majestic soaring and gliding flight, and can remain in the air for hours at a time. Speeds of 128 km/h (80 mph) are reached, although 48 km/h (30 mph) is average. Has very good eyesight, and will dive down to seize and kill prey (hares, small rodents and birds) with curved talons. A golden eagle pairs for life and tends to have territories of up to 56 km^2 (35 mi^2). Probably most numerous eagle of its size in the world.

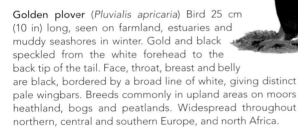
Golden eagle

Golden plover (*Pluvialis apricaria*) Bird 25 cm (10 in) long, seen on farmland, estuaries and muddy seashores in winter. Gold and black speckled from the white forehead to the back tip of the tail. Face, throat, breast and belly are black, bordered by a broad line of white, giving distinct pale wingbars. Breeds commonly in upland areas on moors heathland, bogs and peatlands. Widespread throughout northern, central and southern Europe, and north Africa.

Kestrel (*Falco tinnunculus*) Most common and widespread of the falcons, both in the UK and throughout Europe. Its wingspan is 70–80 cm (25–30 in). Scans the ground by hovering at a height of 7–12 m (23–40 ft). Feeds mainly on voles but also insects. A familiar raptor seen near highway verges, it is quite common in dense woods and open country throughout Europe, north Africa, Russia, Turkey.

Kestrel

Lammergeier, **Bearded vulture** or **Old World vulture** (*Gypaetus barbatus*) Huge bird 1–1.1 m (3.3– 3.6 ft) long with a wingspan of 1.9–2.7 m (6–9 ft). Found in wild mountainous areas throughout southern Europe, north Africa and Asia. It soars on thermal updrafts of air looking for offal and carrion to feed on; sometimes breaks bones to reach the bone marrow by dropping them on rocks.

Merlin

Martial eagle (*Hieraaetus bellicosus*) Large, powerfully built eagle, up to 85 cm (35 in) long, dark brown above and pale below with a short crest on nape. At close range appears slightly spotted below. Usually silent, but can make far-carrying call. Widespread in open areas, usually seen soaring, often alone; may make long daily flights in search of prey. Found in South Africa.

Merlin (*Falco columbarius*) Smallest of Europe's raptors, 25–30 cm (10–12 in) long, its wingspan 55–65 cm (20–25 in). Quite common (though declining), it breeds in open hilly, mountain or moorland regions. Nest made from sticks in cliff, tree or on the ground. Makes swift low dashes to make surprise attacks, feeding mostly on small birds. Widespread in Europe, Russia, north Africa, and Turkey.

Peregrine falcon

Peregrine falcon (*Falco peregrinus*) Large falcon with dark gray/brown wings and back; underside striped white and brown. Has fairly short tail, sharply tapering wings and down-curved beak. Breeds usually on cliff faces; feeds mainly on medium-sized birds caught in flight. Known for its impressive diagonal downward stoops with closed wings over hundreds of meters. On impact it knocks out prey with its feet. Common in Europe (except Iceland), Russia, north Africa, and Turkey.

Ptarmigan (*Lagopus mutus*) Bird with red mark above the eye and three plumages: all white in winter; male blackish gray on head in spring; in summer brown/gray over whole back. Call is a distinctive hoarse croaking "uk uk." Noisy flight with fast wing beats followed by gliding on down-turned wings. Breeds mainly in higher mountains. Widespread and common above 600 m in Scotland, Norway, northern Scandinavia, parts of Russia, Iceland; pockets in Alps, Pyrenees.

Ptarmigan

Raven

Raven (*Corvus corax*) Bird with all black plumage, larger than a buzzard, with a wingspan of 125 cm (50 in). Breeds fairly commonly on rocky coasts, in mountains and in extensive woodland. Maintains lifelong pair bonds, and often seen in pairs. Feeds on small animals, carrion and refuse. Often performs half-rolls in play. Widespread and common throughout Europe, north Africa, Russia, and Turkey.

Ring ouzel (*Turdus torquatus*) Bird with similar size and behavior to a blackbird; white, crescent-shaped breast band distinguishes adult. In the UK breeds fairly commonly on hilly moorland with rocky outcrops and scrubby areas, on the continent in Alpine spruce forest. Widespread and common throughout northern, western and southeast Europe (except Iceland).

Ring ouzel
(spring male)

Short-eared owl (*Asio flammeus*) Sub-Arctic owl that nests on moorland and bogs. Much the most likely medium-sized brown owl to be seen by day. Has conspicuously long wings, with which it soars, wheels and glides like a harrier. Feeds mainly on voles. Widespread and common throughout Europe, north Africa, Russia, and Turkey.

Short eared owl

Skylark (*Alauda arvensis*) Very common breeding bird in open country; nests on the ground. The song is an endless outpouring which starts at dawn and continues all day. Sometimes seen performing a parachuting motion from 10–15 m (30–45 ft) to ground level. Widespread and common throughout Europe (except arctic Europe, including Iceland) and east into Russia.

Snow bunting (*Plectrophenax nivalis*) Small bird 15 cm (6 in) in length identified by its white wing markings. Often seen around picnic tables in ski resorts. Prefers snowy regions. Widespread and common throughout northern Europe, including Iceland.

Skylark

Willow grouse/Red grouse (*Lagopus lagopus lagopus/Lagopus lagopus scoticus*) Willow grouse of continental Europe is bigger and slightly more elongated than the ptarmigan. In Britain and Ireland the species is represented by the red grouse, which lacks the white winter plumage and has reddish-brown wings throughout the year. The male's somewhat hysterical laughing note often surprises the mountain walker. Breeds mainly in moorlands. Red grouse widespread and common in Scotland, Ireland, northern England and Wales. Willow grouse widespread in Scandinavia east to Russia.

Willow grouse

Birds and waterfowl of lochs, lakes and streams

Arctic tern (*Sterna paradisaea*) Remarkable bird that migrates from the Antarctic to breed in northern and Arctic Europe. Has a coral-red bill and a black cap, which extends from the bill, through the eye to the back of the neck. Wings and back gray; white underside and forked tail streamers. Favors coastal areas but also found around mountain lakes. Has been known to attack walkers approaching its nests by dive-bombing. Widespread and common throughout northern Europe, including Scotland, Ireland, Iceland, Denmark, coastal Scandinavia and Svalbard.

Arctic tern

Black-throated diver (*Gavia arctica*) Bird distinguished, as name suggests, by a black patch on the throat. Its length varies, at 60–75 cm (25–30 in). Nests mainly in clear deep lakes in tundra and open moorland. Fishes in lakes or at sea; often found in mountainous areas. Common in northwest Scotland, Scandinavia (excluding Iceland) and Russia.

Black-throated diver

Dipper (*Cinclus cinclus*) Bird easily identified by its conspicuous white front and habit of constantly bobbing on rock in midstream. Common in fast-flowing streams and rivers in hills and mountains. Can swim both on and under the water surface, and walks on the stream bed in search of invertebrates. Widespread throughout Europe.

Whooper swan (*Cygnus cygnus*) Large swan 145–160 cm (55–65 in) long that nests in marshy lakes in tundra and forest country. Migrates south in family groups when the lakes freeze over. Feeds on aquatic plants, but also grazes on the shore. Common in northern England, Ireland and Scotland, Scandinavia and Iceland.

Common frog

AMPHIBIANS

Common frog (*Rana temporaria*) The commonest frog, up to 10 cm (4 in) long. Found in woods and mountainous areas wherever there are ponds to breed in. The skin is smooth and brownish-green with darker bands, but very variable. Males have blue chin in breeding season and thick black "thumbs." Feed on invertebrates and are prey for birds and large fish. Very vocal in breeding season.

Common toad (*Bufo bufo*) The largest and commonest toad, up to 15 cm (6 in) long, and can inflate itself to nearly 15 cm (6 in) wide when threatened. Drier, wartier skin than frogs and dark brown; pale and spotted below. Lives in drier habitat than frogs and often far from water. Feeds on variety of invertebrates. Faint ducklike call in breeding season.

REPTILES

Adder or **Common viper** (*Vipera berus*) Snake 50–65 cm (20–25 in) long with a large head and rounded snout, red-brown eyes with vertical elliptical pupils, and a distinctive zigzag pattern along the back. Found in heathland and mountains, bogs, open woodland, hedgerows, moorland, sand dunes and riverbanks, preferring undisturbed country-side. Uses venom to immobilize prey such as amphibians, nestlings, small mammals and lizards. The most northerly distributed snake (the only species found within the Arctic Circle), and one of the most widespread. Found throughout Britain (the country's only venomous reptile; absent from Ireland) and common throughout Europe and across Russia and Asia to north China.

▼ *The Common or Viviparous lizard is unusual in that the female will give birth to between 8 and 11 live young (hence the alternative name Viviparous), instead of laying eggs, which is more common in lizards.*

Common or **Viviparous lizard** (*Lacerta vivipara*) Common and widespread lizard up to 17 cm (6.5 in) long. Found even inside Arctic Circle, in mountains in southern Europe and other open habitats. Feeds on small insects and spiders.

Females produce up to 11 live young in summer. Mostly brown above with darker stripes and bands, males brighter color below. Sheds tail if captured, but grows new one in time.

Copperhead snake (*Denisonia superba*) Large glossy snake attractively patterned with red-brown, yellow and orange markings; basks in the sun in open rocky areas. Can reach a length of 1.5 m (5 ft). Has a fatal bite. Found in the mountains of southeast Australia and Tasmania.

INSECTS

African monarch butterfly (*Danaus chrysippus*) Large, colorful butterfly with warning orange and black colors; the larvae feed on poisonous milkweed plants and retain the poison as adults. A migrant species likely to turn up in many places from Africa, through western Asia to Australia. Several nonpoisonous species mimic its markings.

African monarch
butterfly

Midge (*Culicoides impunctatus*) Tiny two-winged fly (wingspan less than 2 mm/0.08 in), one of the many biting midge species, its mouth able to pierce skin; related to the mosquito. Most biting midges feed off farm livestock, deer or birds, some attacking humans. *Culicoides impunctatus* makes most attacks, the Scottish variant allegedly more aggressive than its counterpart elsewhere. Found worldwide in the uplands, and particularly infamous in northwest Scotland.

Mountain emerald dragonfly (*Somatochlora semicircularis*) Dragonfly 45–50 mm (1.5–2 in) long with a brilliant shiny metallic green-gold body; has a distinctive lobe on the hind margin of each compound eye. Adults may pursue small insect prey underwater. Prevalent around ponds, marshy bogs and upland streams, especially those with surrounding vegetation. Found in northwest USA, from Alaska south to California and Colorado.

Rocky Mountain wood tick (*Dermacentor andersoni*) Member of the hard tick family which is named from the hard plate on top of the body; 2–4 mm (0.08–0.16 in) in length. A major carrier in the USA of Rocky Mountain spotted fever (*Rickettsia rickettsii*), a bacterium transferred to humans from small rodents via ticks. Ticks feed on two or three hosts, primarily on large mammals (including humans), requiring a blood meal before developing into its next life stage. Found only in the Rocky Mountains in the USA and southwestern Canada.

▲ *A male Emperor moth.* The Emperor moth, with its four large eye spots, is one of the largest and most distinctive of Europe's moth.

Moths

Emperor moth (*Pavonia pavonia*) Male moth has brown and white forewings and orange hindwings, both with prominent eyespot; wingspan is 60 mm (2.3 in). Female wings (larger, at 80–mm/3.1 in span) are generally gray and white with similar eyespots. The black and orange larva becomes green with black rings and yellow and red spots later. Takes food from heather but also bramble, hawthorn, blackthorn, sallow and meadowsweet. Associated with moorland and heathland, it occurs throughout Europe and is the only member of its family found in the British Isles.

Netted mountain moth (*Semiothisa carbonaria*) Moth with gray-black abdomen and variable white flecks on the wings, which span 23–25 mm (0.9–1 in). Active late April–early June, its appearance dependent on weather and altitude. Flies most in the sun, preferring flowering plants in moorland such as bearberry. Common in areas of Norway, Sweden and Finland; found on central European mountains, the Alps and northeast Siberia; rare in the UK, known only in the central Scottish Highlands.

Mountain People

INTRODUCTION

Mountains are home to at least 12 percent of the world's people, with more than 70 million living above an altitude of 2,000 m (6,500 ft). A further 14 percent live very close to mountain areas, and well over half of the world's population depends on mountains for water, food, hydroelectricity, timber, and mineral resources. In order to support the world's growing population it is necessary to protect mountain ecosystems and enable mountain people to sustain and improve their way of life.

Mountain peoples have been the guardians of the mountains for thousands of years, evolving ways of living and working in harmony with their environment. Their idiosyncrasies have been regarded as backward by lowlanders, urban dwellers and other outsiders, but these apparently eccentric ways are the efficient and effective means of surviving the harsh and challenging realities of mountain existence. All over the world, the pressures to increase productivity, generate income, diversify activities (by engaging in growing industries such as tourism, forestry and mining) and adapt to the challenges brought about by increasingly easy access into formerly remote communities are affecting mountain ecosystems, bringing mountain people into increasing contact with lowland and urban dwellers, and increasing poverty levels in both mountain and lowland areas.

Approximately half of the world's mountain peoples live in the Andes and the Himalayas, although the population density in these regions is not as high as in some of the tropical mountain ranges, such as parts of Mount Kenya, the highlands of Papua New Guinea, the Vale of Peshawar in northern Pakistan, and the Virunga volcano region of Rwanda, each of which has more than 400 people per km^2 (400 people per 0.4 mi^2).

Many mountain areas are relatively inaccessible and where there are few roads the area can be home to hundreds of tribes, each speaking its own languages and with its own traditions and belief systems. Mountain areas can also provide a form of sanctuary to threatened indigenous peoples, ethnic minorities and refugees, especially when near a border. These people will often have little political or commercial power. Even in developing countries, many mountain people typically live on the economic margins as nomads, hunters and foragers, traders, subsistence farmers and herders, loggers, miners, waged-workers, or in households headed by women while men pursue seasonal or

▲ *It is estimated that somewhere in the region of 12 percent of the world's population live in mountain regions—in remote villages and towns such as Mucuchies, which lies nestled in the Andes Mountains of Venezuela.*

even permanent work in the lowland towns and cities. A study undertaken for the United Nations showed that three-quarters of total income for the average mountain family comes from pensions, money sent from outside the area or earned by working for others away from the mountains. The rest came from selling surplus crops and livestock, working for other local farmers, from selling handicrafts or providing services.

In economic terms, very many mountain people exist in material poverty. More than 60 percent of the rural Andean population live in extreme poverty, and most of the 98 million Chinese—considered to be among the world's absolute poor—are ethnic minorities who live in mountains. Although these statistics do not reflect the value of barter trade and communal property (most mountain communities, for example, have shared forests and pastures), the characteristics of poverty still remain.

MOUNTAIN SETTLEMENTS

Of the nearly 200 countries of the world, fewer than 50 have no mountains or high plateaus. On the other hand, more than 20 countries have substantial areas above 2,000 m (6,500 ft)—classed as high mountains—with significant urban populations. These towns and cities often comprise an eclectic mix of people, offer the same access to facilities and services (although these will be provided at varying standards), and have the same range of rich and poor areas as would be found in major towns and cities in lowland areas. Mountain people who have moved from their villages to live and work in these mountain conurbations often do so for unskilled or semiskilled jobs. In return they receive a wage that is often used to support their families back in the remote mountain communities. Some younger people move away to better their education and gain life and work experience, but never return to their mountain homes on a permanent basis.

URBAN MOUNTAIN DWELLERS

Countries having significant populations living in towns and cities in high mountain areas are found at all stages of development, economic success and security. Some key facts about each of these follow.

▼ *The central highlands* of Afghanistan, in the east of the country, reach a height of more than 7,600 m (24,900 ft), and make up a total of about 75 percent of the country's entire landmass. The villages that scatter these high regions are remote and many are almost inaccessible.

Afghanistan

Afghanistan is a land-locked, mountainous country in the Hindu Kush area of south-western Asia. About three-quarters of the country is virtually inaccessible and even though agriculture is the main economic activity, up to two-thirds of available farmland is uncultivated. The majority of its population live in high mountain areas, and fewer than 20 percent in urban settlements, many of them in or around the capital, Kabul. Until the late 1990s Afghanistan was a war zone and much of its infrastructure and economy is being rebuilt with the help of outside agencies.

Andorra

Andorra is a tiny land-locked principality lying between France and Spain, high in the eastern Pyrenees. Its inhabitants number around 60,000, 95 percent of whom live in small towns along the river valleys; half of

▲ **With around 75 percent** *of its land lying in mountainous regions, Austria offers some of the most spectacular scenery in Europe, such as the setting for the village of Heiligenblut, which lies in the forested Holltal Valley in southern Austria. With tourism generating around seven percent of the country's GDP, over six percent of the entire population work in tourist-related industries.*

the country is classified as high mountain. Andorra's spectacular scenery and Alpine climate have made tourism, especially skiing, its main source of income; the high mountain population provides services for this market. Water is a major resource with hydroelectricity providing for all domestic needs; the country, however, needs to import the majority of its raw materials, power for commerce and industry, and certain foods, as the soil and the climate support mainly cereals, potatoes and tobacco.

Austria

Austria lies in the heart of Europe, and is dominated in the west by the Alps. All of Austria's industries, particularly its strong tourism, benefit from the sophisticated communications and transportation network developed as a result of the country's central geographical position. The population is roughly evenly split between urban and rural settings, with a number of major towns located around the foothills of the

Alps, while others such as St. Anton, Kitzbuhler and Lienz are major upmarket mountain resorts. Half a million of Austria's population of eight million have jobs associated with the tourism industry, which accounts for around seven percent of Austria's GDP (one third of which comes from the winter sports industry).

Azerbaijan
Azerbaijan lies on the west coast of the Caspian Sea bordered by the Upper Caucasus in the north and the Lesser Caucasus in the west. Its neighboring countries are Iran, Georgia and Russia. The population is split more or less evenly between urban and rural centers and there are many large towns in the mountain regions. War in the 1990s, however, and a continuing refugee problem are hindering the country's economic development.

▼ **Larches with fall foliage** cover the slopes of Odaray Plateau and surround Lake O'Hara in the mountainous landscape of Yoho National Park, British Columbia, western Canada. This region of Canada is home to both the Rocky and McKenzie mountains and offers almost unlimited scope for hiking, skiing, climbing and cycling.

Bhutan

Bhutan is a small country situated in the Himalayas between India and China. Mountain forest covers almost three-quarters of the country and although Bhutan has very fertile tropical lowlands and valleys to the south, most of it falls within the high Himalayas, inhabited by seminomadic yak herders. Bhutan's topography ensures that the climate is tropical in the south, and cold and harsh in the north; the country relies on the summer monsoons for its rain. Less than 10 percent of Bhutan can be cultivated for arable crops, but the land's fertility allows almost any crop to grow. Its population of less than two million is almost all rural, with few permanent settlements and only two of these having more than 10,000 residents. Ninety percent of the population depend on subsistence farming in the highland and mountain regions, the country relying on Indian workers to fill many of the public-sector jobs from construction to teaching.

Bolivia

Lying land-locked high in central South America, Bolivia boasts the world's highest capital city, La Paz, as well as the world's highest golf course and ski run. Over half of the population lives on the altiplano, the windswept plateau 3,500 m (11,000 ft) above sea level that sits between two ranges of the Andes. The lowland regions in the east are tropical, but sparsely populated and underdeveloped. The population is split almost equally between rural and urban areas. Two-thirds of the population are indigenous, speaking their own languages (Aymara and Quechua), and they largely lead their own lives, with little intermixing. Rich in mineral wealth having deposits of gold, silver and zinc, Bolivia is also the world's largest producer of tin, which is mined around Oruro and Potosí in the high mountains. Oil and natural gas deposits are now being exploited.

Canada

The west coast of Canada is bounded by the northern peaks of the Rocky Mountain range, which, together with the Mackenzie Mountains, make up the two states of Yukon Territory and British Columbia. Several large townships have developed in the mountains including Calgary, a major settlement of over half a million people, and Whitehorse, the capital city of Yukon Territory. Discoveries of gold in the Yukon River in the 1860s sparked the gold rush made famous by the Klondike gold strike of 1896. Around four percent of Canada's population of around 30 million are indigenous people, many of whom live in the Yukon Territory and retain their own language and culture. The Inuit successfully settled their land claim with the Canadian government, leading, in 1992, to the Inuit Nunavut area becoming the first part of Canada to be governed by indigenous Canadians in modern history. The major industries in the mountain areas are mining, metallurgy and tourism, especially trekking and skiing.

Chile

Chile is perhaps the longest and thinnest country in the world, extending some 4,500 km (2,800 mi) down the west coast of South America, separating the Pacific from the Andes. Most of the population of around 20 million live in towns around the fertile plains of the capital, Santiago, with almost one-third living in and around the capital itself. The majority of the population is of mixed Spanish-Indian descent, but there are around one million indigenous Mapuche Indians living almost exclusively in the south of the country. Chile is the world's biggest copper producer with enormous mines in the mountains at Teniente and Chuquicamata; it also has flourishing fishmeal and wine industries, and a range of manufacturing and engineering sectors operating in the capital.

China

China covers a vast area of eastern Asia, bordered by 14 countries on three sides and with a long Pacific coastline in the east. Two-thirds of China is upland or high mountain, including the Tibetan Plateau in the southwest. Two-thirds of the population live in the lowlands to the east, and the remaining 400 million people have their homes in mountainous areas. With more than 20 percent of the world's population to feed from only seven percent of the world's farmland, China makes great use of complex irrigation systems and intricate terracing of mountain areas. Although the official language is Mandarin, six other Chinese languages are also recognized and spoken by significant numbers of the country's inhabitants. About 93 percent of the population are Han Chinese, the remaining 92 million belonging to one of the 55 minority nationalities or recognized ethnic groups, many with their own language and culture. Some minorities are marginalized because of the border areas in which they live. The strict one-child policy for most Han Chinese living in urban areas has been relaxed for some rural and mountain communities and ethnic minorities. China is self-sufficient in food and has vast mineral reserves supporting an increasingly diversified industrial sector. It is the world's largest producer of molybdenum,

titanium and tungsten. Tourism has become very important to China since the easing of restrictions in the 1980s.

Colombia

Colombia lies at the northern tip of South America where the Andes divide into three ranges, with the capital, Bogotá, situated high in the mountains. Colombia's main industries are coffee, emeralds and gold; the small tourist industry is limited mainly to the Caribbean coast due to the country's economic and political uncertainties and the relative inaccessibility of its other regions. Colombia's population is mixed: just over half are European-Indian, 20 percent are white, 20 percent are European-African, with the rest being black or Amerindian. The mountain areas are also the richest

▼ *Hebei Province*, *China, is home to one of the country's famous highland retreats—the Mountain Resort of Chengde, once the largest summer residence of the Qing Dynasty (1644–1911).*

and most productive, with coffee and other cash crops being grown for export in the Bogotá and Medellin regions, while coal is mined for export to the UK and the USA.

▲ *Coffee plants* growing in a plantation near Armenia, Colombia. Coffee is grown in the lush mountain regions of the country and the crop is Colombia's major export, bringing much needed income and work for the country's farmers.

Ecuador
Ecuador was part of the Inca Empire before its colonization by the Spaniards in 1533. The country sits between Colombia and Peru with the Pacific on its eastern coast. More than half of the population is of Indian-Spanish descent and Spanish is the national language. Around 50 percent of the population live in the high mountains along the Andean Sierra. Ecuador is the world's biggest producer of bananas, most of which are farmed in the equatorial lowlands. Tourism, a major industry, is directed largely at the Inca sites of cultural and archaeological interest in the high mountains.

Ethiopia
Ethiopia is a land-locked, mountainous country in northeast Africa. It is subject to devastating droughts and famines as its rainy seasons are unpredictable. There are 76 nationalities in Ethiopia speaking almost 300 languages. Few of the population of 55 million live in urban settlements, and the majority are in rural villages and communities; with a poor transportation infrastructure, most travel takes place using pack animals, primarily donkeys. There is accordingly very

little communication or mixing among sectors of the population, and so tribal distinctions are maintained. Three-quarters of the population is engaged in farming, mostly for subsistence, but growing coffee for export is also an important source of income. Tourism is slowly increasing as scenic and cultural packages are made available to the pilgrim centers of the Ethiopian Highlands.

India
India is the second most populous country in the world, separated from the rest of Asia by the Himalayas. In the northern mountainous states of Jammu, Kashmir, Assam, Arunachal Pradesh and Himachal Pradesh the temperature can reach 40°C (104°F) during the hot season; monsoon rains break in June and continue through to September or October. Only four percent of India's one billion people live in these high mountain areas, which sustain a range of industries from petroleum production and tea plantations in Assam, mining and woodwork in Jammu and Kashmir, textiles and handicrafts in Himachal Pradesh, to forestry and wood products in Arunachal Pradesh. In the northern mountain regions tourism represents the largest industry, with many Hindu pilgrims and increasing numbers of foreign visitors journeying to the major sacred and cultural sites.

Italy
The Alps and Dolomites form a natural northern boundary to Italy, while the Apennine Mountains create a ridge down the center of the country. More than three-quarters of Italy is covered by mountains, which include the highest summit in Europe, Mont Blanc, at 4,807 m (15,771 ft). The south is literally a hotbed of seismic activity, most notably the volcanoes of of Vesuvius and, on the island of Sicily, Mount Etna, the largest active volcano in Europe. The high mountain regions are made up of the Dolomites, where there are significant mountain settlements. The regions classified as "mountain districts" constitute over half the area of Italy and have a resident population of over 10 million people, almost one-fifth of the Italian population. Italy's constitution includes a specific clause on mountain areas emphasizing the importance of their protection and considerate development through Upland Development Authorities. Local community cooperatives have also been in existence in the mountain regions since the late 1800s, and are the key to the successful sustainability of these fragile areas. The main mountain industries are climbing, winter sports and forestry, although the impact of volcanic activity around Pompeii also attracts many visitors.

Kenya

Kenya sits on the equator on Africa's east coast, its central plateau split by the Great Rift Valley. Most of the population of 25 million live around the high plateau, with only a quarter in permanent townships or around the capital, Nairobi; the rest live in smaller villages in tight clan or family groups. Kenya's wide ethnic diversity comprises about 70 different groups, and these strong extended family bonds, coupled with poverty and one of the world's highest population growth rates, are causing increasing racial and ethnic tensions. Coffee and tea are major cash crops and tourism is the largest foreign-exchange earner. Most of the broad agricultural and manufacturing base is situated on the high plateau.

Kyrgyzstan

Kyrgyzstan is a small and very mountainous nation in central Asia with a population of only 4.5 million. It is the least urbanized of the ex-Soviet republics with only 40 percent of its people living in towns. The population is roughly half

▼ *Despite lying on the equator,* Mount Kenya's elevation of 5,199 m (17,057 ft) ensures its summit is dusted with snow all year round. An extinct volcano and the second highest mountain in Africa after Mount Kilimanjaro, Mount Kenya lies in southwestern Kenya's highland region where the majority of the country's 25 million inhabitants live.

Kyrgyz, 20 percent Russian, 13 percent Uzbek; the rest comprises other minority groups. Kyrgyzstan is rich in minerals, particularly gold and mercury, which it exports. The vast majority of its people, however, are subsistence farmers living and working in the mountains of Tien Shan.

Lesotho

Lesotho is a mountainous and land-locked country situated within the borders of South Africa, making it entirely dependent upon its neighbor for all land transportation links with the outside world. Around 20 percent of the population of about two million live in urban areas, the vast majority being subsistence farmers in small villages around the high plateau. As the majority of men of working age travel to South Africa to work in the mines, over 70 percent of households in the rural population are headed by women, who also carry out the work around the settlements. Diamonds mined in the northeastern mountains are a major source of export income.

Mexico

Mexico sits at the southern tip of North America, with coastal plains running along its Pacific and Atlantic seaboards. The land rises sharply into an arid central plateau, which includes the world's biggest conurbation, Mexico City, built on the site of the Aztec capital, Tenochtitlan. The Pacific coast has a tropical climate, which results in the plateau and high mountains remaining warm almost all year round. Tourism is Mexico's largest industry as the country has many World Heritage Sites in the mountains as well as excellent beach resorts. Mexico has significant mineral resources including oil and silver, the latter being mined in the mountains at Durango.

Nepal

Nepal is located on the shoulder of the southern Himalayas, bordered by India and China. It is one of the poorest countries of the world and its largely subsistence agricultural economy is heavily dependent upon the monsoon each year. Only 10 percent of the population of 20 million live in urban areas, mainly in and around the capital Kathmandu. The most famous of the mountain peoples are the Sherpas in the north. The negative impact of tourism in the north—through trekking in particular—has resulted in the setting-up of the Annapurna Conservation Project to try to find ways of sustaining the valuable income from tourism without destroying the land and livelihoods of the mountain people.

▲ The Karakoram Highway is the highest trade route in the world, winding through spectacular mountain scenery. It runs for some 700 km (430 mi) from Islamabad through the Karakoram Mountains and into China.

Pakistan

Pakistan is naturally divided in to six major regions. Its northern border, or North Highland Mountain Region, lies against the mountains of Afghanistan and China, and the country's northern tip is in the Hindu Kush mountains. The mountain ranges that make up this region include the Himalayas, the Karakoram as well as the Hindu Kush, and contain 35 giant peaks over 7,300 m (23,950 ft) high, including the world's second-highest summit, K2. Even the mountain passes are at heights greater than that of the summit of Mont Blanc, with several over 5,500 m (18,000 ft). The Karakoram Highway, which passes through these mountains joining east to west, is the highest trade route in the world. In among these high peaks are huge glaciers, enormous lakes and lush green valleys that are host to industries such as forestry and tourism. However, the majority of agriculture and manufacture takes place in the vast fertile lowland regions of the country. Living in the high mountains are small tribes of people whose ancestry can be traced back 3,400 years and who preserve their own language and culture, subsist in small communities and produce beautiful handicrafts and woven goods. One of the larger mountain settlements is Quetta, renowned for its carpet weaving; here the traditional craft has developed into a village industry.

Papua New Guinea

Papua New Guinea occupies the eastern end of the island of New Guinea in southeast Asia; much of the country lies above 1,500 m (5,000 ft). The country is one of the most linguistically diverse in the world, supporting approximately 750 languages and many tribal customs. In a country with little infrastructure and a largely isolated interior, this diversity is not surprising, especially given that most of the indigenous population still live by hunter-gathering in very small village tribes. The religious background is equally diverse, the biggest group (comprising over one-third of the population) holding indigenous beliefs. The island contains extensive copper resources, as well as much gold and other minerals. Oil and gas reserves are becoming an increasingly important resource.

Peru

Peru lies just south of the equator on the Pacific coast of South America, rising from an arid coastal strip to the Andes and dominated in the south by volcanoes. About half of Peru's population of around 25 million lives in the mountains and is engaged mainly in subsistence farming or producing cocoa as a cash crop. Peru's border with Bolivia in the south runs through Lake Titicaca, the highest navigable lake in the world. Peru has abundant mineral resources, including oil, and produces for export both coffee and cotton—the latter supporting a well-developed textile industry.

Rwanda

Rwanda is a mountainous land-locked country in east-central Africa lying on the equator. Its climate is tropical,

▼ *Lake Titicaca*, the highest lake in the world, lies on the border with Peru and Bolivia. Local inhabitants use the plentiful supply of reeds to construct dwellings.

91

though this is tempered somewhat by its high altitude. Two wet seasons, when the rain does come, allow for two harvests each year, though internal ethnic conflicts have meant that food production has suffered in the past. Only around eight percent of the population of eight million live in urban settlements, mainly in and around the capital Kigali. The rest are subsistence farmers and herders who live in small villages or work on the tea and coffee plantations that bring in export income. Other cash crops include corn, beans, rice, millet, wheat, sweet potatoes and bananas, and the main manufacturing industry is largely based on food processing. The other significant industry is the mining and processing of the mineral Coltan (Colombo-Tantalite); it has heat-resistant properties when refined and is used in electrical applications.

Switzerland

Switzerland is a land-locked country at the center of western Europe and although many of its population of seven

million live along the river valleys and lakesides throughout the Alps, there are some large villages in the high mountains in the south of the country. Switzerland is one of the world's most prosperous economies, with tourism being its third largest industry. Perhaps the country's greatest significance as a mountain region is that it is the source of western Europe's largest rivers—the Po, the Rhine, the Rhône and the Inn-Danube—and is therefore often referred to as "Europe's water tower."

Tajikistan

Tajikistan lies on the western slopes of the Pamirs in central Asia, although the Tajik language and traditions are more similar to those of Iran than those of neighboring Uzbekistan. The majority of the country is high mountain. Of the one million or so people living in the mountain areas, almost a quarter of them are found in the Gorno Badakhshan region, the country's largest and most mountainous province. Settlements there start at an altitude of 1,000 m (3,300 ft), while the town of Murgab is at a height of 3,200 m (10,500 ft). Only 30 percent of the population of six million live in urban areas, with the rest in smaller village settlements. Only six percent of the land is arable and much of the interior is inaccessible. Vast glaciated fields cover around six percent of the country's landmass (over 9,000 glaciers containing almost 600 km^3/145 mi^3 of ice). Tajikistan's main industries are the mining of uranium—although the value of this fell with the end of the nuclear arms race—and aluminum processing. Hydroelectric power provides three-quarters of the country's domestic energy needs. Carpet making is a major village industry.

◀ *The spectacularly picturesque village of Grindelwald lies at the foot of the Swiss Alps, which make up around 60 percent of the country's landmass. Switzerland's highest peak is Monte Rosa at 4,634 m (15,217 ft). Scenery such as this, combined with good transportation infrastructure and mile upon mile of excellent skiing, have made tourism the country's third largest industry.*

RURAL MOUNTAIN PEOPLE

People living in the high mountains in villages, communities, clans, tribes or even just as individual families often display a rich cultural diversity not found in the towns and cities. Many mountain inhabitants, particularly the indigenous peoples, have their own languages and beliefs. These may be peculiar to only a relatively small geographical area or even a single group of people. However, although the world's mountains are home to several thousand different tribes or ethnic groups, there are many games and pastimes, crafts and skills that have evolved in villages and which make use of local landscape and resources but which are known, with only slight variations and by different names, in mountain regions the world over.

FOOD AND DRINK

Nutrition is a major issue in many mountain areas as the availability of food is highly dependent upon weather and other natural factors. Diet also varies according to the way of life and the terrain. Herders who are largely nomadic, or who have permanent settlements only at certain times of the year, will eat mainly meat and milk products—not having easy access to cereal, fruit or vegetables. Subsistence farmers on the other hand will have much greater access to cereal, vegetables and perhaps fruit, supplemented with eggs, chicken and domesticated farm animals—these last being kept mainly for their dairy produce.

Mountain people throughout the world, however, have experimented in varying their often meager resources to provide as interesting a range of food and drink as possible in order to sustain their families and provide the nourishment needed to live and work in sometimes extreme environments, without any waste. Even though recipes have evolved in different villages, on different mountain ranges many thousands of kilometers apart, often very similar dishes are produced.

Ethiopia is said to serve the hottest, most peppery food in all of Africa. A traditional meal always includes injera, a sourdough pancakelike bread made from a cereal called tef, served with wat, the hot and spicy curries made in every family kitchen. Often the injera will be made large enough to cover the whole table and the various dishes put straight on to it. The family will sit around the table and pull off small squares of bread to wrap around portions of the curry before rolling it up and eating it—rather like a series of small pancakes. The traditional drink with this meal is tej, a honey wine, and a coffee ceremony follows.

Kenyan food on the other hand is much plainer, and designed to be filling and economical; it consists mainly of soups or porridges made from a variety of pulses or cereal and thinned with water or milk. This is often served with barbecued meat, usually chicken or goat. A good range of fruit is usually available together with a variety of beers.

A feature of Chilean cooking is its sauces, which are home-made, stored and then used in a multiplicity of ways to flavor other dishes. Peculiar to Chile is the orange-red colored sauce called color, which is made by heating a mixture of garlic and paprika in fat or oil for a time and then cooling it. Color can be made according to a family's taste from very hot and spicy to very mild, and several strengths can be found in many kitchens. The flavoring pebre, comprising tomatoes, onions, vinegar, oil, garlic, chili and cilantro, is

◄ **A flock of goats** in the Elburz Mountains of Iran. For many mountain inhabitants around the world goats provide a valuable source of milk and meat, while their skins, and in the case of some breeds their coats, are also used to make a variety of items, from clothing to water bottles.

made in the same way. Chile also has a national dish made predominantly of cereal and pulses made interesting with the addition of herbs and spices. Porotos granados contains beans, corn and squash, flavored with onion and garlic. Chileans use corn in much of their cooking and one of the most popular dishes is a type of meat pie, its crust made from fresh ground corn rather than pastry.

Mexican food uses the same staples as other South American mountain regions but the Mexicans have made the thin round patties made of pressed corn or wheat-flour into a national dish now known the world over. The basis of many Mexican meals are these tortillas, nachos and tacos that can be stuffed, filled or dipped into any of the mince and bean dishes, usually flavored with chili.

A variety of hot chili peppers grown in Peru forms the basic seasoning or ingredient for many Peruvian dishes. Other staples of this region are rice and, of course, the potato. The potato was introduced to the rest of the world having been discovered in Peru and over 2,000 varieties now grow there, each mountain village often having developed its own variety suitable for the particular micro-climate of the area. Peruvians use the potato's variety of tastes and textures in all kinds of dishes—from appetizers to desserts.

In Kyrgyzstan the food in the villages has developed from the subsistence diet of the nomads. Meat is accordingly central to all Kyrgyz cooking, and this includes all parts of the animal, with milk and milk products, bread and sometimes potatoes served alongside. It is a feature of the region that cooking should preserve the taste and appearance of the meat, and so very little chopping or mincing takes place, and very little added in the way of spices or herbs. The characteristic dish is kebabs, where the meat is simply cut into chunks and roasted over a wood-fire. Other parts of the animal can be cut up and boiled or fried and served with rice or noodles. A classic type of cheese called qurut is made in the high mountain villages from sour cream dried in goatskin. In a region where fresh food is difficult to get, this method successfully preserves food for either times of shortage or severe weather, or for when the men go into the mountains for days to herd their animals or hunt.

▼ *In Tajikistan the chaikhona (teahouse) is often the focal point of a village, where important village and national issues are often hotly debated. Many are highly decorated, which helps to emphasis their social significance.*

In the lush forests of Papua New Guinea sweet potatoes are the staple food, supplemented with meat caught in the highlands such as wild pig, bats and tree kangaroos. Birds, eggs and a large range of fresh fruits are also collected to add variety to the diet.

In the Kalash mountain region of Pakistan the unleavened flat bread typical of many mountain regions is stuffed with crushed walnuts and goat's cheese for festivals, when it is eaten with roast goat.

The cuisine in Tajikistan is typical of much of central Asia, but the act, or art, of drinking tea is much more than a social ceremony. The chaikhona, or teahouse, is the center of village life and is often highly decorated by skilled woodcarvers and painters, becoming a work of art in itself.

▲ *The yam*, *or sweet potato, is an important source of nutrition in many mountain regions, particularly those of Papua New Guinea.*

CLOTHING

Another feature of mountain life that depends on both climate and available materials is clothing. Nomadic herding tribes that travel across high plateaus often in subzero temperatures need to clothe themselves in many layers usually made from the hair, fur, wool and skins of animals. Villagers on the fertile plains or in tropical mountain forests use natural grasses, leaves, reeds and other materials. The women in a family of sheep farmers will have been taught how to spin, weave and knit at an early age. Essentially, the textile industry has evolved from village skills being passed down through generations.

Archaeological digs in the Andes have uncovered remains of fibrous objects that have been preserved for almost 10,000 years. Significant numbers of fabric items discovered throughout South America are now in collections and span 5,000 years, forming the longest continuous textile record in history, and establishing evidence of the use of woven fabrics in daily life from as long ago as 3,000 BC. Analysis of the discoveries showed that wool, cotton and a plant-based fiber called cabuya, or agave, were the basis of much woven material that was then made into a wide range of clothing; these fibers are the basis of many textile industries today. These threads were also fashioned into fuses for guns and combined to make thicker cord for sandals and ropes. Indigenous weavers from the Otavalo region of Ecuador still produce some of the most outstanding textiles and clothing, and use a special twisting and dying technique to produce the intricate designs that characterize their work. The Otavalo Indians are also famous for their hand-knit sweaters, and it is considered a disgrace in their culture if a girl can't or won't learn the craft.

▲ **Masai** man
and woman in
traditional clothing.

The ubiquitous woolen poncho, thought to have originated in Chile, developed in form throughout the Andean Sierra to reach the stage where, in Ecuador, the poncho can identify the wearer's origins and status. This use of pattern and color in a garment or in jewelry to identify family relationships or tribal ancestry is a common feature in mountain areas. In Papua New Guinea and some of the Kenyan tribes, such as the Masai (where traditional dress is primarily identified in the accessories worn), belts, armbands, necklaces, aprons, nose pieces and chest bands are made from a mix of animal skin and fur, seeds, dried berries, bark, bone, tusk, snakeskin and woven grasses. In Papua New Guinea many patterns and items are unique to a single tribe or a very small area and will immediately identify "strangers." The patterns and colors used in the beadwork of the Masai signify importance or seniority within the tribe.

The Basotho people of Lesotho are a farming community renowned for their skill in textiles. With herds of sheep and goats in abundance, the women are skilled in weaving, knitting and crochet with fine wool and mohair. The traditional Basotho dress used to be capes made from animal skins, but more often today these have been replaced by lengths of woven fabric wrapped around the body. The Lesotho

► **Traditional Tibetan**
*folk costume is colorful
and the designs are
often intricate.*

blanket is now famous, its patterns reflecting political and social changes affecting the country; certain patterns are reproduced for use in special ceremonies and festivals, such as a boy's circumcision, a wedding or the birth of a first child. Lesotho also produces a range of sheepskin products: slippers and jackets, bags and belts as well as whole skins. Perhaps the most famous feature of Lesotho national dress is the Basotho hat—a woven hat in the shape of Mount Qiloane, which also appears on the country's flag. The hat is worn by locals and is also used as a decoration in village homes.

Bolivian women wear bowler hats as part of their national dress. Bolivian dress is as colorful as the dress in most of the Andean regions, but is more likely to have been woven than knitted and then made into shawls and skirts. The material is made in long strips and then sewn together in horizontal bands. Finer material is made into underskirts, or petticoats, so that layers can be added or removed depending on the season.

Bhutanese men and women are required to dress in national costume on a daily basis in an attempt to preserve their cultural heritage. Men wear the gho, a long robe hoisted to the knee and held in place with a belt. The pouch of cloth that hangs over the belt is used for carrying essentials. Women wear a kira, a floor-length rectangle of woven cloth that is wrapped around the body over a blouse (wonju) and also held around the waist with a belt.

The nomadic families and herders in the mountain villages in central Asia are very skilled in the art of weaving strips of fabric on traditional looms. This fabric has a variety of uses, from lining the frame of a yurt (or ger as they are called in Mongolia), the traditional tent of the nomads, to making blankets and covers, clothes, hats, bags and saddle-cloths.

All over the world women use natural plants to produce the dyes to color their fabrics.

◄ **Women at market**
*in the El Alto
neighborhood of
La Paz, Bolivia. While
the colorful shawls
and bags are typical
of the Andes, the
somewhat incongruous
bowler hats worn only
by the women are
unique to Bolivia.*

DWELLINGS

Houses, huts and traditional homes in most high mountain areas are made of the natural resources and materials available in the immediately surrounding area, as most of these materials need to be carried to the site where the house is to

be built. Sometimes there are oxen or donkeys to transport bundles of rushes or baskets of stone, animal dung or mud, but in many cases the villagers themselves have to carry everything they require.

The Masai of Kenya and other highland tribes on the African plains live in permanent villages in a collection of bomas, or loaf-shaped huts, made from mud and cow-dung pasted on a frame of bent poles. These will often be surrounded by a thorny thicket to give some protection from wild animals.

Another way of protecting a family where suitable wood is available is to build the hut on stilts. This also provides shelter for animals in colder regions, and the heat from the animals below can help warm the people in the hut above. Traditional huts built on stilts are seen in many areas of China, Africa and South America.

The hunter-gatherers of Papua New Guinea make shelters under the trees in the tropical mountain forests with thatched roofs and woven reed mats and walls.

The Kalasha people who live in the mountains near the Afghan border in Pakistan live in unique houses built of stone and wood stacked on top of each other against the hillsides. As the houses get higher, so the roof of the lower one becomes the veranda of the upper one. In each village a special communal house, the bashleni, is built for women to move into when they are about to give birth.

The tentlike structures occupied by nomadic tribes are known as yurts across central Asia, and as gers in Mongolia. Designed to be moved quickly and easily, and transported on the backs of pack animals, the traditional yurt is a simple wooden structure consisting of three major parts: the tunduk or shanirak—the round wooden structure at the top of the yurt through which the smoke from the fire inside can escape; kanats—foldable wooden frames which make up the walls; and the uuks—long wooden poles connecting the main body of the yurt with the kanats. The outside covering is a strip of waterproof felt made from sheep or camel's wool. The inside is decorated with woven cloth, which also serves as blankets and seat covers. Similar conic structures are seen in the wigwams of the native American Indian; here hides are

◀ *Typical African hut*

▼ *Several gers* stand together forming a small community near hills in the Gobi region of Mongolia. Gers are an ideal form of shelter for many of the nomadic peoples of this region— they can be erected and dismantled quickly, and they are light enough to be carried on the backs of pack animals.

used to cover the wooden frame, which again is constructed in order to be easily taken down and moved when necessary.

Some of the highest mountain villages in the world are those built by the Sherpas in Nepal, where traditional wooden huts with corrugated aluminum roofs are now being upgraded to have solar heating and modern plumbing—each panel and toilet seat being carried up the mountain in a bamboo basket on the back of a porter!

CULTURAL IDENTITY

Of the many indicators of cultural identity (such as customs and traditions, indigenous practices, values, world views, beliefs, music, arts and crafts), language and folklore are among the best recognized. The development of language is often associated with the system of beliefs upon which a community is founded, giving meaning to words and phrases

often not understood by those outside that community. Other influences on language come from the particular environments and how people have evolved or survived within them. The relative isolation and remoteness of many mountain communities means that rich language systems have evolved, which are specific to very small geographical areas, even to particular family groups. Communication within cultures has also provided rich visual resources for understanding and appreciating past civilizations.

Before the written word, Mexican creativity was expressed through carving and rock art. The Olmecs' monumental stone heads and the murals at Teotihuacan and Bonampak are notable examples of preHispanic art. There are approximately 1,000 rock art sites throughout Bolivia, mainly in the highlands. In Kenya, the Kamba engraved images on calabashes, or gourds, to imbue them with mystical or spiritual meaning. In China, bronze vessels were made and decorated in a similar way, their size and intricacy signifying status and power. The Moche people of Peru sculpted and painted ceramic pots in a style known as huacos-retrato, or portrait pottery, which suggested emotions and states of the human soul (such as happiness or anger) and even depicted diseases and their treatments with very realistic images.

Another Mexican tribe, the Huichols, had no written language until the 20th century, relying only on oral tradition. They preserve their ancient beliefs, rituals and folklore by making elaborate and intricate yarn paintings, just as they have done for thousands of years. These paintings are regarded as sacred offerings, believed to ease entry into the spiritual world. Regions in China produce wax prints, a form of batik, where patterns are created on white cloth using a knife and hot wax.

Tapestry-making is another rich tradition serving to portray images, beliefs and culture in a pictorial way, and is common to many regions. The Salasaca women of Ecuador have made tapestries as a historical record for centuries, and now use more modern looms to increase the production of decorative tapestries for sale to tourists and for export. In some regions of Peru tapestries were produced reflecting the indigenous culture, and tapestries themselves were regarded as worthy of sacrifice. The Incas would take the best tapestries woven by the most skilled weavers to a site in Cuzco and burn them as sacrifices to the sun.

The Incas were expert in using fabric to record and communicate data and details and used everything from colored knotted strings, the quipu, to complete sets of textiles with recognized patterns and symbols woven into them—in

▶ *Papua New Guinean*
performers wearing
traditional costumes
and face paint during
the Mount Hagen
Cultural Show. There
are numerous and
subtle significances to
the various elements
of such traditional
costumes; often they
identify the individual
as belonging to a
certain tribe, but they
can also signify seniority
and status within a
particular group.

essence performing the same function as an early form of filing system.

As spoken languages evolved, so the relative isolation of many mountain peoples meant that languages and dialects could often survive unchanged to the present day. Quechua was the language of the Inca state spoken throughout the Andes before the coming of the Spaniards. Today, there are three main varieties of Quechua spoken by millions of indigenous people, but each of these has dialects understood by certain tribes that are unintelligible in other parts of the region. Similarly, in China, although Mandarin Chinese is the official language and six other Chinese languages are recognized, hundreds of other languages are spoken by over 50 minority nationalities and tribes, with perhaps thousands of dialects existing in some of the more remote mountain regions. In Papua New Guinea, around 650 languages have been identified, of which only around 400 seem to be related. Some languages are spoken only by a few hundred people. In Ethiopia 83 languages are current; the country also boasts its own unique script.

Storytelling is a cultural feature of many tribal groupings across Africa, South America and Asia. Rwanda has a rich tradition of stories and folklore and good storytellers are honored and admired. Most stories carry a message and were used to teach values that were fundamental to successful tribal existence. Others told of heroic exploits or the wrath of evil spirits. Central Asia has a wealth of songs, poems and stories told by akyn, or itinerant minstrels. The Kyrgyz have an entire cycle of oral legends, not unlike the Sagas of Icelandic culture, and equally lengthy, telling of a superhero called Manas. In China, puppet theater has developed as an art form through which to relate ancient tales and fables.

National dress is a very recognizable feature of culture and identity and can be distinctive at a very local level in some regions. In Africa, Papua New Guinea and the altiplano of the Andes the costumes, jewelry and body painting are indicators of not only family or tribe, but also seniority, status and power. In Ethiopia both men and women wear tattoos, in Kenya they wear body-paint, and in other regions of Africa and South America body ornaments such as lip disks and ear and nose piercings are prevalent. In the Kalash region of Pakistan at festival time girls wear a traditional headdress made with braids, shells, coins and beads, which can weigh several kilograms.

BELIEFS, RITUALS AND FESTIVALS

For many mountain cultures the cycle of seasons, the success of crops or the welfare of animals is dictated by the extent to which the gods or spirits look favorably on them. Rituals, festivals and ceremonies in these communities are therefore numerous.

▲ **Terracotta head,** Nigeria

There are over 40 ethnic groups in Nepal, each celebrating different gods and phases of the moon. The two main religions in the country, Hinduism and Buddhism, have coexisted for centuries, with temples and shrines often sharing the same sites and worshipers regarding the same god but with different names. Different dances have evolved to be performed for a variety of religious purposes—from simple rhythmic stick dances to trance-inducing rituals. Dances involving masks are a feature of many cultures including Nepal, Bhutan, Papua New Guinea and Africa. Masks—symbolizing the ancients or clan spirits—would be used in

▲ **Mask,** Papua New Guinea

initiation rites so that the young men could communicate with their ancestors. In Bhutan the sacred mask dances go back to the eighth century; just to watch a dance is considered a spiritual experience. Performers represent saints, wise men, gods and animal forms, this last being at the heart of many indigenous belief systems.

The Huichol tribe in Mexico tries to ensure the successful continuation of its fragile lifestyle through an elaborate series of ceremonies, each linked to a previous one in an annual cycle related to the seasons and stages in crop growing. For example, the ceremony to bring rain for the corn crop is performed by sprinkling the corn with the blood of a deer. However, the deer can only be sacrificed after it has eaten peyote, which in turn must be collected by making a pilgrimage to Wirikuta. The Huichol also believe that animals speak to man, arrows carry prayers and that serpents bring rain. Their artwork captures many of these beliefs and passes them on down through the generations.

In Chile a number of ceremonial dances exist in which the performers imitate animals to make it easier for the hunters to catch them. A more romantic form of ritual, however, is the cueca, a courting dance for couples performed with a handkerchief. For this lively and vigorous dance the men of the Huaso tribe often wear spurs.

It is during the Kalash festival of Choimus in northern Pakistan that single women have traditionally found themselves husbands. Special dance halls exist in the villages for dancing at festivals and these are highly decorated. The music and dances particular to the festival are the cha, or clapping song, accompanying a very energetic circular dance, and the drajahilak, more of a long, slow, storytelling type of song often with numerous verses and chorus. A performance can sometimes last for up to two hours.

Music plays a big part in most tribal systems. The instruments, evolved over centuries, reflect the materials indigenous to the areas where the tribes are established. Rwanda and Ethiopia each have string instruments, flutes made from reeds or bamboo, and drums made in a variety of sizes to

▲ *An Andean musician* from Peru plays the zampoña, a traditional bamboo version of the pan-pipes. The existence of such pipes can be traced back to the ancient Greeks (hence the reference to the Greek god Pan). Similar pipes are found in just about all regions of the Andes.

▲ The rag-dung is a copper horn used in Tibetan rituals.

produce different tones. These are made from hollow logs and plants, such as gourds. Many styles of drum are found in Papua New Guinea where trees are abundant and can be hollowed and carved into a great variety of shapes. The drums are then covered with skins of various animals including snakes, lizards and tree kangaroos, depending upon the tribe and area. A rhythmic drumbeat is the distinguishing feature of much tribal African music.

Andean music is characterized by pan-pipes, percussion and guitar. Bolivia, Ecuador, Chile and Peru all have a particular version of the pan-pipes, a set of cane tubes without holes, played by blowing across the ends of the different length of cane.

Mountain villages in China also have a form of pan-pipe called the lusheng, made from bamboo rather than cane, but almost identical in construction and sound.

At festivals Bolivians play a guitar that is traditionally made by stretching strings across the shell of an armadillo. In Azerbaijan, to construct the stringed instrument called the kobuz the skin of a camel's throat is stretched across a heart-shaped chamber carved from a single piece of wood. The play the instrument a bow is drawn across strings threaded above the chamber.

The religious dances of Bhutan are accompanied in the main by drums and percussion consisting of cymbals and bells, horns and shells.

SPORTS AND PASTIMES

As with so many other aspects of mountain life, sports and games in villages have developed to make the most of the surrounding landscape and the materials to hand. From the Highland Games of Scotland to the wild horse chases in Kyrgyzstan mountain people have played sport from time immemorial.

Traditional games played by people in the small communities of the Scottish Highlands were, by necessity, only those able to take place in rugged mountain landscapes. Tossing the caber (a tree trunk) is one of the spectacular heavy sports, along with putting the shot (a stone often unique to each Gathering or community weighing between 6 and 13 kg/13 and 29 lb), throwing the weight (a 13-kg/29-lb ball on the end of a short chain) and throwing the hammer—

formerly a sledgehammer but now more often an iron ball on a long wooden shaft. Each event tested strength and accuracy and was accompanied by music played on the bagpipes.

Wrestling, a sport found in most regions around the world, was probably once associated with rites of passage. In central Asia alone several forms exist. In Pakistan, the malakhara is a fast and frantic game with much spinning around and flailing of arms and legs. The wrestlers wear baggy trousers and turbans and wrap the sundhro, a long belt, around their waists. The game's objective is for a wrestler to grab the back of his opponent's sundhro and throw him to the ground. Another form of the sport found near the Afghan border is called rhiji, which though similar in dress and rules is a much more considered game (more like a slow waltz with the contestants hanging on to each other), which culminates in a quick flick to floor the unsuspecting opponent. Oil-wrestling in the Taurus mountains of Turkey involves contest-ants dressed in tightly fitting black leather trousers and a belt and then spread liberally with olive oil, which makes gripping the opponent almost impossible. The winner must grab the opponent's belt or inside of the trousers and throw him to the ground. A time limit is imposed in case this also proves to be impossible.

In Bhutan the national sport is archery, which originated in hunting but then developed as a competitive sport. Many other countries have games based around the throwing of sticks, spears and javelins.

► *The traditional Highland sport of tossing the caber relies on great skill as well as strength. The throw is not judged on distance but rather on direction, with the ideal throw resulting in the caber turning over lengthways exactly in line with the competitor. The length of cabers varies from 5.5 m (18 ft) to 6 m (20 ft).*

Games on horseback are another popular form of sport played with variations around the high plateaus of the world. Some of the simplest are those that test a rider's agility and accuracy, in which horses are raced to a target in the ground—which has to be speared—and taken back to the start. In Pakistan this is known as nezabazi. Pig-sticking and boar-hunting, the live versions of this, are still practiced in some parts of India.

Where teams of horsemen chase the same quarry a version of the game of polo is recognized. It is thought that polo originated from a form of hunting and across central Asia variations of this game are played with everything from balls to dead animals. In Pakistan and India the traditional form of polo is played in many towns and villages; in Afghanistan the national sport buzkashi is of a similar nature to polo, the winning team being the first to pitch a headless goat, or dead calf, across the opposing goal line. The game is very much free-form with few rules and can last for up to a week. As in polo throughout the world, the horses, which are specially trained for the game, are much prized and command enormous sums of money, even in relatively poor countries.

A number of versions of horseracing also abound, some of the most interesting being from nomadic culture. In Kyrgyzstan the horseracing tradition is such that children are taught to ride almost before they walk. The Kyrgyz have a saying that if you only have a day to live you should spend half of it in the saddle. Nowadays a game called kyz kumay, (kiss the girl) is played at gatherings across the country. This originated as part of the marriage ceremony at traditional weddings. Carried out on horseback, the bride-to-be riding in full wedding dress is given a small headstart and then chased at a furious pace by the groom who, before a particular point was reached, had to catch up with her and kiss her while still galloping along. If the groom failed to catch the girl, she could then chase him back to the start and if she caught up with him she could use her riding whip across his back. It is likely that this entertainment began as a formalized alternative to abduction, the traditional nomadic way to take a bride.

Other traditional sports common to many regions are animal fights, which are now banned in many parts of the developed world, but which still abound in the more remote regions. They comprise everything from bird fighting in Pakistan to camel wrestling in Turkey.

DECORATIVE ARTS AND CRAFTS

As access to remote regions improves and tourists find ways into villages and communities once undiscovered, more is becoming known about the indigenous arts and crafts of mountain people. Many of the items made for sale to tourists today, providing a source of additional income for villagers, are in fact clothes, household products and decorations that would be found in daily use in the homes. Other products are developed from forms of traditional art and artifacts for which a wider market has been found. These include paintings, batiks, gold, silver and other decorated metalware, sculpture, beadwork and jewelry.

Traditional woodcarvings from Ethiopia, Rwanda and Kenya are renowned. The Kamba in Kenya are particularly known for their blackwood carvings of everything from miniature animals to life-size Masai warriors. The range of carvings is now targeted more for the tourist market, though the carved spoons, ladles and stools represent traditional items. Another feature of Kamba craftwork is the use of coiled wire, in jewelry and also inlaid into their woodwork.

A particular form of carving can be seen in masks, created for use in rituals as well as for decoration in all mountain forest areas. Across Central Asia, in China, Africa, South America and in Papua New Guinea, highly decorated masks are carved and traded and now sold in the tourist markets.

As well as the traditional clothing of Ecuador and Bhutan, these countries' leatherware—in the form of patterned belts, bags, sandals and other small items—is increasingly popular, as is beadwork from Africa, Ecuador and Mexico. With their rich colors and patterns, carpets, tapestries and rugs from villages in Pakistan, Ecuador, Kyrgyzstan, Afghanistan, Peru and Azerbaijan are much sought after, the traditional handmade rugs being unique. Additionally basketry and woven reeds that can be formed into many household articles from wall-hangings to table-mats are produced in many African countries.

China has one of the most varied arts and crafts histories: weird and wonderful kites; paper cuttings to decorate windows, mirrors, lamps and lanterns; silk garments and paintings; jade figures and ornaments; lacquer ware; cloisonné or enamelware; fantastic landscape, flower and bird paintings, and puppets can all be found.

▼ **This close-up** picture shows a knot being tied as an Afghan boy weaves a carpet in his home in Kabul. It takes a month to make a standard-sized 5-m (16.5-ft) carpet, for which a family will get about 12,000 Afghanis ($250)—a rare bright spot in the economy of Afghanistan, one of the world's poorest nations.

THE FUTURE

Policy decisions affecting mountain people and resources are usually made in centers of power far away from mountain communities. The people in these communities are often unrepresented in political forums, even suffering open discrimination in some countries; many receive little or no compensation for changes in their lifestyle and livelihoods as a result of policies that affect the mountain resources upon which they depend, or the services and products that they have provided for generations. Climate change, natural disaster, war, refugee movement and resettlement, migration, poverty and the environmental impacts of commercial and industrial development all threaten the complex human and biological interaction that makes life possible in these fragile ecosystems.

In addition, the crucial role of mountains as the watersheds of the world is being threatened by glacier melt, destruction of the watershed topography and the political tensions surrounding land use and degradation around massive hydroelectric schemes, the latter often running along countries' borders and impacting upon millions of mountain people both socially and economically.

It is imperative that the views, expertise, skills and experience of the people who have lived and worked in the mountains for tens of thousands of years are taken into account when formulating policies for the sustainability of mountain ecosystems in the future. Such people need to become part of the solution at a micro level, as policies and actions in one mountain area can yield very different results and have negative consequences in another mountain range or even on another slope of the same mountain.

As well as sustainability of the biodiversity and resources, policies and development need to address sustainability of the communities. Over 60 percent of the rural Andean population and around 98 million of the Chinese population living in mountain areas are considered to be living below the poverty line, although economic measurement does not always take into account the value of barter trade or the use of communal assets, both crucial to the survival of small, remote communities.

In many countries, policies in the pursuit of development have actually undermined the sustainability of subsistence farming of mountain communities by moving toward ever larger holdings of fertile lowland areas using intensive production methods, including the use of pesticides, fertilizers and large-scale machinery. This in turn drives subsistence farmers toward higher, less stable or fertile ground, which reduces the genetic diversity of both crop seed and native wildlife, thereby increasing the likelihood of disease, poor productivity, soil erosion and landslide.

Some countries have been addressing the issues associated with sustainable mountain development for over 100 years. Yellowstone in the USA was the world's first National Park created in 1872, followed by Yosemite and, in 1887, Tongariro in New Zealand. Tongariro was gifted by the Maori people to Queen Victoria in an inspired attempt to protect their indigenous lands, which they held sacred, against colonists and settlers. It is now estimated that around 10 percent of all mountain areas are protected in this way, but the areas covered do not necessarily correspond to those under the most threat.

Nongovernmental organizations and, more recently, international partnerships and cooperation such as those formed under Agenda 21 and the UN Committees are now coming together to develop integrated approaches to conservation and development, taking cognizance of local knowledge to develop strategies to achieve the formerly competing goals of equity, empowerment, indigenous rights and local management of the natural resources of the world's mountain regions. Many of the initiatives are deliberately on a small scale—their impact and success will lie in the long-term commitment of these organizations, having support from the highest levels of government, not only to implement but also to see through programs that can bring success and sustainability for, as well as protect the identities and cultures of, the mountains and their people.

▼ *With hundreds of millions* of people of mountain regions thought to be living below the poverty line, numerous government and nongovernmental organizations are attempting to encourage sustainable economic development and conservation programs. By working closely with local mountain communities it is hoped that their expertise and knowledge of their environments are central to the initiatives.

Mountain Economy

INTRODUCTION

Mountains cover around one quarter of the Earth's land surface, with almost one fifth of this being in high mountain regions (2,000 m/6,500 ft above sea level). Around 10 percent of the world's population, over 500 million people, live in mountain areas. Mountains are responsible for the climate in many parts of the world, supporting in addition a multiplicity of micro-climates, or zones, from base to summit. Often representing the border between countries, mountains can be rich in mineral resources, have a wide diversity of plant and animal life and are centers for the fastest-growing and largest industry of our time, tourism. For these reasons the economic and even political importance of mountains cannot be underestimated.

Mountains' relative isolation and remoteness, however, their topography and the fragile balance between development and tradition can mean that sustaining commerce, industry and independence is a challenge for the people living in mountain locations. Tools and technologies are often unique to mountain areas. Practices that would seem irrational and unwise in lowland areas, such as plowing furrows running down the mountainside and maintaining many very small and geographically diverse plots of land, are often the only practical or sustainable means of undertaking some activities, and have evolved over generations.

A sense of community is essential in sustaining mountain villages. As villagers move away to more urban areas, communities are broken up and indigenous knowledge and practices are lost. Governments have recognized that this outmigration of workers and young people adversely affects the ability of those left behind in already fragile communities to be self-sustaining or to tend the land sufficiently well to maintain its productivity in the longer term. Agricultural land or terraces in the high mountains will fall into disuse and disrepair, and will revert to wild mountainside that will be difficult to bring back into cultivation in the future. World leaders have agreed that more formal agency and international partnership is necessary to support the sustainable development of mountain communities in the future. To this end a Mountain Chapter was incorporated into Agenda 21, the action plan adopted by more than 178 governments at the United Nations Conference on Environment and Development (UNCED), the Earth Summit, held in Rio de Janeiro in Brazil in June 1992.

The Mountain Chapter—"Managing Fragile Ecosystems: Sustainable Mountain Development"—defined two program areas, critical for identifying and addressing the issues regarding the sustainability of mountain regions. These were:

a) Generating and strengthening knowledge about the ecology and sustainable development of mountain ecosystems, and;

b) Promoting integrated watershed development and alternative livelihood opportunities.

In the first program area six objectives addressed the collection, storage, sharing, analysis and use of information on all aspects of mountain ecosystems. The second program area defined three objectives addressing land and resource use, income generation and infrastructure development, and the impact of natural disasters. The Commission on Sustainable Development (CSD) was created in December 1992 to ensure effective follow-up of the UNCED, monitoring and

▶ **The problem** facing many mountain communities today is that many of the young people are migrating to cities in the hope of finding better-paid work. This results in increasingly aging local populations who are often unable to manage the land, which in turn sees once-productive agricultural land fall into disuse.

reporting on implementation of the agreements at local, national, regional and international levels.

In 1997, an Earth Summit progress review was made by the UN General Assembly meeting in special session, during which participating countries filed progress reports. And in 2002 the full implementation of Agenda 21, the Program for Further Implementation of Agenda 21 and the Commitments to the Rio Principles were strongly reaffirmed at the World Summit on Sustainable Development (WSSD) held in Johannesburg, South Africa.

The Mountain Partnership, a voluntary alliance of partners dedicated to improving the lives of mountain people and protecting mountain environments around the world, was launched at the World Summit for Sustainable Development in 2002. Presently, 45 countries, 14 intergovernmental organizations and 58 major groups (civil society, NGOs and the private sector, for example) are members of the partnership.

The intention of the Mountain Partnership is not to create a new entity; but rather to build on the global alliance of individuals and organizations involved in mountain issues that have grown up since the Earth Summit in Rio. It captures the momentum created during the International Year of Mountains in 2002, when national committees were formed in 78 countries to raise awareness about mountain issues and initiated concrete activities to improve mountain livelihoods and environments.

AGRICULTURE
Mountain landscape
Successful and productive agriculture in mountainous areas is far from straightforward, but the mountain people's knowledge, skills and understanding of their particular conditions and environment have enabled them and their subsistence lifestyles to survive for centuries.

Mountain landscape is characterized by zones that are partly dependent upon altitude but locally dependent upon many other factors including the slope of the terrain, the direction in which the land is facing, the prevailing weather systems and the underlying biochemical systems.

High mountains generally contain within short distances a number of tightly compressed natural vegetation belts, which range from warm valley floors through grasslands, coniferous forests and tundra, to permanent snow and ice at the summit. These meadow and tundra zones are known as Alpine wherever in the world they occur.

In order to make the most of these conditions mountain farmers have evolved many specialist techniques to maximize the productivity of the land, not least a system of working together and respecting common areas.

Lifestyle

Although output varies according to country and mountain range, the lifestyle of mountain farming communities around the world is strikingly similar. The farming involves a careful combination of animal husbandry and crop cultivation using the different altitude zones for different purposes depending upon the season, and diversifying the production by plant and by geography as widely as possible. The threats of landslide, forest fire, flooding, adverse weather, crop failure, disease or even human error are therefore minimized.

Technology for the mountain farmer is often handmade and, having evolved over centuries, is simple but practical. Equipment such as short-handled hoes and scythes and the Andean foot-plow is unique to mountain farming in places where tractors and other vehicles, or even animal-drawn plows, could not function.

In lower areas, permanent villages are frequently surrounded by fields enclosed with stone walls and each family will have its own cultivated area, growing a wide variety of fruit and vegetables, mainly for the family's own use or for

▼ *Successful cultivation* and management of mountain regions relies on local knowledge and experience that has been gained and passed on for generations. To develop sustainable agricultural practices it is essential that this local knowledge is central to any initiatives.

local trading. The fields will be used for cropping during the summer and grazing in the winter. Crops that do well in mountain areas are tea, coffee and corn, and the export of these crops from the Andes, Himalayas and East African Highlands to developing countries provides much-needed income for mountain farmers.

Above the villages land is used for haymaking, for growing hardier grains (suited to the local environment) and for vegetables such as potatoes, a staple of many mountain diets and a food source that now has over 3,500 varieties to ensure maximum yield whatever the terrain.

The higher the land, the less suited it will be for commercial agriculture, and where foodstuffs can be grown, most of the production will be for winter fodder. These fields will more generally be used for seasonal grazing.

Biodiversity

The grazing of animals both in the high meadows and on the valley floors adds to the biodiversity of mountain regions. Scientists have found that in some mountain areas many more plant species exist in mountain forests than in a much larger area of tropical rain forest. When animals were banned from grazing to prevent damage to the flora, some plant species died because the surrounding overgrowth blocked out light and used up necessary nutrients. When

▼ *China alone* has approaching 100 million people living in mountain regions who are recognized as living below the poverty line. Even the use of summer pastures as here in the Pamirs, western China, needs to be carefully managed if the land is to retain its biodiversity and remain productive in the long term.

◀ **Terracing** has been practiced in many mountain regions for thousands of years, as here in these terraced rice fields on the island province of Bali, Indonesia. Terracing, combined with often complex irrigation systems, is an excellent way of increasing the productivity of fertile soil.

animals were reintroduced the rare plant species recovered. This balance of farming, cultivation and natural biodiversity has been understood by the indigenous populations for centuries and has allowed them to harvest many of these plants for medicinal, culinary and cosmetic purposes, again generating much-needed income. Some plants and extracts can command high prices, especially as many of the plants are restricted to single mountain ranges, and in some instances, single mountains.

Maximizing yields

On steep slopes a very recognizable feature of mountain agriculture is terracing. This raising of level banks of earth brings into use fertile soils in otherwise inaccessible places

117

and, combined with intricate irrigation systems, is widely used in China to grow rice, and in the Himalayas, for everything from crop production to grazing.

Whether the land is terraced or continuous, it is usual for farmers to own or cultivate up to 100 tiny individual plots that can be spread over tens of kilometers. In such fragile and challenging environments dispersion of plots reduces the risk of total crop failure. Planting a wide range of crops in different localities and at different altitudes means that a poor yield in one part of the mountain will not necessarily be repeated elsewhere. If plots in one area are destroyed through frost, fire, hail or landslip, the other plots will remain productive and the farmer will not have lost a season's harvest. Higher or sunnier plots mature earlier than others, enabling farmers with labor-intensive means of crop collection to phase their harvesting over a period of time, thus preventing the loss of valuable crops. In addition, splitting the productive land area among families ensures that each farmer will have access to a variety of soil types.

To maximize yields still further many mountain communities practice a complex system of crop rotation, much in the same way as lowland farmers do, but more dependent upon organic processes due to restricted access to fertilizer or other artificial means of enhancement. Depending upon the number and range of crops that the soil and climate support, up to seven stages in the farming cycle can be identified. The planting and growing of the various crops, grazing (hence natural fertilizing by livestock) and then leaving the land fallow to ensure soil recovery follow in strict rotation.

Forests

Forests cover over nine million km^2 (three and a half million mi^2) of the world's mountains and, aside from supporting the forestry industry, perform useful functions associated with mountain agriculture. Agroforestry is the practice of creating ecosystems similar to the area's natural ecosystems, but comprising species that are useful to man. For example, planting trees to provide shelter for crops and to anchor soils on slopes or terraces that also yield edible fruit, berries and seeds (while providing fodder or useful compost material) maximizes the productive value of the land.

Livestock

The less fertile zones of Alpine tundra tend to be used for grazing. Sheep, goats, llamas, deer and yak are best suited to high altitudes and rough surfaces, and the livestock herded in these regions have developed not only thick coats but bigger

▲ **Yaks and goats** are well adapted for living in high mountains. Their thick coats protect them from the cold, while large lungs and strong hearts enable them to breath the thin air of high altitudes. Livestock are crucial to the survival of many mountain peoples, who are careful to use almost every part of an animal for food, clothing, tools and even to make handcrafted items to sell to tourists.

lungs and more powerful hearts to enable them to breathe the thinner air more efficiently. These animals are bred for wool, milk and meat, but also for their skins and bones. Mountain people utilize as much of an animal as possible in the provision of their own clothing, tools, household articles and furnishings; these items are also sold to tourists.

Sustainability

As the pressure on mountain agriculture increases as a result of depopulation, increased industrial and commercial activity encroaching on mountain communities, the demands of tourism and the need for greater productivity to yield higher income levels, the sustainability of these communities is in danger. The International Center for Integrated Mountain Development (ICIMOD), working in partnership with governments around the world, has identified a number of agriculture-related technologies and practices specifically suited to mountain conditions, which have had some measure of success in areas of the Himalayas. These include angora rabbit fiber and meat production, beekeeping, water harvesting, the use of plastic film and polytunnels, the use of sunflower stalks as a by-product to provide alternative supports for vegetable growing, and the production of fodder supplements to increase the food value of the limited feed resources available for livestock over winter.

INDUSTRY

Many of the world's mountain regions are rich in minerals, forestry, agricultural land or in some instances a combination of these. Some have large urban settlements within the mountains or nearby. Others are primarily inhabited by large numbers of people living in villages or small communities. The industrial make-up of these regions is in part dictated by the mix of these factors.

Mineral processing

In countries with a significant mining industry there are often extensive mineral-processing operations. Metallic minerals such as tin, copper and iron as well as the precious metals silver and gold are processed in smelters and foundries throughout South America, earning significant export income for several countries. Trace elements and rare minerals are derived from the salts in Bolivia, and Tajikistan has a large aluminum-smelting industry. Colombia's varied chemicals industry produces fertilizers, insecticides and other derivatives of their mineral wealth.

In areas with mining operations for nonmetals (such as limestone, sandstone and clays), the products are often used in construction. And cement and ceramics earn both domestic and foreign income in countries including Bhutan, Colombia, Kyrgyzstan, Mexico and Nepal.

Precious gems are also extracted and refined in some mountain areas—emeralds in Colombia and diamonds in Lesotho for example.

Forest products

Countries with forests within easy access of transportation routes and urban centers have built up a range of industries dependent upon the timber from these forests. Wood pulp and paper, chipboard and wood veneer are manufactured throughout the forested regions of Bhutan, Columbia and Mexico, where in the more urban areas everything from furniture to matches is produced for both the domestic and export markets.

The danger of timber-based industries is that, unless the forestry is managed properly, the industry destroys the very resource upon which it relies. In addition, especially in mountain areas, good forestry management is essential to prevent damage to other resources from soil erosion, land-slide and changes in water retention, and to preserve the communities that need the mountain for their livelihoods.

Food processing

Mountain areas supporting agriculture or livestock farming beyond subsistence level often have a well-developed food-processing industry. Those with mineral resources or forestry operations frequently develop the manufacturing base to produce the packaging too.

Austria's mountainous west specializes in milk and milk products operations, as does Switzerland with its tradition of producing fine chocolate.

Many tropical mountain regions in Africa and South America produce coffee and cacao, and Asia, China and India grow tea as a cash crop. The processing and packaging of these crops takes place on farms and in factories across these countries prior to export. Much has been done in the last few years to ensure that the smaller farmers in these countries receive a fair income for their crops so that they can exist alongside the multinational companies managing huge estates.

Textiles

In many mountain regions textile production has grown from a village industry into a major manufacturing sector, utilizing the spectrum of natural resources from cotton, sisal, jute and peyote, through silk, to a wide range of animal fur, hair and wool from sheep, goats, camel, llama, alpaca, yak and mohair. It is an activity that has traditionally employed the women of the tribes and villages.

◀ *As well as* their agricultural potential, many mountain regions harbor important natural mineral resources, such as the Muzo emerald mines of Colombia. Emeralds have been mined here since before the arrival of the Spanish in the early 16th century, and Muzo emeralds are today recognized as some of the finest examples in the world.

The production of tapestries, carpets and rugs is a major industry in many central Asian countries where the mountain plateaus are ideal for herding the large flocks of animals that provide some of the raw materials. Afghanistan, Kyrgyzstan, Azerbaijan, Nepal and Tajikistan are among those countries now benefiting from the export of these products, along with Ecuador and Peru in South America. These regions also produce high-quality woven materials, which are manufactured into clothing and household products.

The production of superior cotton yarn and cloth is a significant manufacturing sector in both Pakistan and Tajikistan. Silk and silk products are major industries in Afghanistan and China, with the latter also producing fine examples of silk paintings and embroidery.

Lesotho blankets, handwoven from a mix of cotton and sheep's wool, are world-famous, being made in a variety of traditional and popular patterns and colors, and of which some are for special occasions.

Jumpers, sweaters, shawls and ponchos, the traditional warm wear for the people of the high plateaus, have been woven, knitted and crocheted in traditional patterns and styles for generations—and are now much sought after.

Handicrafts

Although often operating only on a small scale in village homes or workshops, the handicrafts sector is significant in the income it brings to small mountain communities, both in local trading and increasingly to the tourist market.

In developing countries where livestock farming is predominant, leathercraft and creating sheep or goatskin products are key activities. Belts, bags, sandals, shoes, hats and other accessories and decorative artifacts are produced in indigenous styles and patterns.

Villages with access to cane, bamboo, rushes or the variety of cereal straws left after harvesting will often produce a wide range of basketware, woven mats, wind instruments, dolls and toys. Villagers in mountain forest areas create woodcarvings and engravings, as well as a range of wood-based musical instruments.

Over the centuries, pots, dishes and other vessels have been produced for daily village life from a variety of muds and clays. Ceramics is now a major craft industry; modern techniques are used, but the patterns and glazes are in many cases traditional.

Jewelry is an important part of the dress of many tribes and family groups in mountain areas, and has been a valuable trading commodity among tribes and villages. In more

▲ *In many mountain villages* locally manufactured goods, such as these metal artifacts from Nepal, are an important source of income. Such goods are either sold directly to tourists traveling through the region or sold for export to Europe or North America.

developed societies it is also an adornment signifying wealth, seniority or status or simply for decoration. The portable nature of jewelry makes it very popular in tourist areas as a souvenir. Items are made from many materials, though traditionally from resources close to hand. These include horn, feathers, bone, seeds, dried plants, tortoise-shell, bark, skins and teeth as well as silver, gold, bronze and copper. In some mountain areas precious stones such as emeralds, rubies, garnets and lapis lazuli are locally available and will be used.

Nonwood forest products

In recent years concern over the impact of deforestation on mountain communities has prompted research and development into sustainable activities that depend upon nonwood forest products. Projects in the Hindu Kush region of the Himalayas, for example, which involve the harvesting of a variety of plants growing within the forests that have high medicinal or culinary qualities have shown promising signs. Similar studies are being carried out in the high forests of the Andes, although these specialize more in herb and spice production.

MINING
History and development

Millions of years ago, the forces that built the mountains created rich deposits of minerals that have been used for millennia, starting with clays for making vessels. The discovery of copper marks the period when metal began being used to make hunting tools, domestic utensils and other artifacts. Evidence of this activity 5,000 years ago comes from the Nal Cemetery in Quetta, Pakistan, while China was working bronze, a copper-tin alloy, around this time.

In Kumaun in the central Himalayas, miners used to collect the ore in large bags on their backs before washing it to remove the soil and mixing it with fresh cow-dung to make small pellets. These pellets were the dried in the sun and put into a furnace or crucible. While smelting the ore, the crucible was covered with ash, and the molten liquid copper settled at the crucible's base. The cooled metal was then worked locally.

As mining became more commercial so the techniques changed. The first established mines in the mountains were

very labor-intensive operations. Ore was collected with pick and shovel, and then crushed, ground and processed near the mine at great altitudes. The copper concentrate was taken down narrow mountain tracks, originally by pack animal, then by trucks, covering often huge distances to smelters or to ports for export. Poor weather, landslides or accidents could kill both pack animals and men or destroy the track, while snow in winter could cause delays. The steep-sided mountain valleys near the mines were used to store the tailings (the rubble residue after ore separation); this required the construction of high dams on account of the significant wastage, often as much as 98 percent of extracted rock. There was a high risk of damage further down the mountain if the dams failed, and the leaching of chemicals and minerals into the watercourses was dangerous.

Following technological advances in the late 19th and early 20th centuries, the ore was transported by aerial cableways—the forerunner of the cable-car mechanism used to transport skiers up the slopes today. Large buckets ran on two cables, one going up the mountain empty and the other running down, full.

With operations becoming more mechanized so the volume of material handled has increased. Open-cast mining is carried out by bulldozers and large-capacity trucks, while conveyor belts are used to move the rock and crushed ore around the mine site.

More modern methods of processing and transportation have improved not only productivity and efficiency but also safety, and have benefited the environment and mountain communities. Today, large machines called concentrators are used to process the ore (at a rate of up to 70,000 tons per day) to the stage where it can be mixed with water and transported down a pipeline to a smelting plant or port for export.

At one of the world's largest copper mines at Antamina, Peru, a 300 km-(190 mi-)long pipeline runs from the mine at 4,300 m (14,100 ft) to the port at sea level. Pipeline technology is available wherever flotation can be used.

Mining in the high mountain countries

Mining has taken place throughout the Andes for centuries, and thousands of working mines exist. It is one of the most strongly mineralized mountain chains in the world, with major deposits of tin, silver, gold, antimony and lead, as well as copper. Many developed countries have a mining interest in South America, including the USA, Canada and Britain.

Before the Andean range existed, the future mountains of the high plateaus were underwater. Thick layers of salt were

▼ *The Inti Raymi gold mine, one of Bolivia's most lucrative mines, is located along the altiplano, a high plateau along the Andes Mountains. As well as gold, Bolivia also has significant deposits of silver-tin and antimony, used to make semiconductors.*

stored in the ocean bed, and eventually covered by more than 3,000 m (10,000 ft) of sediment. When the mountains were uplifted a basin was formed into which rivers flowing down the surrounding volcanic rocks drained. This formed an inland sea trapped between the eastern and western ranges of the mountains and, after a complex process of volcanic activity, erosion and evaporation, the salt was mineralized and formed the Uyuni and Coipasa salt-flats. Lake Titicaca is a remnant of this vast inland sea, and its waters are still slightly salty.

There is a series of 11 salt and sediment layers, representing former lakes, which may extend to 500 m (1,600 ft) underground. The lithium and potassium deposits located in the brines of the Uyuni salt pan are believed to be the largest of their kind.

At one time Bolivia mined about one fifth of the world's antimony, used in flameproofing compounds and semiconductors, and the country also sits on major silver-tin deposits along the eastern Andes. The discovery of ore in Cerro Rico prompted the foundation of the city of Potosí in 1545 at the foot of the hill. Large-scale excavation began and the mine became the largest in the world, producing around one half of the world's silver over the next 200 years. In 1672 a mint was established and Potosí became one of the largest and

◀ *Even the remote* and
tiny kingdom of Bhutan,
lying nestled between
India and China, has
deposits of numerous
minerals, including tin,
tungsten and zinc, as
well as major deposits
of limestone, clay,
graphite and slate,
for which the country
is famous.

wealthiest cities in the world, its mineral wealth enabling the Spanish to continue their conquest of the indigenous peoples of South America. Today the mines of Oruro, Lallagua, and Morococala are more important, producing high-quality gems and crystals, and many rare minerals.

Afghanistan has reserves of a wide range of mineral resources, including iron, chrome, copper, silver, gold, barite, sulfur, talc, magnesium, mica, marble and lapis lazuli, though extraction is mainly limited to energy-related resources such as coal. Surveys have also revealed deposits of asbestos, nickel, mercury, lead, zinc, bauxite, lithium and rubies. The iron and copper reserves, among the world's largest, are located at Hajji Gak, in the Hindu Kush, at an altitude of almost 4,000 m (13,000 ft). The mining industry holds great potential for the Afghanistan economy now that there is some political stability following the fall of the Taliban in 2001, and international efforts to improve the infrastructure and economy are yielding results.

In India, minerals form up to 15 percent of annual exports, the country being among the world's largest producers of mica, coal, lignite, barites, iron ore, bauxite, manganese ore and aluminum. A further development opportunity in the mining sector is that of placer gold resources on the Himalayan border.

The Qinghai-Tibetan plateau is an area of great natural resource for China. The regions is abundant in salt, petroleum and natural gas, nonferrous metal minerals and nonmetal minerals, as well as being a significant site for hydroelectric power. However, all of the resources are situated at high or extreme altitudes. The gold mines at Tok Dschalung are at 4,880 m (16,010 ft) in the Western Himalayas. Open-cast mining for coal is at an altitude of 5,250 m (17,220 ft) at Machala in eastern Tibet. Also, the Tibetans work at altitudes of up to 6,000 m (20,000 ft) in central Tibet in the Tanggula range, mining quartz for half of the year. These are higher than the mines of Cerro de Pasco (4,330 m/14,210 ft) and Morococha (4,540 m/14,900 ft) in Peru, and similar to the Aucanquilcha mine in Chile. China's current problem resembles that of America in the gold-rush days—millions of individuals living in poverty will exploit mineral reserves as soon as they are identified, and cherry-pick the easily accessible material, leaving a much more difficult resource for the State to mine economically. India has a similar problem in that hundreds of small-scale slate mines have stripped much of the topsoil and forest from the Khaniara region of the Himachal Pradesh, triggering landslides and destroying valuable mountain resource.

Bhutan has a varied mineral industry, the major extraction being of limestone and clay, though production includes marble, dolomite, graphite and slate, this last being identified as some of the best in the world. In addition, deposits of copper, gypsum, lead, tin, tungsten, zinc, coal, beryl, mica, pyrites, tufa and talc have also been found.

Crushed rock, and sand and gravel

The igneous rocks making up many mountain chains are, or have the potential to be, major sources of crushed rock for aggregate purposes. Crushed rock is used locally for construction and road building in developing areas, but unless sources are close to the coast the transportation of crushed rock material is not economic. Many small quarries are often opened up, operated and then closed near the site of construction, particularly for important buildings or major routes. Crushed rock is normally quarried, as opposed to mined, with the waste used as back-fill.

Sand and gravel, another important material used in construction, is found in significant quantities in many river valleys that have been glaciated. There are deposits in mountain areas, but again this material is not economic to dry, sort and transport great distances.

Mountain-top removal mining

In open-cast mines over large areas rock layers at the peaks of mountain ranges are systematically removed to uncover coal beds so that they can be mined, starting from the top of mountain ridges and proceeding down to a level where it is no longer economic. Rock layers broken up during the mining process take up more volume than the original undisturbed layers and this excess material is placed in the steep heads of streams along the mountainside and fills adjacent valleys. As mining is completed, some of this excess material should be used to try to recreate the original contour of the ridge tops. Water exposed during the operation is often stored in slurry compounds and used in coal-washing operations. The resulting liquid waste is toxic as a result of the chemicals used in the process, as well as the particles or dust, known as coal fines, which are washed off the coal, laden with heavy metal compounds such as arsenic and mercury and held in suspension in the waste water.

This practice is causing major controversy, especially in the Appalachians. Removing the surface soil destroys habitats and vegetation unlikely to regenerate in other parts of the mountain or return after mining ceases. The blasting process to extract the coal, as well as creating noise pollution and potentially dangerous vibrations in the Earth, can lead to "fly rock"—rock particles raining down onto neighboring settlements, in a similar way to a volcanic eruption. The cleared sections also impact upon the rate and direction of runoff following rainstorms, creating the potential for flooding and landslides. A break in the storage system of the liquid slurry can result in millions of tons of toxic waste being released into watercourses and onto neighboring land. Even when restoration does take place, the original contours can never be recreated because of the volume of material that has been removed.

The environment

Mining clearly benefits mountain communities, but it can damage ecosystems and mountain cultures, both in the mountains and for the surrounding lowland communities. Despite recent improvements and regulations now in force, many environmental issues remain. Adverse impacts on the extremely fragile mountain ecosystems can be difficult or impossible to rectify. Among the most serious environmental consequences are damage to water quality and quantity,

▼ **Open-cast mining,** as practiced at the Grasberg Mine in Irian Jaya Province, Indonesia, while being commercially a successful way of extracting vast amounts of coal is extremely controversial. The practice can have a huge impact on the local environment and nearby communities.

▲ **Porters pass** an area of deforestation while at Lanjura La on the Everest Trail. Deforestation is a major problem in the Everest region since most people use firewood to cook rather than kerosene. Ecologically minded tourists are encouraged to stay in teahouses that use fuels supported by a National Parks' scheme.

loss of biodiversity and vegetative cover and the effects of pollution. The visual effects of mining are the most obvious (surface dumps, slag heaps, valley fill and open pits) but the serious side-effects of deforestation and mining operations take the form of flooding, mudslides and landslides. Some operations have a human impact, not just in the fatalities and injuries that occur annually, but also in displacing local residents or taking over agricultural or grazing land for mining purposes without reinvesting profits into the local economy.

Agenda 21 of UNCED called for governments and mining companies to reduce the environmental and social effects of mining, and a number of initiatives since then have begun to have a positive impact. New techniques in blasting and processing have helped to reduce environmental damage from chemical waste, and mining associations have begun to address the problems of global warming. The International Labor Organization Convention on Safety and Health in Mines has established a principle for national action on the improvement of working conditions in the mining industry, toward which increasing numbers of countries are working.

ENERGY

Some form of energy is essential at high altitudes—for cooking and particularly heating. As tourists reach ever more remote communities so their demands for facilities and services increase the pressures on limited energy resources, and many alternative technologies such as hydroelectric, solar and wind power are being adopted as a result.

Traditionally, the two most accessible sources of power for mountain communities have been water and wood, and although hydroelectric power is efficient, clean and in common use in most mountain areas, burning wood fuel is becoming unsustainable. Air pollution is destroying surrounding ecosystems and adversely affecting the health of people and animals. Also, as wood is collected and forests destroyed, villagers (usually the women, who sustain family and village life) need to travel further and for longer to collect the wood fuel. Other biomass sources have been used in the place of wood, especially in nonforest areas, but the use of animal dung and crop waste for generating energy means that these materials are diverted away from use as fertilizers to enrich often poor soil, which in turn affects crop productivity and grazing.

Where wood is the only available resource for generating energy, introducing sustainable fuelwood forests and using the wood through more efficient means is helping to slow the rate of deforestation and reduce pollution levels.

▼ *Many alternative sources* of energy are being sought to help reduce the reliance on precious fossil fuels and also to provide heat and power to remote mountain locations. Arrays of photovoltaic cells, which turn sunlight into electricity, are being tested in a number of regions; they enjoy the benefits of reliability, longevity and ease of use.

For remote mountain regions the alternative energy solutions that are being developed are small, efficient and decentralized—thus overcoming the difficulties of distance, capital costs and demanding terrain, and avoiding the problems inherent in energy distribution over a network.

The potential for solar power is significant, though it is not yet as widely taken up as hydroelectricity. Solar photovoltaic systems are attractive for small-scale use: they are reliable, having no moving parts; the cells degrade very slowly; and the systems are simple to use. The intricacies of the mountain environments need to be understood (prevailing weather, relief, altitude, slope and aspect), but then an effectively positioned installation will yield many benefits to the community. Solar cooking is already taking place in the mountain areas of China and India, with further developments in Nepal and Pakistan. Solar heating is being installed in public buildings in Tibet and India, while in Nepal all remote airport and telecommunications facilities are powered by solar energy.

Wind power is one of the fastest-growing forms of energy, and mountain chains and valleys have some of the characteristics that give rise to extremely strong winds. These winds include the föhn of the Alps, the chinook of the Rockies and the zonda of the Andes. However, the occurrence of rime and ice at higher altitudes, and the effects of turbulence in these areas, are potential problems; small-scale turbines are therefore increasingly appropriate in mountain contexts.

Mountain communities that live around the geological hotspots of the world (such as Japan, Mexico and Indonesia) benefit from the geothermal reservoirs close enough to the Earth's surface to be reached by drilling. Unfortunately, however, this form of energy does not travel well and is most efficient near major centers of population.

In many remote communities animals still fulfill an important role in generating the power required for driving equipment or providing the fats for burning.

Hydroelectricity

Mountains are often referred to as the "water towers of the world," with fresh water rising in them providing the water needs of as many as half of the world's population. This water is used for drinking and other domestic use, for fisheries, irrigation, industry, recreation, transportation and to generate energy.

Hydroelectricity is a form of power that uses the energy stored in water held at a height then released under gravity to turn a turbine, which in turn produces electricity. It is a mature and proven technology, perhaps the oldest method

► *The Diablo Dam* in the North Cascades National Park, Washington, USA, was built between 1927 and 1936 and provides hydroelectric power to the Seattle region. Hydroelectricity provides in the region of 20 percent of the world's power generation, and many of the projects have no or little environmental impact. However, some projects, particularly ones in which large rivers are dammed, can cause massive environmental damage and result in the displacement of local populations.

of harnessing renewable energy. The first water wheels were used for irrigation over 2,000 years ago. Within 200 years they were being used to turn millwheels and by the time of the Industrial Revolution, in the mid 1700s, their use was extensive. They had been replaced by the late 1800s by water turbines, which were smaller, more compact, more efficient and ran at higher speeds than the water wheel and, more importantly, were particularly suitable for electricity generation. Today, hydroelectric power provides almost 20 percent of the world's total electricity supply in over 150 countries, a third of which rely on it for more than half of their electricity needs.

While many industrialized countries have developed most of their possible productive sites, most developing countries still have enormous potential. In mountainous areas significant hydroelectric power can be generated utilizing the steep gradients, relatively high levels of rainfall and storage of water as snow and ice at higher altitudes. Steep valley sides and gorges allow the storage of large amounts of water in deep reservoirs behind dams that have relatively modest construction requirements and remove the risk of flooding large surface areas. The stored water can also be used for irrigation and to supplement the local water supply.

Size of hydroelectric scheme

Large hydroelectric projects account for about 20 percent of the world's power generation. During the past two decades, major controversies have arisen over the human and environmental impacts of such hydroelectric schemes as the Narmada Project in India, Three Gorges in China and the Great Whale Project in Canada. These massive projects consist of dams built on major rivers to create reservoirs, flooding many thousands of square kilometers of land, displacing entire communities and wiping out habitats of indigenous species of plants, birds, animals and

▼ *A highway* cuts through the arid hills of the Atacama Desert in northern Chile, bounded by snow-capped volcanoes. This road is part of the Pan-American Highway, a network of roads that almost connects Alaska in North America with

fish. Downstream the quality and quantity of water available for irrigation and urban use is decreased, and these problems are exacerbated when the river also forms the border between two countries and water shortages cause political tensions.

Improvements in small turbine and generator technology mean that micro-hydro schemes, those producing less than 100 kW, are becoming an attractive means of producing electricity. Useful power can be produced even from a relatively small stream. Mountain villages and even isolated farms could benefit from small plants that generate sufficient electricity for domestic needs, or from larger plants that could supply the needs of localized irrigation systems or other commercial activity.

Hydroelectric power requires the source to be relatively close to the place where the power is to be used, or to a grid connection, although in most mountain regions regional or national grids do not exist and the value of small hydroelectric schemes lies in their potential to provide electricity locally. However, if a main grid connection is not available, seasonal variations in the water flow may affect the power supply and the impact of this must be considered.

Pumped storage systems

One way of overcoming seasonal variation or supplying instant power at times of peak demand is to use pumped hydroelectric energy storage systems. This type of technology has been in use since as early as 1929, making it the oldest kind of large-scale energy storage technology. Indeed, before 1970 this was the only commercially available option for storing energy.

A pumped hydroelectric storage system consists of two large reservoirs located at different heights. During peak demand, water is released from the upper reservoir, dropping down high-pressure shafts; it passes through turbines located at the base of the shafts, generating electricity and finally gathering in the lower reservoir. The same technology operates in traditional hydroelectric plants; the difference here is that when demand drops, or the grid can supply demand, the water from the lower reservoir is pumped back up to the upper reservoir ready to be released when next required. The Dinorwig plant near Llanberis in the mountains of north Wales is one of the best-known plants in the world, constructed in the 1970s within a cavern built into the mountain. The plant is second in size only to the Tianhuanping pumped storage system in China, though Dinorwig benefits from its reservoirs being an extra 50 m (165 ft) apart.

Chile in South America. The only gap in the link exists between Colombia and Panama. Known as the Darién Gap, this is a 87-km (54-mi) stretch of harsh mountainous jungle, which some nations believe should be left undeveloped.

TRANSPORTATION AND COMMUNICATIONS

Transportation

It is indicative of the varying expectations of communities around the world that one of the measures of an appropriate road network in Switzerland is that everyone should be able to drive home, whereas in Ethiopia every village should be within one day's walk of a road.

Since people have used pack animals to carry loads they have traded with others—bartering necessities or trading surpluses with neighboring villages. To extend foraging areas or open up trading opportunities, or even to reach spiritual sites, tracks have been built into, through, across and around mountains.

Economic development and military strategy have often pushed these roads further into remote regions and across borders, made them wider and with better surfaces, and able to support passenger, freight and military vehicles. However, in many mountainous areas with difficult terrain, "hub and spoke" systems of transportation still remain—

◀ **Unsurprisingly, bridges** are an essential form of communication and transportation in all mountain regions. In some Buddhist countries bridges have assumed an almost spiritual significance. A bridge's form and structure relies on the skills of the local workforce and the raw materials available.

centers of economic activity developing around road ends and railheads, with porters and pack animals providing the necessary carriage service into the smaller villages.

In the high mountains and across plateaus some major highways link major cities and population centers. These include the Transoceanic Highway from Peru to Brazil, the Karakoram Highway between Pakistan and China, the Atacama desert route between Argentina and Chile, and the 20 road and rail routes forming the Transalpine network connecting eight countries and 11 million people in central Europe.

It is both difficult and extremely expensive to construct good road networks in mountainous areas to connect smaller villages, and countries have arrived at different solutions to these problems. In Yemen there is a grading and points system to determine which rural roads get the go-ahead. Indonesia has a community solution. All available men from the villages along the route help in the construction process. The skills they learn are then used in their own villages to build the smaller connecting roads. Each village as a result is able to maintain its own section.

The steep valleys and gorges of many mountain areas make construction of roadways or even tracks impossible. In these areas there has been a long tradition of bridge building, which in Buddhist countries has an additional spiritual significance—the building of a bridge being seen as removing an obstacle. The size and shape of a bridge depends upon locally available materials and the extent of local skills and knowledge. A combination of rope, log, bamboo arch, cantilever, iron chain and bamboo/cane bridges are found in the Himalayas and parts of the Andes. Bridges are so important to the communities of Nepal and Bhutan that the countries' governments have developed strategic bridge-building projects: Nepal with more state intervention linked with local initiatives; and Bhutan with extensive community participation.

The mountain transportation probably most familiar to tourists are the rope-ways seen in ski resorts the world over. Arguably the most ancient technology for crossing difficult mountain terrain (their existence dates back to the third century BC in China), a rope-way allows people and goods to be moved around the mountains safely and economically.

In many parts animals still provide the only means of moving around either vast plateaus at high altitudes or negotiating difficult mountain tracks without access to fuel or spare parts. Horses, donkeys, mules, oxen, yaks, llamas and camels remain widely in service depending upon the task, climate and terrain; and throughout history animals from elephants to camels have been used as military transportation.

What's New

The Mountain Forum bulletin has recently been relaunched. Mountain Forum members worldwide submitted news, opinions and updates.
Click here to download your copy.

ON-LINE
LIBRARY

Mountain Forum's Annual Report for 2004 is available online.
Click here to download your copy.

APMN and **InfoAndina** have elected their regional board members. To learn more, please go to APMN election and InfoAndina election.

E-MAIL LISTS

ABOUT US   MEMBERSHIP   REGIONAL NETWORKS   CALENDAR   SEARCH

HOME | ABOUT US | MEMBERSHIP | REGIONAL NETWORKS | CALENDAR | ON-LINE LIBRARY | E-MAIL LISTS | SEARCH

PHOTO CREDITS

Light aircraft are increasingly employed to link small communities in mountain regions, even above the snow line where ski-planes can be used. As well as passenger and cargo transportation, they provide emergency services and a mail network.

Communications

As alternative technologies bring electricity to more remote areas and satellite technology opens up the airwaves, so access to the internet and to international communications systems penetrates deeper into and higher up mountains.

Pressure from tourists wanting contact with the outside world has been instrumental in establishing some sites, including Everest base camp, but the benefits for remote communities in health, education and commerce have been the focus of governments in driving projects forward. Bolivia, Nepal, Pakistan and Venezuela are among countries that have taken part in projects to assess the factors affecting the development of the internet in different environments.

▲ *The Mountain Forum is a rapidly expanding global network that connects disparate mountain communities with one another. Its aim is to disseminate information that may be relevant to mountain inhabitants, no matter in which part of the world they live.*

Bhutan again involved the whole community, deciding to bring internet access to its entire population, and developing an extensive internet education and training program. Bhutan is also linking with countries that have similar internet projects (Philippines, Nepal, Papua New Guinea and Vietnam) to assist local information providers and governments by putting content on the web, accessible in local languages.

The new data-communications and satellite technologies enable ambitious educational developments in parts of the world where mountains make more formal access to education difficult. The UHI Millennium Institute is a Higher Education Institution providing university-level education and research throughout the Highlands and Islands of Scotland, by linking a network of 14 colleges and research institutions, as well as around 100 community-based learning centers. Lectures are delivered by a combination of online access to materials and resources and videoconference meetings between students and tutors. E-mail and telephone communications largely supplant face-to-face contact. Course development and administration take place by videoconference and e-mail, connecting staff sometimes hundreds of kilometers apart and bringing in experts from universities in countries experiencing similar challenges, especially throughout the Arctic Circle. In this way, thousands of students can fulfill educational ambitions without having to leave their communities.

The future

Although technological developments have brought better transportation routes and increased access to communication networks, this merging of boundaries and nationalities often has a cost measured in terms of the adverse effects on mountain ecosystems and cultural identity. Future developments must take place in the context of sustainable mountain communities.

Ironically, communication technologies and the internet could provide a means of doing this. The remoteness of mountain people, with limited access to public resources, means that they can greatly benefit from using the internet to communicate with other mountain people all over the world. It can also be a resource to capture information on cultures, traditions, crafts and skills for the wider world to see. The Mountain Forum is an innovative global network established for communication and information sharing through the collaboration of nongovernmental organizations, multilateral agencies and the private sector (linking over

2,000 individuals and 50 organizational members in over 100 countries to date). The use of communication technologies could also lead to greater trade and commercial possibilities within mountain communities, thereby increasing the communities' financial security, and resulting in less migration to lowland and urban areas.

TOURISM

Although tourism is thought of as an activity of modern times, millions of people have visited mountain areas for many centuries. The earliest visitors were religious pilgrims, but during the 19th and 20th centuries mountains became synonymous with health and recreation. Today, with easier travel and access, more remote mountain areas are opening up as tourist destinations in themselves. Revenue from tourism has become the main source of income for many mountain communities. Over 50 million people visiting mountain regions spend around $650 billion a year. In the Uttar Pradesh region of India almost half of the state's income comes from tourism. However, the increasing numbers of visitors to these remote and often fragile ecosystems could destroy the very features that attracted them in the first place. It is important that governments and communities continue to work together under the auspices of Agenda 21 and within the Mountain Partnership to find ways of making tourism sustainable in mountain regions.

Pilgrimage

Almost every religion identifies individual mountains or specific places around mountains as sacred. Pilgrims travel to these sites to do penance, for spiritual healing and to participate in worship, either individually or at appointed times in their religious calendar. Mount Kailas in western Tibet is the most sacred mountain for over a billion Buddhists, Hindus, Jains and Bonpos, and many thousands of pilgrims visit every year to meditate and to travel around the mountain. The Himalayas are home to many sacred sites in all of the bordering countries. Almost 10 million pilgrims annually visit Dev Bhumi, the land of the gods, in the Garhwal region of India.

The Chinese phrase for pilgrimage means literally "paying one's respect to a mountain," and in China's ancient recorded history mountains were believed to support the heavens above the Earth. Taoist belief is that five mountain summits across the country perform this role, one of which is Mount Tai Shan in the Shandong province of eastern China. This

► **Pilgrims** on the Stairway to Heaven climb the 7,000 steps to reach the Gateway to Heaven Temple at the top of Mount Tai Shan, Shandong, China. The mountain, visited by millions of pilgrims each year, is thought to be the son of the Emperor of the Heavens and is considered a god in its own right.

mountain is considered to be a deity in itself, the son of the Emperor of the Heavens, and millions of pilgrims visit each year, climbing the 7,000 steps of the Stairway to Heaven to pray and to worship at the temples at the summit.

Other notable mountain pilgrim sites include Mount Sinai in Egypt, Mount Ararat in Turkey, Mount Kilauea in Hawaii (believed to be the birthplace of Pele, goddess of volcanoes), Mount Olympus in Greece, Mount Fuji in Japan, and more than 50 sacred sites at summits of peaks along the Andes in Colombia, Ecuador, Peru, Bolivia and Chile. One set of ruins on the summit of Llullaillaco in Chile is the world's highest archaeological site. However, although the ruins are of Inca origin, dating back to the 15th century, it is known that the mountains were worshiped for thousands of years before the arrival of the Inca and their rise to power in the region.

Health and wellbeing

For centuries, people have traveled to the mountains for their health, and letters still exist from the early 1500s describing the healing and restorative powers of mountain air and the mineral-rich waters of mountain springs and glaciers. One of the first documented areas reputed to be health-giving was the Alps, when in the 18th and 19th centuries the rich and famous traveled to the high lands of Austria, Switzerland and Italy to escape the polluted cities and towns across Europe. Today there is a burgeoning business in health spa vacations across Europe and North America, stressing rest and relaxation. Locations in more remote areas, usually associated with the more strenuous activity vacations, are now realizing the benefits of providing vacation bases where people can simply enjoy the local culture and scenery. A study of visitors to the Himalayna Kinnaur region in 1995 found that, whereas tourists coming to the region when it was opened to tourism in 1992 were attracted in the main by trekking and climbing vacations, most later visitors came for the scenery and environment, and were spending longer at a chosen destination to soak up the atmosphere and meet the local people.

Recreation

Activity-based tourism has boomed in mountain regions since the advent of cheaper air travel and easier access. This has grown from the more traditional areas of North America and the European Alps to remote areas of central Asia, the Himalayas, the Caucasus and the Andes. There are even packages to view the mountains of Antarctica.

Many recreational vacations are chosen by people wishing to visit key cultural and historical sites and even to recreate particular events or journeys. Millions visit religious sites each year as tourists rather than pilgrims. Archaeological sites also hold a special interest. Many cultures in the Andes, China, Africa and Asia used mountains as burial sites, and the tombs discovered and excavated during the 19th and 20th centuries hold a continued appeal.

More active forms of recreation are found in traditional mountain sports such as hiking, skiing, snowboarding, canoeing, climbing and birdwatching. Over recent years more extreme sports, such as bungee jumping, hydrospeeding, rafting, paragliding and canyoning, have become popular. Many companies now specialize in sport and recreation packages, and local economies benefit from the provision of hotels, shops, restaurants and from the supply of services associated with mountain sports, such as equipment hire and training.

Sustainability

Tourism is often seasonal, and in providing many of the facilities and services required for relatively large numbers of people over relatively short periods of time, local land and resources can be damaged. The provision of heating, food and water for large groups of people, for example, can result in small-scale deforestation, which would otherwise allow building in local communities or provide shelter for animals or crops. Outside the tourist season the indigenous people will then need to travel further to gather the resources needed for burning or building. The tourist season in many remote areas coincides with periods best suited to local agriculture, and the attractions of extra earnings can lure some people away from the land at key times, leaving others less suited to the work to tend the farms. This can adversely affect farm productivity and even its sustainability in the longer term. In addition, external companies often control the tourist business, preventing local communities from benefiting from increased opportunities.

Tourism is also extremely volatile, sensitive to security alerts, natural disasters and adverse media reports. Certain incidents and events can significantly reduce tourist numbers overnight, dramatically affecting the income of some mountain communities.

◀ A hiker peers from the doorway of a stone hut, fronted with a bed of blooming flowers, at the Himalayan village of Gurung, Annapurna Sanctuary, Nepal. Annapurna, like many other mountain regions, has become a popular destination for hundreds of thousands of tourists each year. The massive seasonal influx of visitors can cause great environmental damage if not properly managed.

Ecotourism is defined by the International Ecotourism Society as "responsible travel to natural areas which conserves the environment and improves the welfare of local people." International agencies and many of the world's governments agree that ecotourism is the best way forward for sustainable tourism. Strategies to encourage ecotourism are being considered by members of the Mountain Partnership and signatories to the Agenda 21 action plans that will bring into partnership all stakeholders with an interest in mountain development. Stakeholders include not only national governments and international agencies but also the mountain communities and businesses. Communication, cooperation and partnership among all of these groups can ensure that conservation and development is linked to good practice, local employment opportunities, maintaining biodiversity and the recognition and support of indigenous cultures.

Mountain Sports

INTRODUCTION

Prior to the first mountaineering conquests in the Alps in the 18th century, mountains were believed to be the abode of dragons; they frightened people but at the same time held a certain fascination, mystique and intrigue. Gradually as the myths and legends were dispelled, the drive to explore and climb the world's tallest peaks has come to inspire generations of amateur and professional climbers and explorers. As the number of people who head to the mountains for recreation increases, so has the number of sports and pastimes that they come to pursue. The list is growing and today includes climbing and mountaineering in its many forms: ice climbing, snow climbing and rock climbing (together on the same route known as mixed climbing), scrambling, Alpine climbing, big wall/aid climbing, Himalayan climbing, rappeling, via ferrata (a form of rock climbing using fixed ladders and steel ropes); skiing (Alpine or downhill skiing, ski jumping, ski slalom racing, Nordic or cross-country skiing, telemark skiing, snow blades); snowboarding; skating; toboggan and bobsleigh; gliding (fixed-wing aircraft); paragliding; hang-gliding; angling; camping and hiking; mountain biking; fell-running; orienteering; spelunking; canoeing and kayaking; motor cross and off-road or four-wheel driving. The list is no doubt

▼ *Paragliding* is one of the more recent sports to be enjoyed in the mountains. The list of recreational activities that are now available in mountain regions grows year by year, and with air travel becoming less expensive, an increasing number of people from all over the world are enjoying the many varied mountain sports.

▶ **Skiing** wasn't always as glamorous as the modern-day pistes of the French Alps or the well-tended slopes of Colorado; and equipment and clothing have changed beyond recognition. But as this image testifies the recreational fun to be had on the snow was recognized many years ago.

incomplete, and it will be growing all the time. This chapter will explore some of the more popular mountain sports and their attraction, cover some technical details and discuss the sports' impact on the mountain environment and people.

SKIING

Skiing as a sport developed in Norway, first among Norwegian troops who were taught by an Army Captain Jens Emahusen of Trondheim in the early 1700s. In 1868 Sondre Norheim demonstrated a revolutionary skiing style in Christania (Oslo). In 1888 the famous Norwegian explorer Fridjof Nansen achieved, in a mere 46 days, the first crossing of Greenland on skis. Mathias Zdarsky is probably the true founder of the ski school. He set up a military-style school in Lilienfeld near Vienna in 1896. In 1911 Hannes Schneider of Austria and Vivian Caulfield, a British engineer, wrote a revolutionary ski instruction manual called "How to Ski and Not to Ski." It was Schneider who, between 1907 and 1918, conceived the basis for what we now know as "the ski school" for recreational skiers.

▲ **When we think** of skiing today, most of us think of downhill, or Alpine skiing. In as little as 75 years after the first hardy souls ventured onto the slopes of the European Alps, Alpine skiing has become a huge international pastime, with an estimated 40 million skiers taking to the slopes each year in over 40 countries.

With the rising popularity of the sport, National Ski Associations appeared in turn in Russia (1896), Czechoslovakia (1903), the USA (1904), Austria and Germany (1905) and Norway, Finland and Sweden (1908). Between 1910 and 1924 a Skiing Commission supervised the development internationally of skiing as a competitive sport. Today 40 million Alpine skiers use around 300 major Alpine resorts in mountainous areas within 40 countries. Many thousand ski slopes stretch north to south, and east to west across the globe—from the French Alps to Korea on the Pacific rim. Some more unusual locations for Alpine skiing include India and Antarctica.

The International Ski Federation (Fédération Internationale de Ski/Internationaler Ski Verband; abbreviated to FIS), which governs the sport of skiing, was founded in 1924. There were then 14 countries involved; now membership is comprised of 101 National Ski Associations. FIS disciplines currently include as Olympic sports: cross-country (15 km/9 mi, 30 km/19 mi, 50 km/31 mi, pursuit, team and sprint); ski jumping; Nordic combined; Alpine skiing (downhill, slalom, giant slalom); freestyle skiing (moguls, aerials); snowboarding (parallel, halfpipe), and as World Cup sports: speed skiing; grass skiing; telemark and masters.

Cross-country or Nordic skiing

Cross-country or Nordic skiing is also known by the Norwegian term Langlaufen the world over. For this sport boots have flexible soles and are attached at the toe only by various systems that involve pins (which locate into three holes in the boot) and clamps which hold the toe of the boot to the ski. In other systems cables extend around the heel of the boot to keep the boot securely in the binding. Such lightweight cross-country ski equipment is designed for skiing on preprepared tracks on relatively flat terrain.

The skis do not have metal edges so are not effective for making turns. Skis for cross-country use are generally longer than those used in downhill skiing; the bases may be waxed (with different waxes for different snow temperatures) to attain a suitable balance between grip and glide, or the part of the base below the foot in the ski's center may have "fish-scales" which grip the snow on moderate uphill ascents. The poles involved are slightly longer than those for downhill skiing as they are used far more for

▶ **Cross-country**, or Nordic skiers enjoying the picturesque scenery around Aspen, Colorado, USA. Cross-country skiing is the oldest-known form of skiing, and there is evidence to suggest that primitive types of ski were in use in Norway more than 5,000 years ago.

pushing the skier along, and maximizing speed when racing. In more hilly terrain slightly shorter skis with metal edges are used and on descents, the telemark turn—a smooth turn on the outer ski—has evolved. Telemark skiing is now a popular branch of skiing in itself, where skiers may use taller plastic boots, still with flexible soles, and short carving skis to ski both on and off piste.

Ski mountaineering (also called ski-touring)

Ski mountaineering is a branch of the sport practiced by mountaineers in order to gain easier and faster access to their climbs in winter (and in summer too in high mountain areas). It is practiced off-piste. The equipment used combines principles from both the Nordic (cross-country) and the Alpine (downhill) branches of skiing, allowing the skier to negotiate much steeper terrain. The boots are plastic and double-layered with a traditional stiff vibram-type sole (with grips) which are flexible enough around the ankle for walking and climbing, but sufficiently stiff for skiing steeply downhill. They can also be fitted with crampons for climbing. Skis used are wider and shorter than for cross-country skiing, making them easier to turn on descents and also increasing their surface area on the snow—this helps minimize the amount of sinking into the powder snow. Bindings are fixed at the toe where a hinge mechanism facilitates walking; the rear part of the foot plate, however, can be clamped to the ski for descents, so that the ski then operates like a downhill ski. To obtain grip on ascents, artificial "skins" are stuck to the base of the ski with a type of glue. The skins have minute backward-pointing hairs, which grip snow crystals on ascents.

Downhill or Alpine skiing

Downhill or Alpine skiing is practiced on specially "pisted" runs where large snow-cat machines used in ski resorts compact and smooth the snow on runs to optimize skiing conditions. Increasingly these days snow resorts have snow cannons on the lower runs to make artificial snow. This can help to increase the length of the ski season and improve the skiing experience. For downhill skiing skis are usually as long as the skier is tall, though recently a trend for shorter-shaped skis with more sidecut (called carving skis) has evolved. These modern designs make the ski easier to turn. The boots are plastic, well insulated and stiff, to give the foot and ankle maximum support and some flexibility. They clamp into bindings at both the toe and heel. Bindings must be specially adjusted both to hold the boot securely most of

the time, but also to be able to release the boot and skier in the event of a fall when excessive forces could result in injury to the skier. Drag lifts or chair lifts around ski resorts convey skiers uphill to the top of the prepared runs. In some resorts telecabins, gondolas, funicular railway and even underground trains now speed skiers to the mountain summits. Modern downhill ski techniques are based on the "central theme," which is a progressive coaching system whereby skiers first learn to snow plow and then progress to parallel turning. Downhill racing is a popular Olympic event in which competitors complete a slalom course.

Ski jumping

The FIS Ski Jumping Committee provides detailed standards for the construction of ski jumping hills, landing hill profiles and judges' tower. Hills are divided into five classes from small (20–49 m/66–161 ft) to Flying (185 m/607 ft or larger), and the starting point from which the ski jumper begins is determined by a jury. The jumper is not allowed to use ski poles or any other assistance. Jumpers are judged on both the distance jumped and on style. The judges award style points for the utilization of the aerodynamic shape of the body and skis, the posture of arms and legs, the position of skis in flight and the succession of movements during the landing and outrun. The length of skis used is determined by the competitor's weight,

▲ *One of the most thrilling* ski disciplines both to watch and participate in, ski jumping as a sport began in the late 19th century—the first ski jumping competition taking place in 1862 in Norway. The aim of the jumper is to get his or her body into a position that will provide as much lift as possible thereby helping the jumper to travel as far as possible.

and ranges from 2.1–2.9 m (6.9–9.5 ft)—a great deal longer than in the other ski disciplines already discussed.

Freestyle skiing

Freestyle skiing competitions consist of five events: aerials, moguls, dual moguls, ski cross and halfpipe. Aerials are different acrobatic jumps stressing takeoff, height (referred to as "air"), proper style, execution and precision of movement (referred to as "form" and "landing"). Final scores are multiplied by a degree of difficulty factor. Mogul competition consists of free skiing on a heavily moguled course (a mogul being a mound of hard snow creating an obstacle), stressing technical turns, speed and aerial maneuvers. In dual competitions the winner progresses to the next round. In ski cross, competitors ski a downhill course with a slope of 12–22° and negotiate a series of colored gates set at right angles to the competition line. The halfpipe is a trough-shaped channel of specific dimensions constructed in snow into which skiers drop at speed. They perform tricks within the halfpipe and judges award scores based on difficulty and successful execution of maneuvers.

▲ *Freestyle skiing was first organized into a disciplined event in Canada in 1974. Since then the sport has grown in popularity and new events and disciplines are being constantly added.*

Snowboarding

Snowboarding originated in the USA in the 1960s. The first boards were very rudimentary but more recent designs reflect the variety of riding styles that have emerged within the sport. There are two primary styles of snowboarding: alpine/carving and freestyle/freeride, and each style requires its own specialized set of equipment. Freestyle snowboarding has an emphasis on park and pipe riding and involves a lot of tricks; generally shorter boards with soft boots are used. Alpine/carving refers to riders who use carving boards, hard boots and plate bindings. This is a snowboard specialty that concentrates on carving and is the opposite of freestyle in which riders use soft boots and concentrate on tricks.

Snowboarding competitions have taken place since the 1980s, and include events such as the halfpipe, boardercross, slopestyle and parallel giant slalom. In 2000, snowboarding was the fastest-growing sport in the USA (followed by skateboarding), adopted by around 7.2 million people. Some argue that snowboarding helped start a revolution in the ski industry by inspiring ski manufacturers to make the shorter, more manoeuvrable skis called carving skis, which have deeper sidecuts.

For freestyle the snowboarding boots used are soft and flexible, and are clipped and tightened into bindings. Control of the speed of descent is achieved by edging the board to make it turn. Boarders do not use poles. Drag lifts and chair lifts in ski resorts are used in the same way as by downhill skiers. Snowboarding became an Olympic full-medal sport at the 1998 Winter Games in Nagano, Japan—the competitions being the halfpipe (men's and women's) and the parallel giant slalom (men's and women's).

The origins of the snowboarding half-pipe competition lie in skateboarding, for which the halfpipe was invented. In the early days of snowboarding, the 1980s, natural snow-filled gullies served as the first "halfpipes." Then riders began hand-digging "trenches" to ride in, and finally the trench grew into a half-pipe, a run made out of snow that is semicircular in cross-section. Snow-boarders perform similar tricks inside a halfpipe to skateboarders. A basic trick is a "grab," where riders go up into the air off the side of the halfpipe and grab their snowboard. Skateboarders have to grab their board in order to keep it with them; snowboarders—their board fixed to their boots by bindings—have adopted the grab for style and stability in the air. Halfpipe technology advanced with a grooming machine, called a pipe drag-on, which cuts a near-perfect, uniform halfpipe without the need for a team of people using shovels. Later came the superpipe, a super-sized halfpipe, which was used in the 2002 Olympic Winter Games in Salt Lake City. Off-piste snow-boarding is now an increasingly popular branch of the sport.

▼ *Snowboarding* presently is broken down into two distinct types: freestyle and carving. Freestyle involves performing elaborate stunts while carving utlizes a slalom course.

◄ **Grass skiing** was developed in the late 1960s, and as its name suggests involves skiing down grass slopes. The techniques employed are very similar to Alpine or downhill skiing, however, the sport has never quite captured the imagination as much as Alpine, Nordic skiing or snowboarding.

Grass skiing

Grass skiing was invented in Germany in 1966 and is, as the name suggests, skiing on grass. Without the need for snow, it is a more accessible form of skiing. Grass ski centers are available in Europe and other mountainous areas and while the sport has grown somewhat in popularity, it is still far from being mainstream. In Japan, Taiwan and other Asian countries, grass skiing is emerging as more resorts, teachers and equipment become available. During the 1980s, grass skiing started to be used for ski training in preparation for Alpine skiing.

Grass skiers use shorter skeelerlike skis with caterpillar tracks that are specifically designed to work well on grass. Some of the tracked skis nowadays can go fast and can be steered accurately. Ski poles are used in the same way as in Alpine skiing. In addition, padding on the legs and elbows is worn to protect the skier from falls, which are more danger-ous than on snow. Helmets are also recommended in grass skiing, and are becoming more widely used in other skiing disciplines, especially by younger skiers. The FIS holds World Cup competitions in grass skiing—in sprint, slalom and giant slalom at present.

TOBOGGAN AND BOBSLED

Toboggans are sleds that have no steering mechanism, whereas bobsleighs have a purpose-built steering mechanism incorporated into the design. Bobsleigh was invented in Switzerland in 1890, and races, with riders lying in the prone position, were soon taking place on natural ice courses and later on specially made tracks with banked curves. The early wooden racing sleds were later replaced by lighter and stronger steel and aluminum composite sleds known as bobsleds—the name stemming from the crew's "bobbing" back and forth to go faster on the track's straight sections. Some of the first competitions required teams of five or six people, one of whom had to be a woman. However, by the 1930s the requirement was changed and the present two- and four-man events emerged. These races take place down ice tracks that are at least 1,500 m (5,000 ft) long, with at least 15 banked curves. Bobsleighers are highly trained athletes, some of whom are drawn from other sports in order to execute a fast start at the beginning of the run (or lauf). The total weight of the crew is limited and bobsleigh teams include a pilot, whose responsibility it is to steer the bobsleigh down the track in the most time-efficient way possible, and a brakeman in the two-man event; two further crewmen/pushers are added for the four-man race. All the crew push the sled for up to 50 m (165 ft) from a standing start, and this

▼ **Team USA 2** races past spectators at the World Cup Bobsleigh race in St. Moritz. Developed in the late 19th and early 20th centuries, bobsledding is a high-speed event in which speeds of up to 135 km/h (85 mph) can be reached. Today the two-man and four-man events are the recognized disciplines.

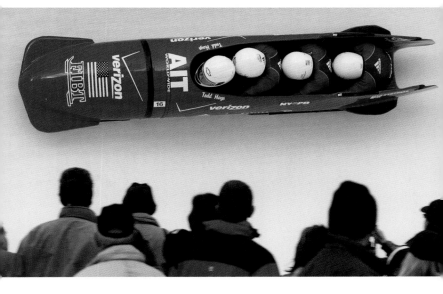

distance is often covered in less than six seconds at speeds of over 40 km/h (25 mph) after which the crew loads into the sled. Differences in start times of tenths or even hundredths of a second separate the top crews, so a fast start is critical. A 0.1 second lead at the start usually translates into a 0.3 second advantage by the end of the race. During a typical one-minute run, crews are subjected to over four times the force of gravity while speeds of more than 135 km/h (85 mph) can be reached.

The world's top teams train all year round to compete mainly on tracks of artificial ice, on high-tech sleds made of fiberglass and steel. The sport began among the Alpine nations but has expanded internationally, now including southern-hemisphere countries such as Australia and New Zealand. In the early 1990s women raced for the first time at events in North America and in Europe. The Fédération International de Bobsleigh et Tobogganing (FIBT), based in Milan, Italy, controls the sports at all international events.

MOUNTAIN BIKING

Cycling as a pastime, means of transportation and competitive sport has been around for many decades. Mountain biking as a sport developed from the style of cycle racing known as cyclo-cross. This new form of cycle racing developed in California in the 1970s and used extremely light but strong bikes with fatter tires and a suspension system to help riders over very uneven, difficult courses. Known as BMX (bicycle motocross) as an indoor competitive sport, outdoors it developed into mountain biking. Such bikes can be used to tour, compete, get fit and explore the countryside.

Modern mountain bikes have evolved into specialist machines that are strong, light and durable; they can withstand the forces created by negotiating uneven mountain terrain and even jumps. The frame size is generally 5–7 cm (2–2.75 in) smaller than the equivalent road bike for the same rider, and is made usually of a high-specification alloy steel or aluminum/steel, or even carbon-fiber/steel or aluminum combinations. The frame is the heart of the bike and while needing to be strong enough to cope with the stresses of rough terrain it must be sufficiently light to be carried over those parts of the route where it may not be possible to ride. Wheels are normally made of light alloy capable of taking heavier-duty molded tires that provide both grip in wet and muddy terrain and which give the rider a smoother ride on uneven ground. Wheels are strengthened by stainless-steel spokes and alloy rims. Brakes may be center-pull cantilever arrangements or, following recent developments in mountain-bike braking systems, through disks incorporated on both wheels or just the front. These may be operated by cable or hydraulic fluid in the same way as motorcycle brakes and work better in wet conditions than traditional rubber brake-blocks, which rely on friction with the wheel rim. Gears, of which there may be ratios of 15, 18 or 21, are used to ascend steeper grades, their purpose being to permit a greater number of pedal revolutions per wheel revolution, so easing the muscular strain required to get up a hill. The aim is to achieve a constant speed of pedaling. Both front and rear suspension help to even out the bumps, giving a smoother and faster ride. Downhill racing bikes have even larger tires and reinforced frames, often with the rear wheel being smaller than the front to make the riding angle on steep descents safer.

Riders wear helmets since the risk of a fall in which the head is struck has severe consequences. Clothing worn usually conforms to the layer system of clothing used in most outdoor activities—a base layer next to the skin to

▼ *Mountain biking*
developed in California,
USA, in the 1970s, and
as a recreational activity
is among the fastest-
growing sports. It
combines a pleasurable
way of getting fit with
often exciting downhill
freewheeling, all in
potentially breathtaking
scenery, as here in
Waimea Canyon,
Hawaii.

◄ Mountain biker
Scotty Rinckenberger
bikes over a rocky trail
in the central Cascade
Range. Competitive
cross-country mountain
biking has developed
into a popular sport all
over the world and
became a recognized
Olympic sport during
the Atlanta Olympics of
1996. Competitors need
to be supremely fit to
make the long and
arduous climbs, and
have nerves of steel to
navigate safely at speed
the often alarmingly
steep downhill sections
of the course.

wick away moisture, a "midlayer" (a warmth layer such as a
fleece) and a "shell-layer," the outer windproof or perhaps
waterproof (but breathable) outer layer. Strong footwear
appropriate for walking and cycling, glasses and gloves
complete the rider's personal clothing needs. Some mountain bikers prefer to carry a small backpack with repair kit
and water; others fix these to the bike's frame or make use
of handlebar bags, bags which sit on a rear rack or panniers
(popular when touring).

Mountain bikes have been used to access some of the
world's highest mountain areas, and specially designed
courses are being developed all over the world where
recreational mountain biking and competitions take place.
In 1993, cross-country mountain biking ("vélo tout terrain")
became an Olympic discipline, making its Olympic debut in
the program of the 1996 Atlanta Olympics.

CLIMBING AS A SPORT

Climbing is taken to mean an ascent of rock, snow or ice that generally requires the use of hands for progress or for safety. Climbing is neither an art nor a science but an activity that is a combination of both. There are few hard-and-fast rules; rather, there are general principles that are usually followed, but sometimes even these may have to be abandoned. Climbing is unlike most other sporting activities in that it takes place in an inherently dangerous environment, be it on a rock face or a high mountain. Part of the attraction of climbing can be the sense of danger; to remove this risk would alter the activity itself. Climbing and mountaineering have a long and fascinating history, which is well documented in the next chapter. In this chapter we will be outlining the different aspects of the sport that have now evolved.

Bouldering and rock climbing

Bouldering and rock climbing are at the core of all aspects of the sport. Almost without exception climbers who progress to other branches of the sport, such as Alpine and Himalayan climbing, will have started their climbing careers by bouldering and rock climbing, and will usually continue these aspects of the sport, perhaps for training or enjoyment. Bouldering involves climbing solo (without ropes) at relatively low levels, protected from a fall only by a crash mat positioned beneath the particular technical move that the boulderer is attempting. Apart from this mat, the equipment a boulderer uses includes special rock shoes, the same as for rock climbing. The soles of these tight-fitting shoes are made from soft or "sticky" rubber affording the climber a high degree of friction with the rock being scaled. Boulderers and rock climbers sometimes carry a chalk bag into which they dip their fingers. Chalk increases friction with the rock giving the climber a better grip on the holds. Many good bouldering areas now have guidebooks to help climbers isolate areas of particular technical challenge, and bouldering competitions are now widespread.

Rock climbing extends the principles of bouldering to greater heights and usually, therefore, involves the use of a rope, a harness and devices for anchoring the rope to the rock for safety. Climbers may also wear special helmets. People usually climb in pairs, though it is sometimes done in threes. The principle is that the first climber (the "lead" climber) ties one end of the rope to the harness he or she is wearing and begins to climb the pitch (a section of the climb which must be shorter than the length of the rope being used). Climbs that consist of one pitch are called single-pitch climbs, while

others with more than one pitch are multipitch climbs. A rack consisting of nuts, hexes and camming devices called "friends" is usually carried by the lead climber (normally clipped to loops on their harness). At frequent intervals the lead climber will stop to place a nut, hex or friend into a crack in the rock along the line of the route, and clip the rope to it using a quickdraw, which consists of two karabiners with a webbing tape sling between them. Routes in many parts of the world have preplaced expansion bolts fixed into the rock at intervals along the route so the climber just needs to clip the quickdraw into these as they climb past. The rope should pull freely through this placement or protection (also called a runner) so that the lead climber can continue to climb up the route. The number of pieces of protection used in one pitch depends on the length of the pitch, its difficulty and the availability of suitable cracks in the rock to place the protection. Meanwhile, the second climber below passes the rope through a special friction device attached to his or her harness or directly to the rock using slings or camming devices to belay, or make secure, the lead climber. The term "belay" is used in climbing to refer to a point in a climb where the climbers secure themselves to the rock using the

◀ *Bouldering is an extremely physical sport, requiring a combination of excellent body strength and agility. As no ropes or other equipment are used, boulderers rely on the sticky undersurface of their tight-fitting shoes and a bag of chalk into which they dip their hands to help them grip the rock surface.*

rope, slings and/or camming devices. At least one of the climbers should be belayed all of the time. Should the lead climber fall, the second climber below, called the belayer, must jam the rope in the belay device quickly so that it no longer runs out freely. The falling lead climber's weight should then be taken on the rope (which is elasticated) and the fall should be about the distance he or she was above the last runner, rather than all the way to the ground. The lead climber reaches the top of the pitch, and then finds a stance (a comfortable place to rest) before fixing at least one but ideally two or three more runners into the rock face. The lead next ties him- or herself securely to all the runners independently, then using his or her own belay device, brings up the second climber. The second climber removes the items of protection on the pitch placed by the leader while climbing past, and returns them to the lead climber when they meet again at the top of the pitch. Once arrived at the stance, the second climber clips his or her harness into the protection (using quickdraws, a sling or a loop of the rope and karabiner) that the lead climber has placed, so that both climbers are secured safely. At this time the climbing pair may decide to swap the lead, or continue in the same order. The lead climber then unties from the rock and continues up the next pitch, while the second belays them as before. In this way, safe progress is made to the top of the climb, with one or both climbers being secured to the rock at all times.

The term sports climbing is used in areas where the routes are bolted. Bolted routes eliminate the need for the climber to place protection, making the climbing inherently safer. The difficulty of climbs is measured by a grading system, which has evolved independently in several of the world's leading climbing nations. These grading systems broadly overlap, so climbers climbing abroad can easily translate their home country's grades into those of the host nation.

Ice and snow climbing

Ice climbing follows the same principles of leading, belaying and seconding the climb as described for rock climbing. However, the equipment and techniques used are considerably different. Stiff soled, well-insulated leather or plastic boots are worn, to which crampons are fixed. The vibram-type soles are stiffened by the insertion of a metal plate into the sole. Crampons usually have between ten and twelve metal spikes, normally with two front-points protruding 10–30 mm (0.4–1.2 in) from the toe of the boot. In ice climbing these front-points are kicked into the ice and progress is made using a technique known as front-pointing. The climber also holds an ice ax in one hand and an ice hammer in the other. An ice hammer looks almost identical to the ax, except that the adze (the sharp flattened edge opposite the pick used for step cutting) is replaced by a hammer. Modern ice axs designed for ice climbing have angled or drooping picks (which are sometimes adjustable) and shaped shafts for increased efficiency. The climber strikes the points of both the ax and hammer into the ice above his or her head. The climber's wrists are placed through the loop in the leash so that when the ax and hammer are above the head, some of the climber's weight can be transferred to the leash. Always keeping three points of contact, the climber slowly moves upward by alternately kicking in the front-points on each foot and releasing and moving up the

pick of the ax and hammer. Where nuts, hexes and friends are used for protection in rock climbing, ice climbers tend to use ice screws. These are made of steel or titanium alloys and after an initial tap with the hammer, are screwed at an angle of 90° into the ice. A quickdraw is then used to clip the ice screw to the rope. Once the lead climber has placed an ice screw, the second must belay in the same way as described for rock climbing. Ice climbers tend to wear well-insulated clothing in several layers, a wind and waterproof outer layer, gloves or mitts and a helmet.

In snow climbing the angle of the pitches tends to be lower than that tackled by ice climbers. This usually means that one longer ax is more suitable, and a hammer is not normally required. Crampons are still needed, however, and the climber takes care to make sure that all points of the crampons are placed into the snow with each step. If wet snow

▲ *Although ice climbing* uses the same principles as rock climbing in ensuring that a safety rope will always stop a climber from falling farther than when the rope was last attached to the ice face, the equipment and clothing used are very different.

clings to the crampons then the climber takes care to knock off the snow with the ice ax after each step so that the crampons continue to grip the snow. Rubber plates fixed to the crampon's base (called antiballing plates) can help to stop snow sticking to crampons. Where the angle of the snow is steeper, or there is a likelihood of hidden crevasses, climbers may rope up and move together. On steeper slopes they may adopt the tradition of pitching the climb. In hard snow (or névé) an anchor called a deadman may be buried in the snow at an appropriate angle and used as a belay. There are other techniques used in snow climbing such as burying ice axs or making snow bollards from which climbers can belay each other. Climbers who venture onto snow slopes normally begin their training by learning how to carry out an ice ax arrest without and with crampons. An ice ax arrest is a means of stopping oneself sliding down a snow slope using the ax as a brake. An awareness of avalanches and the risks they pose is also required by snow climbers.

In mixed climbing the route may be partially iced (or may have patches of snow) and partially bare rock. A combination of techniques is therefore required. The climbers may wear crampons on some sections of the route and may remove them for others. They may rock climb wearing crampons, placing the front-points carefully into cracks and on holds in the rock. Likewise, they may use their ice ax and/or hammer on some parts of the route, then revert to bare or gloved hands for climbing other sections. Other techniques used in mixed climbing are ax hooking or ax torquing, in which ax picks are placed into slits and cracks in rock, and sometimes twisted to increase friction.

Alpine climbing

For many climbers Alpinism is the next obvious step after climbing on the lower crags and ice cliffs. However, Alpine climbing is inherently different from crag climbing. It demands a high level of mountain awareness (knowledge of objective dangers such as avalanche, rock fall, crevasses, weather etc.), good navigation skills and the ability to negotiate potentially serious situations. Alpine-style climbing covers everything from one-day routes to ascents on 8,000-m (26,000-ft) Himalayan peaks. It is a style of climbing which is as appropriate in New Zealand, Canada, South America and the Himalayas as it is in the European Alps. Alpine ascents are normally considered to be those that are done in a single push by climbers carrying all their own equipment. This may be an ascent of a snowy 3,000-m (10,000-ft) dome in the European Alps, a big face in South

America or a multiday climb on a Himalayan giant. It is difficult to draw a precise distinction as to where big crag climbing ends and Alpinism begins. Perhaps a route which involves an approach (walk-in), ascent and subsequent descent, and which requires navigational, route finding and other mountaineering skills, will qualify as an Alpine route. An Alpine grading system developed by the French classifies routes according to their difficulty and danger. Grades range from Easy to Extremely Difficult.

Climbers often move together on Alpine climbs, joined together by a rope. This is particularly practiced when crossing snow-covered glaciers (frequently necessary in order to get to and from climbs). When snow covers glaciers, it is quite easy for a climber to break through the snow layer and fall into a crevasse in the ice. Climbers therefore practice crevasse rescue techniques so that they can extricate a member of their party from a crevasse quickly.

Since Alpine climbers carry their own equipment, light-weight items are preferred. Sometimes a bivvy bag (bivouac bag) made from waterproof but breathable material is used instead of a tent to save weight. Alpine climbers usually start their routes well before dawn so that they can reach the summit and begin the descent before the sun has had too long to soften the snow. Descending on soft and melting snow is more difficult and dangerous than when the snow is still frozen. A head torch is therefore useful before dawn, as are sunglasses with side panels for when the sun comes out later in the day. If no glasses are worn, the climber risks the painful and debilitating condition of snow blindness caused by the sun's rays reflecting off a snow or ice surface.

▼ *One of the greatest dangers* facing Alpine climbers, particularly when traversing a snow-covered glacier, is falling into a crevasse, a deep fissure in the glacial ice. To combat this danger Alpine climbers usually tie themselves together with rope.

Scrambling

Scrambling is a branch of mountaineering that is halfway between walking and climbing. In general, the hands are

needed on some parts of a scramble. Scrambling routes normally follow rocky ridges or buttresses. Normal walking boots are usually worn and a short rope may be carried and used on the more difficult sections of scrambles.

Artificial, aid or big wall climbing

Artificial or aid climbing developed on the big granite walls of Yosemite Valley in California. The techniques have been successfully transferred to ascents of big walls in many other parts of the world. Climbers armed with large quantities of rock pegs or pitons slowly ascend vertical walls by a system that relies on hammering pegs into cracks. The climber clips or ties onto the peg and hauls up his or her body weight by stepping into a set of loops called etriers. Skyhooks or Fifi hooks and other similar devices may be used to hook ledges on the face to gain upward progress. Ropes are used as in rock climbing to lead and second the pitches. Routes may take several days, meaning that large amounts of water and equipment must be hauled up in special haul sacks at the end of each pitch. At night the climbers will usually clip to several pitons a mobile and collapsible tent platform called a portaledge on which they will spend the night cooking and sleeping.

Himalayan climbing

Traditional Himalayan climbing as first practiced on the expeditions which led Mallory to Everest in 1921, 1922 and 1924 and which led to the successful conquest of Everest by Hillary and Tenzing in 1953 involved establishing and stocking a series of camps at intervals along the route. The lowest camp would be called base camp, the next one up would be advanced base camp, with subsequent camps numbered sequentially. Huge teams of porters (sometimes as many as 100) were employed to carry much of the equipment, while the relatively small climbing team (typically between eight and twelve climbers) forced and protected the route, sometimes by fixing ropes and placing flags as markers. Gradually, over a period of several weeks the higher camps were stocked until the two lead climbers chosen to make the summit bid were acclimatized, supplied and established in the highest camp. From there, the summit team would attempt to climb to the summit and return to the high camp in one day. If the weather held, a second summit team might make an attempt, but rarely would more than two attempts be made. The expedition then retreated along the same route, removing camps as they descended. The whole expedition would have taken three or four months.

▶ *Taken in August 1953,* this photo shows *Edmund Hillary and Sherpa Tenzing Norgay enjoying a light meal after their successful expedition to the summit of Everest. Hillary was to later become involved with the welfare of the Nepalese people, for whom he did much charity work.*

These siege-style tactics are still used today in Himalayan climbing, although improvements in transportation, equipment design and organization since the 1950s mean that expeditions to Himalayan peaks can be faster and lighter. The need to spend time acclimatizing, though, is still essential. Alpine-style climbing has been increasingly applied to Himalayan peaks since the climbing pioneers of the 1970s and 1980s such as Reinhold Messner revolutionized Himalayan climbing with solo ascents and climbs of 8,000-m (26,000-ft) peaks without the use of oxygen. Messner was the first climber to reach the summit of all 14 of the world's 8,000-m (26,000-ft) Himalayan peaks.

The Union Internationale des Associations d'Alpinisme (UIAA) is the recognized International Federation and the acknowledged expert on all international climbing and mountaineering matters.

Via ferrata

Via ferrata is a relatively new sport that developed in France and is now also practiced in Switzerland, Italy, Scandinavia, Austria, Spain and Brazil. Using expansion bolts, steps, ladders, steel cables and other hardware, professional companies

◀ *A climber* works her way up a via ferrata (It. iron way) above the Vandelli hut in the Dolomites, northern Italy. During World War 1, the Italian and Austro-Hungarian armies fought each other over the vertical walls of the Dolomites. To move troops and equipment they had to fix iron ladders and wire cables to the rock. Today, these routes have been converted to recreational trails so people can enjoy in relative safety the world of mountaineering. Similar routes have now been established in many other mountain regions.

establish courses or routes which ascend and descend crags, cross gorges and traverse cliffs. Practitioners use standard climbing equipment (harness, helmet, rock boots or trainers) and remain safely attached to the bolts, ladders or steel cables by means of karabiners and short lengths of rope called cowstails. The sport offers some of the exhilaration experienced by climbers in exposed locations, without the same degree of risk.

Rappeling

Rappeling is really a by-product of mountaineering, rather than a sport in its own right. Having said that, countless numbers of young people may have experienced the "thrill" of rappeling as their first introduction to crags, climbing and exposure to height. The principle is one of sliding down a rope, and it is widely used by climbers as a means of getting down from the top of a climb where the descent path is steep or dangerous, or even nonexistent. Linking rappels can be a speedy way of descending a multipitch long route. Normally climbers use their climbing ropes double so that a typical 60-m (197-ft) climbing rope would allow an rappel of a maximum of 30 m (100 ft). The rope may be passed around a tree or boulder or through a sling secured to another type of anchor such as a bolt, piton, hex or nut. However, unless the climber is going to climb the route again, any equipment used will be left behind.

Climbers who plan to use rappeling as a means of retreating from a climb will carry some spare slings for this purpose. The rope is threaded through the sling and pulled to the halfway point (usually marked on most climbing ropes). Before rappeling, the two ends of the rope are knotted to prevent the climber rappeling off the end of the rope, which could of course prove fatal on a multipitch rappel. Once the climber is ready to begin the rappel, the loop of the double rope is passed through the special figure-of-eight descending device, which is clipped to the climber's harness using a screwgate karabiner. These types of karabiners are safer than the nonscrewgate types mentioned earlier since, once the gate is screwed closed by the user, it cannot open again until unscrewed. The climber then holds the rope below the figure-of-eight and, taking care to get nothing caught in the device (like long hair, long beards or necklaces), slowly feeds the rope through the figure-of-eight while walking backward down the cliff, trying to keep the soles of his or her boots flat on the rock. Where the cliff being descended overhangs, part of the rappel may become a free-rappel—in which the climber loses contact with the rock altogether.

Usually when novices perform their first rappel, a separate safety rope is also attached to the harness and belayed from the top of the rappel. So, if the novice should panic and release the rappel rope, the safety rope would take the weight of the person who could then be lowered slowly to the bottom of the crag. Special nonstretch and more durable ropes have been developed specially for rappeling. Climbers use a variety of other rappel techniques if they do not have a figure-of-eight to hand. For example, it is possible to rappel on a karabiner using a knot called an Italian hitch, or by using a belay plate. Cavers also use various special descending devices for entering deep cave systems.

A History of Climbing

INTRODUCTION

In the past 150 years, most of the world's highest and most difficult peaks have been climbed. In the footsteps of those who pioneered these early routes have come others, determined to follow lines of exquisite difficulty up ridges and mountain faces. Almost every cliff or bare wall of rock throughout the world has been visited, and scaled by climbers. Often it has taken many years of effort, and has cost lives in the process.

So why do it? Why take the risk? "Because it's there" was the reply from the great Everest mountaineer George Mallory. Flippant he may have been, but historically, he was right. Climbing was born out of the drive not for national gain, nor for mineral rights, nor out of a desire to acquire lands—but for pure exploration. The early pioneers of mountaineering wanted to be the first to stand on the summit.

And once the mountain had been climbed, mountaineers on the cutting edge wanted to reach the top by the hardest route possible. In the process, they pitted themselves against rock and ice, against the weather, and against the limits of what their equipment and bodies would allow. And if they succeeded? The next time they would try to complete the route in a bolder way, with lighter equipment and fewer fixed ropes, leaving less of a mark along the way.

At the heart of climbing is a desire to test oneself in the hardest of arenas. And so the limits of mountaineering will always be pushed back. In the past, climbing has been the preserve of a small, well-heeled elite group. Not now. The world's mountains have never been as accessible as they are today. And like the early pioneers, millions of people go to the mountains each year, for the exercise, the views, for the sheer exhilaration. Mountain landscapes are dramatic. No doubt, they will always inspire.

Mount Everest was climbed more than half a century ago, but climbers have not lost interest in it. Every year dozens of people attempt to scale the mountain. Most of them are amateurs on a high-risk break from their day jobs.

And as increasing numbers take to the mountains, extraordinary achievements have been made. The world's highest peak has been climbed in turn solo, without oxygen, by a 14-year-old, by a 69-year-old and via its most difficult faces and ridges. In 2001, the first blind person, Erik Weihenmayer, reached the summit of Everest. This constant daring and pushing back of boundaries shows no sign of abating.

But with people come problems. Mountains all over the world are being loved to death, scarred by millions of

▼ **Early mountaineering** expeditions were often hit-or-miss affairs. Pioneering mountaineers didn't have the benefit of knowledge passed on by previous expeditions, and were usually charting unknown territory with only the most basic equipment. This photograph shows an attempt to climb Pike's Peak, Colorado, in the late 19th century.

footsteps. The South Col of Mount Everest has been described as the highest rubbish dump in the world. In this overpopulated world, preserving the mountain environment is now a pressing challenge.

As mountaineering has developed, climbers have taken its separate disciplines—including rock climbing, ice climbing, Alpinism and high-altitude climbing—and developed each as far as their bodies and technology will allow. As long as people dare to dream, and want to push their own limits, they will always climb.

EARLY TECHNIQUES

The early climbers were restricted by their equipment—but they made up for it with resourcefulness and sheer daring. Many of the first ascents were solo climbs: without modern protection, it mattered little whether the climber was attached to a rope or not. The earliest rock climbers picked their routes with care, often opting to climb mountain gullies

where they could scramble, rather than attempting open faces, which required a more systematic climbing style.

In the late 19th century, teams of climbers commonly used "combined tactics." Groups of mountaineers would climb cliffs and help each other over the hardest sections with a "leg-up," or by clinging to the rock and allowing others literally to clamber over them.

Before the 1930s, climbing teams tended to move together, even on the steepest rock and ice. Few would ever tie themselves on to the rock (the practice called belaying) and climb turn-about. This tactic allowed rapid progress but could be disastrous, as the first climbers to reach the summit of the Matterhorn would discover in 1865. Descending together, one climber fell, pulling three others with him. All four were killed.

Aware of these risks, climbers began developing the systems we see today: moving one at a time, with the stationary

▼ *Taken in 1900*, this photo shows two pioneering mountaineers. Until the development of light-weight synthetic materials, climbers kept warm by wearing layers of woolen clothing. Women climbers wore long, heavy woolen skirts, which must have made climbing extremely arduous.

climber anchored securely to the rock. By the 1930s, wooden wedges and metal pitons, driven into the rock, were being used by lead climbers as temporary anchors along the route. This meant a fall—once invariably fatal—could be shorter and survivable.

As techniques developed, climbing standards rose. Climbers were at last able to move out of the gullies and onto the big rock faces.

Ice climbing, too, was changing beyond recognition. In the 19th century ice climbers, wearing nailed boots and carrying ice axs, were forced to cut steps up their route. This was slow, laborious, and required exquisite balance. Nonetheless, some remarkable climbs were achieved with this technique, including the Alps' hardest north faces. In the 1920s and 1930s, crampons—a framework of steel spikes—were employed for the first time. Their impact was dramatic. These spikes were strapped onto climbing boots and allowed climbers to march up near-vertical ice, with only the front-points of the crampons in contact with the ice.

As ice climbers turned to steeper routes, the disadvantages of the long-handled ice ax became obvious. By the 1950s many Alpine climbers had shortened their axs, and some began to wield an ax in one hand, and an ice dagger in the other. Climbers would stab holes in the ice with dagger and ax in turn. During the 1960s mountaineers realized that they could climb steep ice faster and more easily using a different shape of ice ax. Instead of the flat ice pick, a pick set at 45° was used—then a banana-shaped pick. With just a flick of the wrists it became possible to fix the ax-head in ice, and with another flick, remove it. Climbers were able to race up even the hardest routes in astonishing times. Using such equipment, on 25th July, 1985, the French climber Christophe Profit solo-climbed the three greatest Alpine north faces—the Eiger, the Matterhorn and the Grandes Jorasses—in under 24 hours.

EARLY EQUIPMENT

Few climbers have a death wish. Most want to test themselves to the limit and then return safely from the experience. Good equipment plays a crucial role in achieving that goal. Throughout the history of mountaineering, climbers have constantly sought to develop and improve the gear they depend on to bring them home alive. The last 100 years have seen some extraordinary developments in those designs, but in the early days, climbers had to trust their lives to rudimentary equipment.

The first mountaineers wore stout boots with nails hammered into the leather soles to improve their grip on rock and ice. Different types of nails with names like tricounis, hobs, clinkers and muggers were developed. These were gradually replaced by rubber-soled boots and had all but disappeared by 1960. With the advent of crampons strapped onto their boots, climbers could make remarkable progress up the steepest of ice cliffs.

Climbing pioneers carried a long wooden pole tipped with a steel spike—the alpenstock—to improve their stability on icy slopes. By 1870 the alpenstock was superseded by the long-handled wooden ice ax, which could be used to cut steps. In the last half-century, ice axs became stronger with the introduction of shorter metal shafts, and at the same time the angle of the ice-ax pick changed. By the 1960s, to clamber up the steepest and most difficult routes, mountaineers were using two ice axs, each not much longer than a hammer.

Early ropes were made of Alpine hemp, although silk or cotton ropes were also manufactured. These natural fibers

▼ *Even in the early days* of mountaineering rescue teams would practice retrieving the bodies of unfortunate climbers. The rescue parties were equipped with nothing more than lengths of rope, stout steel-tipped sticks (alpenstocks), leather boots and thick woolen clothes.

were prone to freezing, making them difficult to handle. They were also weaker—the ropes regularly broke if a climber fell too far. Stronger and lighter nylon ropes arrived in the 1950s, heralding in a safer age.

Before the 1960s climbers were reluctant to risk a fall. They made their ascent with the rope lashed around their waist, and falling could result in broken ribs, or worse. Then in the late 1960s, the first canvas climbing-harness was developed. It softened the impact of a fall, and allowed climbers to make the first pain-free rappels. Up to this point, climbers could only slide down the rope, using the friction of their trousers or skin to slow their descent.

The first mountaineers used nothing but a loop of rope to attach themselves to the rock. In the late 1800s artificial protection was developed, in the form of pitons. These metal spikes could be hammered into cracks in the rock. By the 1950s, climbers had begun using temporary chock stones to attach themselves quickly to the cliff as they made their ascent. These allowed climbers to repeat ascents without scarring the rock. In recent years ingenious camming protection has been invented. Climbers jam these spring-loaded, expanding devices into parallel cracks in the cliff face. As a result, climbing routes that were deadly have become far safer.

The pioneers dressed largely in woolen clothing, which is quite windproof and remains warm when wet. Multiple layers were required on the coldest mountains, along with a cotton outer layer. Women would wear long, heavy woolen skirts. By the 1950s, clothing made of down was developed for high-altitude climbing, and the last half-century has seen the development of clothing made from light, synthetic fibers. Breathable shell clothing has made climbing far more comfortable, and nowadays few well-equipped climbers are killed by bad weather alone.

▲ *Modern mountaineering* equipment is a far cry from the days of wooden ice axs and alpenstocks. Today's mountaineers can utilize rock climbing cams and stoppers, attached to colorful slings by karabiners. The purpose of this equipment is to attach climber and ropes firmly to the rock face for safety.

MOUNTAINEERING—THE BEGINNINGS

People have been visiting the mountains for thousands of years. In 1991, the body of the oldest-known European, a Bronze Age hunter, was discovered at 3,200 m (10,500 ft) in the Tyrolean Alps, on the border of present-day Italy and Austria. There is no evidence that Öetzi the Iceman, as he became known, was traveling through this remote mountain path, 5,300 years ago, for any other reason than necessity. Mountainous areas were visited by those who needed to be there—for hunting, migration, grazing animals and trade.

But as people became more familiar with mountain ranges they became curious about the summits that soared above them. With large numbers of people living in their shadows, it was natural that the European Alps would become the crucible of mountaineering.

On 1 September, 1358, a knight of Asti called Bonifacio Rotario set off up Rochemelon, a mountain in the Graiian Alps. Benedictine monks had built a chapel at the foot of this 2,538-m (8,327-ft) peak, and had written about their attempts to climb it as far back as the 11th century. Rotario kept going where the friars had turned back. A small chapel on the summit marks his achievement—the first recorded climb.

In 1492, the French monarch Charles VIII caught sight of the fabulous limestone peak of Mont Aiguille, south of Grenoble. He ordered the ambitious Lord Antoine de Ville to attempt an ascent. This was no easy task: Mont Aiguille had a fearsome reputation and was known in Britain as Mons Inascensibilis! But with the help of what he called "subtle engines" (the noble Lord did not give details) and ladders, Lord Antoine and several of his men reached the top. There the team of pioneering mountaineers built a hut and erected several large crosses.

Other peaks were climbed during the late 18th and early 19th century, most notably by the Swiss monk Father Placidus à Specscha. He made a series of first ascents, in spite of criticism from his fellow monks who believed he was either mad or a French spy. Still attempting high peaks well into his 70s, Father Placidus was the first person to propose the establishment of an Alpine club for climbers.

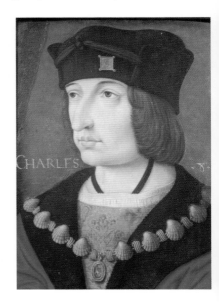

▼ *Charles VIII* of France was an early patron of mountaineering expeditions.

The ascent of Mont Blanc marks the real beginnings of mountaineering as we know it today. In 1760 the rich Swiss scientist, Horace-Bénédict de Saussure, caught sight of the Alps' highest peak, Mont Blanc, for the first time. He wanted to see it climbed, and offered a prize to who- ever claimed the first ascent. Over the next three decades several groups of intrepid climbers attempted to reach the top, only to be forced back. Finally, on 8 August 1786, J. Balmat and M. Paccard reached the summit. At the time it was an extraordinary achievement—at 4,807 m (15,771 ft), Mont Blanc is a giant peak.

▲ *In Chamonix*, France, there exists a statue and plaque to J. Balmat and M. Paccard, the first men to successfully climb Mont Blanc. They made their ascent in 1786, an astonishing achievement.

During the 1800s, political stability and improved transportation links made the European mountains an increasingly attractive place to explore. Particularly in the lat- ter half of the century, there was a burgeoning interest in sci- ence and natural history, and curious naturalists toured the high Alps, identifying new species of plants and animals. Geologists searched for precious stones and ore-bearing rocks. Meteorology and glaciology also led the curious up onto the mountains, and cartographers slowly filled in the blanks on their maps. It was a short step from there to exploring and scaling mountains for their own sake.

Tourism also played a part, with the numbers of British visitors to the Alps soaring during the 19th century. Many came in search of robust physical exercise, and mountaineer- ing suited their needs. Resorts like Zermatt and Chamonix quickly grew up, providing a place to stay and a base for mountain guides. British and German climbers quickly established themselves among the most forceful pioneers of new Alpine routes, although the majority of first ascents were achieved by French, Swiss and Italian climbers, who lived close to the mountains.

The mountains were proving a lure, not only for scientists but also for artists and poets. Their portrayal of climbers as Ulysses-like heroes, challenging nature and achieving dra- matic goals, did much to popularize climbing. Nonetheless, until well into the 20th century, climbing remained an elitist sport, available only to those with money and free time.

◀ **The latter half** of the 19th century is considered the Golden Age of Alpinism. At around this time numerous peaks in the Alps were successfully climbed, with some 100 alone being scaled between 1863 and 1865. This photograph shows an ascent of Mont Blanc in about 1860.

THE GOLDEN AGE

By the 1850s, the Alps had been thoroughly explored and the best unclimbed peaks identified. Through the 1850s and 1860s, mountaineers worked their way through this list with dramatic speed—achieving a rush of first ascents. As a result, the 11 years between 1854, when Alfred Wills made his highly publicized ascent of the Wetterhorn, and 1865, when Edward Whymper climbed the Matterhorn, is often referred to as the Golden Age of Alpinism. In 1865, seven peaks over 4,000 m (13,000 ft) were climbed. Between 1863 and 1865, 100 of the Alps' largest peaks were climbed for the first time.

Throughout this period, it was common for climbers to employ guides to lead them up mountains. The guides were usually local people living in the valleys around Alpine peaks. Many were part-time, and relatively unskilled, but some developed into the finest mountaineers of their time. For decades, it was considered reckless to climb without one. British mountaineers made full use of guides' skills.

During the Golden Age, at least three-quarters of new routes were achieved by British climbers and almost all involved local guides.

But mountaineering was viewed with suspicion, if not derision, by many. The risks in these early days were great, with poor equipment and early climbing techniques reducing safety margins. Deaths were routine on early ascents, as pioneers searched for the safest route up unclimbed peaks. Many thought the risks were unacceptably high.

In 1865, critics howled when four of Whymper's companions fell to their deaths as they descended from the summit of the Matterhorn after the first ascent. The writer Charles Dickens led the charge, writing off mountaineering as reckless vanity: "It contributes as much to the advancement of science as would a club of young gentlemen who should undertake to bestride all the weathercocks of all the cathedral spires of the United Kingdom".

But the criticism did nothing to blunt the public appetite for mountaineering. It simply raised the profile of this dramatic new sport. Whymper's triumph and disaster on the Matterhorn was recounted endlessly in newspapers and magazines. The public was instinctively drawn to the drama of climbs and the boldness of mountaineers. As the sport's profile grew, the number of amateur mountaineers soared: by 1890, Britain's Alpine Club had almost 500 members. Even this, though, was dwarfed by its European counterparts: the Austrian-German club boasted 20,000 members, the French and Italian clubs more than 4,000 each.

As the biggest peaks were climbed, mountaineers turned their attention to smaller mountains and to new, more difficult routes up the biggest peaks. As they did so, standards improved and the impossible became routine. Even climbers of moderate ability became able to reach the highest summits.

By the 1950s, the Italian climber Walter Bonatti was showing how far Alpine mountaineering had come in less than a century. Bonatti made some of the hardest first ascents in the Alps, and then, in 1955, embarked on the most difficult climb he—or arguably any climber—had ever attempted. This involved a solo attempt on the Southwest Pillar of the Petit Dru, a 914-m (2,998-ft) high rock spire soaring above Chamonix, the center of Alpine climbing. It took almost a day of extremely difficult climbing even to reach the cliff's base, via a nearby ridge and a long rappel. Then, for five days, Bonatti pitted himself against some of the steepest and hardest rock-climbing in the Alps. With no partner, any mistake could have been fatal. The climb's steepness and

177

difficulty meant that he was unable to carry his backpack. After completing each section, therefore, Bonatti would lower himself down the cliff face and haul himself and his gear, hand over hand, back up the rope. By the time Bonatti reached the summit, he had climbed the Pillar three times. A huge overhang two-thirds of the way up the cliff was the greatest obstacle. Bonatti swung his away around it, and then, in desperation, lassooed a rocky outcrop with his climbing rope. This move returned him to easier ground, and was the key to one of the greatest ascents of all time.

▲ **The Japanese climber** Junko Tabei became the first woman to reach the summit of Everest. She is just one of a long list of women climbers who have gained the respect of the, largely male, mountaineering community.

WOMEN CLIMBERS

The first women climbers were viewed disparagingly by their male counterparts. But the sexism of the time did nothing to take away from their achievements. In 1808 Marie Paradis became the first female to climb Mont Blanc. By 1929, climbers such as Miriam O'Brien and Alice Dameseme were climbing the highest Alpine peaks, without guides. This was helped by the establishment of several women-only mountaineering clubs. Founding members of Britain's first such group, the Pinnacle Club, wanted to show women that they could lead on even the hardest Alpine routes.

In 1975, the Japanese climber Junko Tabei became the first woman to reach the summit of Mount Everest (this in the same year as the first British men). Then Wanda Rutkiewicz and Alison Hargreaves showed themselves capable of climbing the hardest Himalayan routes. Alison Hargreaves also led the way for women in the Alps, ticking off all the great Alpine north faces, solo, in a single summer. In the 1990s Lynn Hill and Catherine Destivelle established themselves among the leading rock climbers—male or female—in the world. Their skill and balance more than made up for the extra power male climbers could bring to bear.

▶ **Napes Needle** in the Lake District was made famous by the English rock-climbing pioneer Walter Parry Haskett-Smith. Climbing solo, he made the first attempt in 1886.

179

THE SPORT OF ROCK CLIMBING

Alpine climbers always aimed to reach the summit of mountains. But in the Victorian era a new breed of climbers was developing. Their goal was to focus on short, difficult routes on unclimbed cliffs, believing that to be the supreme test of their skills.

In Britain, the sport of rock climbing can be traced back to the efforts of a young student, Walter Parry Haskett-Smith. In the summer of 1881, this trainee barrister visited the Lake District for two months, staying with a group of fellow undergraduates at Wasdale Head. During Haskett-Smith's visit, he began fell-walking and was introduced to simple scrambles—and so his passion was ignited. The next year he returned with his brother and made a series of new rock climbs: Great Gully, Pavey Ark and Deep Ghyll on Scafell are among the climbs he pioneered. He had a brush with death on Pillar Rock, when a loose boulder fell and almost struck him on the head, but Haskett-Smith was not easily put off. He had little interest in reaching mountain summits. Instead he was captivated by the struggle of the climb itself. This view of rock climbing as an end in itself has marked out Haskett-Smith as the founder of British rock climbing.

In 1886 he made his most famous ascent: a solo climb of Napes Needle, a towering pinnacle high on Great Gable in the Lake District. He had a unique style, using, as he described it, "no ropes or other illegitimate means." En route, he threw stones up the cliff to identify holds for his hands and feet, and once on top, he tied a handkerchief to the summit to mark his achievement. British society was astonished, the story making it to the newspapers' front pages. (It would be three years before Napes Needle was climbed again.)

By the 1890s the sport of rock climbing was truly established. Haskett-Smith produced the first guide to rock-climbing routes in England, in 1894. Where he led, many thousands of others would follow, and many of his routes have stood the test of time.

But in its early years, rock climbing was not a sport for the faint-hearted. Winter ascents were made in socks, to give added grip on ice. On one climber's solo first ascent in the Lake District, he trailed a rope behind him in the vain hope of it snagging on the cliff in the event of a fall. Owen Glynne Jones' 1893 ascent of Moss Ghyll sums up the commitment needed: he climbed the route solo in winter conditions, falling en route and breaking several ribs. Patched up, he returned a few days later to complete the climb!

▼ **The peaks around Chamonix** in the French Alps are the focal point of European Alpine climbing. Here ascents that have become the stuff of legend were made during the 20th century.

Others would routinely set off up climbs roped together, hoping that a fall by one would be held by the rest. In the bestselling Victorian guidebook "The Complete Mountaineer," George Abraham describes this tactic: "Vertical and overhanging stretches can be overcome by the leader standing on the shoulders (or even the head) of the second climber until suitable holds can be attained." This tactic sometimes failed, and teams would come crashing down en masse.

Rope-work was casual, too. Modern climbers tie themselves securely to the cliff, using rope and nylon slings, in order to absorb the extreme forces generated by a falling companion. Not so the Victorians. As the leading climber made his way up the route, the second person (the belayer) would simply grip the rope and dig in his or her heels. The golden rule was straightforward, "the leader must not fall!"

Unsurprisingly, most climbs from the Victorian age are of modest difficulty by comparison with the desperate test-pieces

of today. Most climbers stayed well within the limits of their ability. Many of the routes followed the most natural lines up cliffs—the gullies. Only as equipment and skills developed would climbers move out onto the exposed cliff faces.

Nevertheless, the skill and daring of these Victorian pioneers should not be doubted. Many of their routes were extremely exposed. The climbs were dangerous, and often full of loose rock, moss and earth. Retreat was impossible, and falls, if they happened, were long and often fatal. Despite all this, these early routes were bold and often took the best lines up the cliff. To this day, they are among the most repeated in Britain.

These early years of British climbing were recorded on film by two of the finest climbers of the era—George and Ashley Abraham. These brothers were professional photographers who did much to establish climbing in the public eye. It was no easy task: they carried a heavy plate camera with them to capture images. Jealous critics accused them of tilting their camera to exaggerate the steepness of the climbs they photographed.

▲ **This early expedition** to the Himalayas was undertaken by Fanny Bullock Workman and her husband William. A mountaineering pioneer, Fanny Workman made seven expeditions to the Himalayas between 1899 and 1912, and her charts and observations remain an important resource even today.

EXPLORATION OF THE HIMALAYAS

The golden age of Alpine climbing was mirrored in the exploration of the Himalayas, the world's greatest mountain range, and one that offers almost limitless potential for climbing. Owing to the remoteness of many parts of the range, the early pioneers had to map, survey and explore uninhabited areas along the way.

These were not easily accessible peaks. But two of the highest summits—Everest and Kanchenjunga—were visible from Darjeeling, the summer headquarters of British Imperial India. Expeditions were funded to explore this wild and tantalizing terrain. In the late 19th century few dedicated climbers visited the Himalayas, although some early British teams climbed peaks higher than anything found in the Alps. As early as 1852, a survey team established that Peak XV in the Khumbu Himal, on the Nepal-Tibet border, was the highest mountain on Earth. This peak would be renamed Mount Everest, after Sir George Everest, a former Surveyor General of India, and the driving force behind the surveying of the Himalayas.

By 1865 all the major Alpine summits had been climbed. Mountaineers began turning their attention to the world's other ranges, including the Himalayas. In 1892 Martin Conway led the first major expedition to the western Himalayas. His team, which included an artist and naturalist, mapped parts of Baltoro close to K2, and he made the first ascent of Pioneer Peak. At 6,888 m (22,598 ft), this was the highest summit yet climbed.

In 1907, Tom Longstaff reached the summit of Trisul, at 7,101 m (23,291 ft) setting a new height record. A doctor by training, Longstaff was the first to study the effects of altitude, which was proving to be one of the greatest barriers to success in the Himalayas. Many had perished through suffering the effects of high-altitude climbing; one such

▼ *Even today's Himalayan expeditions* rely on Sherpas and their yaks for transportation. Here they are taking equipment to a base camp in Khumu Himal. From there the climbers will begin their ascent of Mount Everest.

was Albert Mummery, the finest climber of his day, during an attempt in 1895 on Nanga Parbat.

At great heights, there is about 65% less oxygen in the air than at sea level, and without enough oxygen the body and brain slow down. Coping with the effects of altitude would be the key to success on the biggest Himalayan peaks, and within 20 years climbers would be experimenting with portable oxygen sets on Everest.

During the early 20th century, British climbers, most notably Bill Tilman and Eric Shipton, were at the forefront of those attempting new routes in the Himalayas. Tilman and Shipton pioneered a style of expedition that traveled light, sought out new ground, and climbed large numbers of virgin peaks. In 1934, with just three Sherpa porters, the pair forced a route into the vast Nanda Devi Sanctuary, traveling over mountain passes and through uninhabited valleys. Eight previous expeditions had failed to reach their goal. On another trip to the Everest area, the pair climbed 20 mountains over 6,000 m (20,000 ft) in just three months. Their light-weight, exploratory style of climbing would inspire later generations of mountaineers.

In 1936, Tilman and Noel Odell climbed Nanda Devi—at over 8,000 m (26,000 ft), it would remain the highest peak to be climbed until 1950. On reaching the summit, Tilman allowed his British reserve to be overcome for a moment: "I think we so far forgot ourselves, as to shake hands on it."

On separate postwar expeditions Tilman and Shipton identified the route through the Khumbu Glacier, to the South Col of Everest. From there the first successful ascent would be made—in 1953.

Nonetheless, success on Mount Everest would elude the early pioneers. The first three expeditions to Everest would claim the lives of 12 people. Bad weather ended three attempts in the 1930s. Only a huge-scale expedition, drawing inspiration from military campaigns, would finally put Edmund Hillary and Tenzing Norgay on the summit.

The 1953 ascent of Everest marked an acceleration of expeditions to the Himalayas. Within little more than a decade, all of the 8,000-m (26,000-ft) peaks were climbed, by teams from all over the world. On all these expeditions, the formula for success was similar: Sherpa porters were used to ferry large amounts of supplies up the mountain; fixed ropes, fixed camps and bottled oxygen then provid-ed the means of ascent; large teams of climbers, trained on Alpine-sized peaks, provided strength in depth, so that losses through injury and exhaustion would not result in the end the attempt.

▶ *The Mustagh Tower* *(7,284 m/24,073 ft) of the Karakoram region of the Himalayas is an awe-inspiring sight. First climbed successfully in 1956, the mountain remains one of the greatest climbing challenges today.*

EXTREME CLIMBS

Before World War II, climbing was largely the preserve of the middle and upper classes. Only the wealthy could afford the equipment, the cost of travel and the time needed to reach mountain areas. But across Europe, as rationing and postwar austerity became a memory, a new breed of climbers came through who refused to be held back by class barriers.

In Britain, the Rock and Ice Club epitomized this movement. Set up by a group of working-class friends in Manchester, the club produced two of Britain's best climbers—Joe Brown and Don Whillans. These men, short, tough and tremendously strong, learned to climb on Derbyshire outcrops, and would go on to conquer some of the greatest Himalayan peaks.

They were among the first to use "running belays," to safeguard their progress up cliffs. Instead of driving pitons into the rock, these climbers would insert pebbles or metal nuts into cracks, and then painstakingly thread rope slings behind them. This sophisticated system allowed them to protect even the hardest routes.

Before the 1950s Alpine and Himalayan climbers generally began their careers on easy routes on big mountains, before moving on to more difficult routes on the same large peaks. It meant that they were mountaineers first and technical climbers second. They had tremendous practical experience of mountaineering, but not all were brilliant climbers. The likes of Brown and Whillans did things the other way around. They cut their teeth on extremely difficult routes on small local outcrops. Even today, their climbs are graded "extremely severe." They moved on to the greatest unclimbed routes in Wales, the Lake District and Scotland. At this time, most cliffs had been climbed, but the boldest lines were beyond the skills of all but the best. In the space of a few years, Brown, Whillans and a few others had pushed rock-climbing standards to a different level.

Brown and Whillans moved on to Europe, climbing the West Face of the Blaitière, one of the hardest new routes in the Alps. Later in their careers, Brown climbed Kanchenjunga and the Mustagh Tower, and Whillans climbed the South Face of Annapurna. They epitomized a new breed of mountaineer, whose technical skills would allow success on the hardest routes on the world's hardest mountains. The best mountaineers of today follow a similar path.

BIG WALL CLIMBING—THE USA

The Yosemite Valley in California is home to some of the most breathtaking rock spires anywhere in the world. From the beginning of the 1930s, these towering pillars of granite, thousands of feet high, have played host to a community of many of North America's best climbers. The style of climbing pioneered there has had an immense impact on the sport's development elsewhere in the world. Soaring cracks in the hard granite rock-faces and routes 900 m (3,000 ft) long demanded new techniques. John Salathe and his companions in the Lost Arrow Club developed equipment equal to the task, including hard steel pitons, prussiking gear (to allow climbers to haul their way up the rope) and haul bags for carrying the food and equipment needed for multiday routes.

In 1958 Warren Harding took 45 days of climbing, with 675 pitons and 125 bolts drilled into the rock, to complete "the Nose" on El Capitan. This route would be among the greatest achievements of "aid climbing." Instead of relying solely on hand and footholds to climb the cliff, aid climbers would hammer pegs and bolts into the rock to help their progress. This did not make aid climbing risk-free: far from it.

Ethics demanded that climbers use the bare minimum of artificial means to overcome extremely difficult obstacles, and aid climbing was the only way that blank or otherwise impossible sections of rock could be climbed. This approach had its critics because in the process pegs and bolts left permanent scar on the rock.

The Yosemite Valley is also packed with shorter routes. On these cliffs, climbers ascended routes more difficult than anything the early pioneers could have imagined. Having tested themselves, these climbers went on to repeat their achievements on the biggest cliffs in Yosemite, and beyond. As a result, in recent years many of the boldest aid climbs have been climbed "free"—without artificial aid.

▶ *Yosemite Valley* with the famous El Capitan in the background. Yosemite is the home to big wall, or aid climbing, in which climbers hammer pegs and bolts into the rock face to overcome sections of sheer flat rock that would otherwise be impossible to climb.

The big wall climbing style has been exported around the world. The huge spires of Greenland, Baffin Island, Patagonia and the Trango Towers of the Karakoram have all been conquered by climbers using techniques developed in California.

▶ *Mount Everest*, *photographed by Doug Scott. He and Dougal Haston were the first British climbers to reach the summit of Everest.*

THE GREAT FACES

With most of the great peaks conquered, mountaineers turned their attention to the boldest routes up the world's great mountains. In 1963, an American expedition achieved the first traverse of Mount Everest, climbing up the West Ridge and descending by the South Ridge. A Chinese expedition reached the summit of Everest from the north. As the obvious ridges were climbed, there remained faces as difficult as anything in the Alps, but many times higher, with extreme altitude adding to the complications.

In 1970, one of Britain's outstanding mountaineers, Chris Bonington, organized an expedition to attempt one of these great climbs: Annapurna's South Face. This wall of rock and ice rises as high as four Alpine north faces. Bonington took with him a team of eight expert climbers, dozens of porters and tons of equipment. Over the course of weeks, climbers fixed ropes up the route, past an ice ridge and the broad Rock Band. Finally, two of the strongest climbers, Dougal Haston and Don Whillans, reached the summit. At the time this was the hardest climb that had been achieved in the Himalayas. Bonington had developed a style that would allow climbers to defeat the most difficult routes on Earth.

Over the next four years a series of international expeditions attempted an even greater challenge: Everest's 2,133-m (6,998-ft) Southwest Face. The crux of the problem was this—how to push a team of mountaineers up to an altitude of five miles, find a route through the extremely difficult Rock Band and then climb 500 m (1,650 ft) higher to the summit? It required logistical strength combined with technical brilliance. The team achieved its goal with remarkable success; fixing ropes and establishing camps all the way to the foot of the Rock Band, they then forged a route through this barrier via a steep ice gully. Dougal Haston and Doug Scott became Britain's first climbers to reach the summit of Everest. The pair even survived a forced bivouac on the South Summit, during their descent.

This expedition marked a high point for large-scale expeditions. It proved that virtually any route, however difficult, could be climbed with a well-led, skilled team and large-scale backup, provided the weather was good. Few climbers, however, could find the funds for an expedition of

this sort, and some felt that fixed ropes and extensive use of bottled oxygen brought the summit down to the climbers. One leading climber described it as "the murder of the impossible." Most mountaineers, Bonington included, turned their attention to smaller-scale expeditions, on the biggest peaks.

TAKING IT TO THE LIMITS

By the 1970s, climbers were seeking out new ways to challenge the limits of what was thought possible. Systematic training and supreme physical fitness helped them succeed. Reinhold Messner, from the Tyrol, Austria, epitomized this new type of mountaineer. As part of his daily training regime, Messner would typically run up a 1,000-m (3,300-ft) hillside in less than 1.5 hours. At the same time, new techniques—particularly the use of two specially-adapted ice axs for climbing steep ice—spurred the revolution he led.

Messner forged a partnership with Peter Habeler, another superb exponent of Alpine climbing. In 1975, the pair climbed the North Face of the Eiger in just ten hours and the Matterhorn's North Face in eight hours. This was breathtaking: in normal conditions, the best mountaineers would normally take several days to complete these routes. The pair then turned their attention to the Himalayas. In the same year they climbed Gasherbrum, 8,068 m (26,470 ft) high, Alpine style—that is, without large-scale fixed ropes or logistical backup.

By this point, Mount Everest had been climbed several dozen times, but always by teams employing bottled oxygen. In 1978 Messner and Habeler achieved the hitherto impossible—climbing the world's highest peak breathing nothing but the thin air around them.

Two years later, Messner would be back on Everest, this time alone. Carrying his home and all his equipment on his back, Messner progressed up the North Face of Everest slowly—"like a tortoise," as he put it. With no porters, Messner could not carry bottled oxygen. Instead he had to

◄ **Reinhold Messner** *is widely regarded as the greatest mountaineer of all time. With his long-term climbing partner Peter Habeler they were able to climb in hours mountains that other mountaineers took days to climb.*

rely solely on his skill and experience. On his third day of climbing, Messner left everything in his tent except his ice ax and camera, and climbed the final few thousand feet to the summit. After barely ten minutes on the top, Messner turned around and descended. He returned to base camp exhausted and dehydrated, having survived a climb which tested him to his limits, and which rates as one of the greatest of all time.

Messner showed that even the biggest peaks could be climbed in small teams, without oxygen—Alpine style. This recipe would be applied with dramatic effect over the next few years, and led to some audacious achievements. But smaller expeditions were naturally more vulnerable to the effects of weather and illness than their larger counterparts. As a result, many of the best high-altitude mountaineers have died young.

EXTREME ROCK

As Reinhold Messner and others were pushing the limits of Alpinism and high-altitude climbing, rock climbers were also taking their sport beyond the realms of what many considered possible. Equipment was improving, with stronger ropes, better harnesses and ingenious protection devices helping climbers test out the steepest routes in greater safety. In the 1970s gym shoes were replaced by rubber-soled shoes with stiff edges, which allowed climbers to make moves on exquisitely small holds. The last two decades have seen sticky-rubber added to the soles of climbing shoes, pushing standards even higher. Almost all of the hardest aid climbs from the 1950s and 1960s were gradually climbed "free," climbers using only their own skill and strength to carry them up the cliff.

As the number of climbers increased, the sport began to borrow ideas from other disciplines. Intensive training came to rock climbing for the first time. Artificial climbing walls were set up in sports centers and converted church halls. For the first time, city dwellers were able to train during the winter, at weekends and after work. Standards soared. Now, the best climbs of the 1950s are within reach of many good weekend climbers.

At the pinnacle of the sport, standards have risen hugely. Climbers have developed gymnastic techniques, using dynamic moves (known as dynos) to leap up bare sections of rock. Improvements in finger strength have allowed climbers to push sustained and desperate routes up the most extreme overhangs.

Leading climbers take many risks now, as they have always done. But modern training and equipment allow climbers to control the risks they take to a greater extent than ever before. As a result, climbing has become increasingly popular: it is now one of the fastest-growing sports on Earth.

GREAT ACHIEVEMENTS
Matterhorn

The Matterhorn—the most recognizable mountain in the world—towers above the Swiss village of Zermatt. At 4,475 m (14,682 ft) high, the Matterhorn is not the highest peak in Europe, nor even the highest in Switzerland. But since the 1850s, the Matterhorn's spectacular shape and stark ridge-lines have drawn climbers like moths to a flame.

The mountain was first climbed on 14 July, 1865 by the British climber Edward Whymper and six companions. Infatuated by the Matterhorn, Whymper had already made eight unsuccessful attempts on the mountain. Many others also wanted to make the first ascent. Aware that an Italian team was preparing to climb the mountain, Whymper assembled a team in Zermatt and went for the summit via the Northeast (Hornli) ridge—a long and complex route, with the threat of stonefall. The team reached the top at 1.40 pm and set off to return the way they had come. But on their descent, three of Whymper's less experienced English companions, including a vicar and a Lord, and their French guide, fell from the ridge, tumbling more than 1,000 m (3,300 ft) to the glacier below. Whymper had claimed one of the greatest first ascents, but he shocked the world in the process.

Eiger North Face

The North Face of the Eiger has a reputation as the most fearsome climb in Europe. The 3,970-m (13,025-ft) Eiger (appropriately, "ogre" in German) is only the 10th highest peak in the Bernese Oberland, but for decades the mountain's vast North Face, the Eigerwand, has been seen as the greatest challenge in the Alps. This huge triangular scoop of rock is almost permanently in deep shadow. Anyone attempting to climb the 1,800-m (5,900-ft) face has to contend with loose rock, snow fields and almost constant stonefall which sweeps the face.

In addition the route is complex, zigzagging up the cliff to bypass impossible sections of rock and ice. To avoid being hit by stonefall, many climbers choose to take on the Eiger in the coldest conditions, when the loose rocks are more likely to be frozen onto the cliff face. Fickle weather also hampers

▶ *The unmistakable Matterhorn* looms over the picturesque ski resort of Zermatt in Switzerland. The mountain has always had a strong hold over mountaineers, but it remained unclimbed until 1865.

mountaineers. Storms can leave the cliff caked in ice, making onward progress, and retreat, virtually impossible.

The Eiger stands above the resort town of Kleine Scheidegg and tourists gather there to watch the game of life and death played out before them, through the telescopes that line the cafés' balconies.

By the 1930s almost all the Alps' great north faces had been climbed. The Eiger remained unconquered until 1938, when a team of four German climbers threaded a route up the face. But the mountain would claim many lives before their success.

In 1935 Max Sedlmayer and Karl Mehringer were the first climbers really to challenge the North Face. They were caught in a storm, and froze to death at what is now called the "Death Bivouac." Their deaths highlit the difficult balance which Eiger climbers had to strike, given the challenge of climbing extremely steep and difficult rock and ice while carrying all the equipment needed for a week's survival. Carry too much, and climbing would be impossible.

◄ The North Face, the "Eigerwand," of the Eiger is one of the most dangerous ascents of Europe. Unpredictable weather patterns, loose rocks and stonefalls have resulted in the death of numerous climbers, some of which have passed into mountaineering folklore.

Carry too little, and risk freezing or starving to death if the weather turned bad.

One of the darkest chapters in mountaineering history occurred in 1936. Four men found the key to climbing the Eiger—but paid the ultimate price for a mistake. Andreas Hinterstoisser, Edi Ranier, Willy Angerer and Toni Kurz set off up the face, reaching a smooth section of rock, which barred their way. Hinterstoisser was able to traverse across this steep slab, and his companions followed behind. Once across, they pulled their rope through. Shortly afterward, they were caught in a storm, and were forced to retreat. They realized too late that without a fixed rope in place, the traverse was impossible in icy conditions. They were trapped. Three of the men were swept to their deaths by an avalanche. After two freezing nights, Toni Kurz tried to rappel to a rescue party below him. His rope jammed, and with hands too cold to free himself, he died dangling over the face, just out of reach of the rescuers. The Hinterstoisser Traverse remains a point of no return on this unforgiving mountain.

This disastrous expedition did little to put off others. Several more attempts were made, some of them fatal, before a team of four climbers finally achieved the impossible. In 1938 Austria's Fritz Kasparek and Heinrich Harrer teamed up with Anderl Heckmair and Ludwig Vorg from Germany, to make the first ascent. Their route was bold—threading past the Hinterstoisser Traverse, across two ice fields and a ramp of rock. The upper half of the face steepens and forms an amphitheater 800 m (2,600 ft) high. Avoiding the heavy stonefall, they climbed out through the loose, easy-angled rock that led to the summit. They had completed the greatest ascent in the Alps.

For decades the Eiger has preserved its fearsome reputation. By the late 1960s, it was the focus of a new generation of climbers, willing to think beyond the classic routes. They had completed direct ascents up many of the great Alpine faces. One of the boldest was John Harlin, an American climber who wanted to achieve a new direct route straight up the Eiger's North Face.

Harlin had established a reputation as an innovative leader of new Alpine routes. Other climbers, uneasy at Harlin's drive and ambition, nicknamed him "the Blonde God." But Harlin was not put off by his critics, and was determined to do the hardest climb yet achieved in the Alps.

Harlin chose his climbing partners carefully. He called upon Dougal Haston, a young and daring Scottish pioneer, known for his skill on rock and ice. And from the USA, he enlisted the help of Layton Kor, one of the world's leading

artificial climbers, who had learned to forge extraordinary direct routes up the sheer walls of California's Yosemite Valley. Their blend of skills would combine with Harlin's drive and focus to make a formidable team.

The Eiger Direct was only possible in winter, since it followed a line normally peppered by falling rocks. Harlin's strategy was to fix ropes all the way up the cliff face. His team could therefore make progress in the short spells of good weather, then retreat to the valley floor to avoid the regular storms. As soon as the weather cleared, they climbed back to their high point and pushed on.

The team set off in late February 1966. The climbing was extremely difficult, and storms repeatedly forced them to retreat to the valley floor.

▲ **From the small** resort town of Kleine Scheidegg, which lies at the foot of the North Face of the Eiger, spectators can use the telescopes found in the town's cafes to watch climbers making their ascents.

Meanwhile, a group of German climbers, led by Jörg Lehne, also began an attempt on the Eiger Direct. At first there was competitive tension between the two teams. But within six weeks, the climbers were working together, to complete their shared objective.

Time and again, they had to retreat from the cliffs. But on 21 March, a spell of clear weather appeared, and the team returned to their high point. Then disaster struck. A fixed rope, already frayed by stonefall, snapped altogether, sending John Harlin tumbling almost 2,000 m (6,500 ft) down the Eiger's North Face.

A week later, Kor and Haston completed the Eiger Direct, along with their four German companions, Jörg Lehne, Günther Strobel, Siegi Hupfauer and Roland Votteler. Renamed the Harlin Route, this climb was John Harlin's legacy to mountaineering. It remains one of the most intimidating ascents in the Alps.

▶ **The classic route** for climbing the North Face of the Eiger, with the infamous Hinterstoisser Traverse.

Everest

In the Himalayas, too, great mountains challenged the boldest mountaineers. However, at the time that peak XV was renamed Mount Everest, in 1865, few thought of climbing the mountain. Apart from the numerous technical difficulties, there seemed no reason to attempt it at a time when helping forge empires gave men all the adventure they could dream of—and could make them a fortune at the same time. Tibet was closed to westerners, and Nepal was a blank on the map.

It was not until 1921 that the first true attempt on Everest would be made. A team led by Lieutenant Colonel Howard-Bury found a route across the Tibetan plateau, via the Rongbuk Glacier, to Everest's North Face. They climbed to the North Col (7,066 m/23,182 ft), hoping to forge a route to

the summit via the Northeast Ridge or North Face. But then the difficulties began. Above the North Col, three bands of steep limestone slabs stretched across the mountain, barring easy progress.

In 1924 a British expedition returned to Everest's north side. One of the leading climbers was George Mallory. His hopes were high: "We shall stamp on the top with the wind in our teeth." Mallory was among the best British climbers of the age—but at 38 he was becoming a little old for hard climbing at extreme altitudes. Mallory was obsessed by Everest, and was determined to reach the summit on this attempt. He and his fellow team members forged the route to the North Col, and set up two further camps, the highest just 700 m (2,300 ft) below the summit. On 8 June, Mallory set out on a clear morning with a relative novice, 22-year-old Englishman Andrew Irvine, aiming for the top and carrying bottled oxygen. They never returned.

In 1999, Mallory's body was found high on the mountain, but the mystery of his death remains. Before his departure, Mallory had told a friend, "We shall expect no mercy from Mount Everest." He received none, but did Mallory and Irvine reach the summit?

Many believe they could not have completed the climb. To have reached the summit, the men would have had to defeat a daunting range of obstacles. First the Yellow Band, steep slabs covered with loose rock; above that, two pinnacles: the first a steep, near-vertical ridge. The so-called "Second Step" is even harder—a 30-m (100-ft) vertical corner. Modern climbers, with good equipment, fixed ropes and systematic training, still struggle up this route. However, there is strong evidence that they did in fact reach the summit. Fellow expedition member Noel Odell was the last person to see Mallory and Irvine from a clear vantage point high on the face. He noticed that they had managed to get above the Second Step, and were on easy angled ground, a short distance below the top.

We may never know whether Everest was first conquered in 1924. Evidence may still be lying out on the mountain, frozen in time. Mallory's pocket camera was not found with his body. Irvine must have been carrying it when he died, and his body has never been recovered. It is clear, though, that it would have taken a lot to prevent Mallory reaching the summit of his ambition.

In the years before World War II, other men would come close to the summit of Everest. In 1938, Bill Tilman's expedition reached over 8,534 m (27,992 ft) on the North Face before bad weather and deep snow forced them back.

In 1921, Mallory had looked over into Nepal, and the

▼ *Despite affording* an almost limitless supply of mountaineering challenges, the mountains of the Himalayan range remained largely unclimbed until the early 20th century. No serious attempt was made on Everest itself until 1921.

southern approach to Everest. He was dismissive—"I do not much fancy it would be possible, even if one could get up the glacier." Thirty years later, he would be proved wrong.

During the prewar years, Nepal was largely cut off from the outside world. Foreign climbers were routinely refused entry to sensitive border areas. But after 1945, relations thawed and a series of expeditions was allowed access to the valleys that lie around Everest. In 1950, Bill Tilman and Charles Houston made a quick visit to the Khumbu Glacier. They had little time to explore, but they could see this could be the route to the summit. The next year, Eric Shipton's reconnaissance group (which included the young New Zealand beekeeper, Edmund Hillary) went to Nepal, and explored into the vast basin known as the Western Cwm, which lies between Everest, Nuptse and Lhotse. From there, the team climbed the Khumbu ice fall, a dangerous mass of collapsing crevasses and ice pinnacles, 600 m (2,000 ft) high. Above them rose the steep side of Lhotse and, far above, the South Col. The team had found the key to climbing

▼ *George Mallory* *(back, second from left) and Andrew Irvine (back, far left) pictured with the rest of the members of Mallory's ill-fated expedition to Everest. His attempt on Everest cost him and Irvine their lives, but although many believe they reached the summit there is, as yet, no evidence to support this.*

▲ *The summit of Everest*, which for so long eluded mountaineers from all over the world, has now been reached by more than 1,200 climbers from 63 different countries. Despite its popularity, the thought of climbing to the highest place on Earth appeals to thousands more.

Everest, but Shipton believed the chances of success for any expedition were as much as 30-1 against.

In 1952 a team of Swiss climbers tried and narrowly failed to climb Everest via the South Col. On that expedition, the outstanding Nepalese climber Tenzing Norgay and his Swiss companion Lambert had reached 8,595 m (28,191 ft)—less than 300 m (1,000 ft) below the summit—before being forced back by storms and exhaustion. It was now clear that Everest could be climbed by this route. But who would make the first successful ascent?

The British Alpine Club met in London to assemble a team to attempt Mount Everest. As expedition leader they rejected Eric Shipton, one of Britain's most experienced mountain explorers. Instead they opted for ex-army officer John Hunt, a comparatively inexperienced climber. The reason was simple: this was not exploration but a brutal battle against gravity, with logistics the key.

For six weeks, the team laid siege to Mount Everest. Three hundred and fifty porters carried ten tons of supplies to base camp at 2,400 m (18,000 ft). Success or failure on such a massive mountain depended on maintaining a supply chain up the route, creating a series of nine camps to within striking distance of the summit. Everything—food, fuel, tents, ropes and climbing equipment—had to be carried by climbers up fixed ropes. For John Hunt, the key to success was teamwork: "Everyone rightly believed that he had a vital part to play in getting at least two members of the team on top."

Between 13 and 17 April 1953, Edmund Hillary and a small group of climbers forced a route through the Khumbu ice fall. This was dangerous work, the ice fall resembling a slow-moving river of ice, filled with fissures and crumbling

▼ *In the early 1950s, following several reconnaissance expeditions, it became apparent that the imposing Khumbu Glacier held the key to a potentially successful ascent of Everest.*

ice cliffs. A rope lifeline and ladders had to be fixed all the way through this labyrinth of ice to safeguard the team of heavily laden Sherpa porters who would follow. By 18 April the route was clear into the Western Cwm, paving the way for over a ton and a half of supplies to be ferried through the ice fall.

Tom Bourdillon and Charles Evans then forced the route up the steep Lhotse face to a height of 7,315 m (24,000 ft). A camp was established on the South Col, the gap between Everest and Lhotse. Meanwhile Tenzing and Hillary showed they had acclimatized well, carrying full backpacks of supplies 1,070 m (3,500 ft) up the face in a single day.

On 26 May Charles Evans and Tom Bourdillon set off from camp IX at 8,503 m (27,890 ft) to make the first summit bid. Just 91 m (298 ft) short of the top, a failed oxygen set forced them to retreat. Three days later, Tenzing and Hillary made their attempt on the mountain.

The route from the South Col begins as a broad snow-covered ridge, but a few hundred feet below the summit the ridge steepens, and the climbers were confronted by a formidable rock-step 12 m (40 ft) high. Hillary scrambled past it, followed by Tenzing. The Nepali's oxygen set mal-functioned—ice had clogged the system, but the pair were able to clear it.

At 11.30 am on 29 May 1953 the two climbers reached the summit. Hillary stretched out his arm for a handshake. This wasn't enough for Tenzing, who threw his arms around Hillary and gave him a mighty hug.

On his descent, Hillary told the story of the climb to a waiting reporter, who was able to rush the story to Britain. It made the front page of the newspapers on 2 June, on the morning of Queen Elizabeth II's coronation.

Since this first ascent, more than 1,200 men and women, from 63 nations, have reached the summit of Mount Everest. In spite of this, the well-travelled route to the summit becomes more popular every year.

SEVEN SUMMITS

In 1985, the American climber Dick Bass reached the summit of Mount Everest and laid claim to a new record: he was the first person to reach the summit of the highest peak on each of the world's seven continents. Around 70 climbers have now completed the seven summits, which are listed on page 204. This challenge has seized the imagination of a growing band of climbers who use mountaineering as an opportunity to explore to the ends of the Earth.

HIGHEST SUMMITS OF THE SEVEN CONTINENTS			
Continent	Mountain	Country	Height
ASIA	Mount Everest	Nepal	8,848 m/(29,028 ft)
SOUTH AMERICA	Aconcagua	Argentina	6,962 m/(22,840 ft)
NORTH AMERICA	Mount McKinley (Denali)	Alaska	6,194 m/(20,321 ft)
AFRICA	Kilimanjaro	Tanzania	5,895 m/(19,340 ft)
EUROPE	Elbrus	Russia	5,642 m/(18,510 ft)
ANTARCTICA	Mount Vinson		4,897 m/(16,066 ft)
AUSTRALIA	Kosciusko	New South Wales	2,228 m/(7,310 ft)

THE GREAT CHALLENGES

With dozens of expeditions forging new routes on mountains across the world each year, what is left to climb? The most pressing challenge for some mountaineers is to climb old routes in a new, bold style. Many of the first ascents of Himalayan peaks were achieved during the 1950s with the help of fixed ropes, bottled oxygen, and large numbers of porters. With better equipment and training, modern-day climbers are attempting these peaks Alpine style: without fixed ropes or oxygen, and taking only what they can carry on their own backs.

▼ *The North Face* of *Jannu, part of the Kanchenjunga massif in the Himalayas, is well known for its unremittingly steep 2,500-m (8,200 ft) vertical face.*

▲ *Nanga Parbat is one of the world's most dangerous mountains, and its Mazeno Traverse remains one of the last great challenges.*

But even now, many new routes still remain to be climbed. Although most of the 8,000-m (26,000-ft) peaks in the Himalayas have received dozens if not hundreds of ascents, few of the more numerous 7,000-m (23,000-ft) peaks have been visited often. On these less massive mountains, there are still hundreds of ridges and faces waiting for first ascents. Many are extremely difficult, partly on account of fickle weather, and call for extremely high technical skills as well as a cool nerve.

THE LAST CHALLENGES

So what are the last great challenges? The world's most desperate unclimbed routes are to be found on the giant peaks of the Himalayas.

The North Face of Jannu (7,710 m/25,925 ft): A 2,500-m (8,200-ft) vertical face, this is the biggest rock wall on Earth. Already the subject of several attempts, and one disputed ascent, it is seen by many as the world's greatest outstanding climbing challenge.

The Mazeno Traverse on Nanga Parbat (8,125 m/26,657 ft): This ridge is 13 km (8 mi) long, at a height of at least 7,000 m (23,000 ft), and runs along Nanga Parbat's West Face. To date, two teams have attempted this route without success. An extremely difficult descent adds huge problems.

The Central West Face of Makalu (8,463 m/27,765 ft): This route is steep all the way, but the most difficult section is saved for last: an 800-m (2,600-ft) rock wall below the summit. Most believe that any successful ascent will require fixed ropes.

The Lhotse Traverse (8,501 m/27,890 ft): From the summit of Lhotse, the world's fourth highest peak, a sharp ridge stretches out. Along its length is a series of formidable barriers: extreme rock climbing, ice pillars and overhanging snow. All this would be challenging enough, but at a height of 8,300 m (27,230 ft), it has so far proven impossible.

The West Face of K2 (8,616 m/26,267 ft): No route is easy on K2, a peak called, with some justification, the Killer Mountain. Several teams have attempted its West Face, without success. This route's extreme difficulty and loose rock, combined with avalanche danger and extreme altitude, make it a desperate challenge.

THE 8,000-METER PEAKS

The Himalaya chain is the giant of mountain ranges, stretching unbroken for 2,700 km (1,680 mi). At 14 points along this huge wall of rock and ice, peaks rise higher than 8,000 m (26,000 ft) above sea level. Many climbers see the sheer scale of these mountains, with their combination of height, difficulty and remoteness, as the ultimate challenge.

THE 8,000-METER (26,000-FEET) PEAKS			
Name	Height	Area	First Ascent
Everest	8,848 m/29,028 ft	Nepal	1953, British
K2	8,616 m/28,267 ft	Karakoram	1954, Italian
Kanchenjunga	8,586 m/28,170 ft	Sikkim	1955, British
Lhotse	8,501 m/27,890 ft	Nepal	1956, Swiss
Makalu	8,481 m/27,824 ft	Nepal	1955, French
Dhaulagiri	8,172 m/26,811 ft	Nepal	1960, Swiss
Manaslu	8,156 m/26,760 ft	Nepal	1956, Japanese
Cho Oyu	8,153 m/26,750 ft	Nepal	1954, Austrian
Nanga Parbat	8,125 m/26,657 ft	Punjab	1953, Austro/German
Annapurna1	8,078 m/26,504 ft	Nepal	1950, French
Gasherbrum1	8,068 m/26,443 ft	Karakoram	1958, American
Broad Peak1	8,047 m/26,400 ft	Karakoram	1956 Austrian
Gasherbrum2	8,035 m/26,361 ft	Karakoram	1958, American
Shisha Pangma	8,013 m/26,291 ft	Nepal	1964, Chinese

▲ *The Makalu region* of the Himalayas is home to one of the last great mountaineering challenges—the Central West Face of Makalu.

Extreme altitude compounds the danger. At 8,000 m (26,000 ft), each breath of air carries only a third of the oxygen found at sea level. Climbers call this the Death Zone. Above 6,000 m (19,500 ft), no human being can recuperate. The body can only survive at this altitude for a few days at a time—and every minute spent there increases the chances of altitude sickness, dehydration and frostbite.

Despite their dangers, all the 8,000-m (26,000-ft) peaks have been climbed many times over. The British climber Albert Mummery was the first to attempt an 8,000-m (26,000-ft) peak, in 1895, and died on Nanga Parbat. In the first half of the 20th century, other expeditions tried and failed to climb the peaks. All the 8,000-m (26,000-ft) peaks were climbed in a short period, between 1950 and 1964. Improved equipment and clothing proved crucial, but bottled oxygen was the key.

Mount Everest is the highest of all the 8,000-m (26,000-ft) mountains. But its popularity—being at the top of the world—has proved deadly. Large-scale expeditions, and a growing trend for climbers to take on Everest without solid Himalayan experience, have led to tragedy: a single storm in 1996, for example, claimed the lives of eight climbers.

The second highest peak—K2—claims the dubious honor of being the most difficult peak on Earth, with around three deaths for every 10 successful ascents. Only about 120 people have climbed this unforgiving and remote mountain. A round trip, from base camp to summit, can take 10 days, allowing for delays and frequent storms. Unlike Everest, there is no straightforward route to the summit.

For many years Kanchenjunga was thought of as the highest peak on Earth. But in 1852 surveyors discovered that it was in fact 262 m (860 ft) lower than Mount Everest. However, it is certainly the most visible of the 8,000-m (26,000-ft) peaks, with its triangular summit dominating the skyline of the Eastern Himalayas.

Lhotse's summit is connected to Mount Everest by the South Col, a ridge that never drops below 8,000 m (26,000 ft).

Makalu, the fifth-highest peak, stands in splendid isolation, 22.5 km (14 mi) east of Everest. It is shaped like a pyramid, with four challenging ridges leading to the summit.

Manaslu was the first 8,000-m (26,000-ft) peak to be climbed by a woman. An all-female Japanese team reached the summit in 1974.

Nanga Parbat is one of the most dangerous mountains to climb. Its first ascent was claimed by Herman Buhl, climbing solo, in 1953—but not before 31 climbers and porters had lost their lives in the attempt. Its Rupal Face, the largest face of any mountain on Earth, rises almost vertically for more than 4,500 m (15,000 ft). This route was first climbed by the brothers Reinhold and Günther Messner in 1970, although Günther was killed by an avalanche during their descent.

Annapurna was the first of the 8,000-m (26,000-ft) peaks to be climbed. The mountain is one of several peaks that together form a huge massif. It now stands as the centerpiece of a stunning National Park.

Cho Oyu and Gasherbrum 2 are seen as the safest and easiest of the 8,000-m (26,000-ft) peaks. A number of companies now offer guided ascents to the summits.

Gasherbrum—or Hidden Peak—was the first of several 8,000-m (26,000-ft) peaks to be descended by ski, in 1982.

Reinhold Messner, widely seen as the greatest mountaineer of all time, was the first climber to complete all of the 8,000-m (26,000-ft) peaks. At least 12 others have repeated this most-demanding mountaineering feat, and 10 more are poised to join this exclusive club.

▶ *Although numerous mountaineering* challenges will always remain, ever-improving equipment, such as artificial indoor climbing walls on which to hone skills, will allow increasingly difficult ascents to be achieved.

THE FUTURE OF CLIMBING

In little more than a century, the sport of mountaineering has diversified into a myriad of disciplines. This process is set to continue and accelerate, as specialists test the limits of every climbing environment.

Artificial indoor climbing walls now allow men and women to climb without ever touching real rock or ice. They also allow climbers to develop skills far beyond those of their predecessors. These technical skills can then be applied to challenges on the biggest peaks in the world. And as equipment continues to improve, safety margins will increase, allowing more difficult climbs to be attempted. Each year, better-trained and equipped climbers make use of smaller

holds to achieve more difficult moves, and create bolder
lines up cliff faces.

Intensive training on local crags and climbing walls allows
Alpine mountaineers to prepare for ever-more desperate
and demanding routes. Climbers now use the skills they
learn on small cliffs to reach the summits of the biggest
mountains. But as difficulty levels rise, the risks remain high.
Climbers continue to push the limits of their abilities.

At the same time, the classic routes are set to be climbed
more often. The North Face of the Eiger had to wait years
before it received a second ascent. Now dozens of teams of
climbers attempt the classic route of 1938 during the few
spells of calm weather every summer.

Environmental challenges, like the effects of global
warming, may also change mountaineering. For the last four
decades, Alpine climbers have noticed mountains "drying

out" as centuries-old glaciers recede and ice fields shrink. In 2004 mountaineers were being warned to take increased care in the Dolomites and elsewhere, because of a heightened risk of rock fall triggered by climate change.

Climbers of every generation believe that they have reached the limits of their sport, but these limits are pushed back relentlessly. The impossible climbs of today will become the great test-pieces of tomorrow.

Meanwhile, the world's highest peak, Mount Everest, is now visited by hundreds of climbers each year, all of them eager to reach the summit. Recent tragedies on the mountain have done nothing to dent the popularity of the peak. If anything, they have made the goal more alluring.

But the picture of novice climbers being led up the mountain "like dogs on leads," as the Himalayan mountaineer Doug Scott described it, is troubling. Can you really be called a climber, when responsibility for your survival on the mountain is taken out of your hands?

The world's leading climbers will continue to look beyond Mount Everest, as the great mountain explorers of the last century once did: breaking new ground on unclimbed peaks, in the wildest and most beautiful places on earth.

▲ *Although still* **dangerous** *and requiring high-levels of fitness and good mountaineering skills, an ascent on Everest is now commonplace, as testified by the large and numerous camps that surround the mountain's base. Some of the more experienced mountaineers question this form of "mountaineering tourism."*

Atlas of Mountains

INTRODUCTION

For hundreds of years, humans have mapped and measured the Earth. Perhaps the greatest challenge in this long process has been to explore the world's harshest environments—the mountains. Reaching them involves many days of travel and coping with extreme cold and altitude. Mountains often form the frontier between nations, and some governments have been notoriously reluctant to allow unhindered access.

Despite these formidable barriers, all of the world's mountain ranges have now been extensively explored and their peaks measured. It would seem their mystery has gone forever. Or has it? More people than ever are drawn to the world's hills and mountain ranges. Most of the world now lives in cities, and natural space unblemished by the hand of man is a crucial counterweight in the lives of so many people. Mountains now act as a venue for them to dare to dream. Vast mountain ranges, with individual peaks of stunning size tucked away among them, are proof that the world is bigger than any one person.

And so the world's mountain ranges are visited by millions each year. All come in search of exhilaration; all want to experience the world for themselves.

But the world's wild places face growing pressures, as increasing numbers of people seek inspiration in the same places. National Parks have sprung up across the world in response to a need to protect the wilderness from those who love it most.

Key to world maps

▲ Mountains
● Cities   ● Capital cities
⊕ Airports

—— International boundaries

▪—▪ International boundaries (undefined or disputed)

▪▪▪▪▪ Internal boundaries

World Maps elevation tints

Height of land above sea level

in feet	in metres
18 000	6000
12 000	4000
9000	3000
6000	2000
4500	1500
3000	1000
1200	400
600	200
0	0

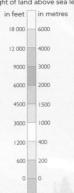

Some of the maps have different contours to highlight and clarify the principle relief features

THE WORLD'S MOUNTAIN RANGES
North America
Alaska Range

◄ The Denali National Park, *Alaska, is home to Mount McKinley, which at 6,194 m (20,321 ft) is the highest point in North America. The extreme cold and isolation of the Alaska Range offer numerous challenges to mountaineering expeditions.*

The state of Alaska is home to the highest peaks in North America. Alaska is isolated and far from the equator, so climbing here is a difficult exercise, requiring a willingness to explore wild and uninhabited areas. The range soars above the surrounding terrain. Over a distance of just 50 km (30 mi), the ground rises by more than 6,000 m (19,500 ft). This change of altitude is seen nowhere else on Earth, except for parts of the Himalayas. Glaciers are common throughout this range, along with avalanches and ice falls.

The biggest peak, as high as many in the Himalayas, is Mount McKinley (6,194 m/20,321 ft). It is increasingly called Denali, meaning "the high one" in the Native American Athabascan language. Because it is so far north, extremely cold conditions are common here: temperatures well below –25°C (–13°F) have been recorded on the summits. The extreme distances involved in the approach to these mountains often compel climbing parties to fly in to base camp.

Southeast of Mount McKinley, in Canada, lies Mount Logan (5,959 m/19,551 ft). Just 50 km (30 mi) from the Pacific Ocean, Mount Logan sits at the heart of the Elias Mountains. It is heavily glaciated and remains a pristine wilderness—as few as 20 people reach its summit each year.

Big walls such as Moose's Tooth (3,150 m/10,335 ft) also attract extreme mountaineers.

Rocky Mountains

The Rockies stretch more than 2,000 km (1,200 mi) down the western side of North America, all the way from southern Alaska, through Canada and continental USA, to New Mexico. The highest mountain is Mount Elbert (4,402 m/14,433 ft). The Rockies are comparatively young, just over 70 million years old, and are the wreckage formed by a collision between the Pacific tectonic plate and two American plates. Their relative youth means that they have suffered few effects of glaciation, and the outlines of many peaks are still magnificently jagged.

The exploration of the Rockies came fairly late—only in 1832 did the first wagon train cross the Rockies through Wyoming's South Pass. Rivers drain off the Rockies in all directions, reaching the Atlantic, Pacific and Arctic Oceans.

The Rockies are not densely populated, and are a popular destination for tourists, walkers and climbers. The most popular summer venues include Glacier National Park, Grand Teton National Park, Yellowstone National Park, Pikes Peak, Rocky Mountain National Park and Colorado's Copper Mountain.

The Canadian Rockies center on the town of Banff. This resort sits in a National Park, which covers 6,680 km^2 (2,580 mi^2) of mountain wilderness. The scenery of this area attracts millions of walkers and climbers each summer. These visitors are spread out over a huge expanse of wild terrain. More than 1,600 km (1,000 mi) of walking trails are found in this National Park alone, and only a few areas are overpopulated by visitors.

The tallest peak in the Canadian Rockies is Mount Robson, at 3,954 m (12,972 ft). The mountain dominates the skyline when approached from the south—little wonder that it is described by many as "the King of the Rockies." The surrounding area is very wild—the first explorers took weeks to reach even the mountain's base because of the long and difficult approach. Today, nearby railroads and highways make it easier.

Many areas along the Rocky Mountains are sparsely populated. Almost 300 km (200 mi) northwest of Vancouver lies Mount Waddington, the highest peak in the British Columbia Coast Range (4,017m/13,180 ft). Located far from habitation, Mount Waddington was known as "Mystery Mountain" until the 1930s because of its extreme inaccessibility. Since then, helicopters and light aircraft enable more people to visit this mountain—but the overwhelming sense of wilderness is still intact.

▼ *Mount Robson National Park* in *Alberta, Canada, is a wilderness paradise for millions of visitors each year, yet because of its vast size few visitors feel part of the crowd. Hikers come to enjoy the breathtaking scenery, while climbers can be found making attempts on Mount Robson itself, the tallest peak in the Canadian Rockies.*

The Tetons

The Tetons lie in the northwest state of Wyoming, in Grand Teton National Park. They rise 2,000-2,500 m (6,500-8,000 ft) above the broad valley known as Jackson Hole, and the Snake River. The Tetons are renowned for their natural splendor, and the area is famous for its glacial lakes and lodgepole pine forests. The mountain range, about 65 km (40 mi) in length, and 25 km (15 mi) wide, is composed of granite and crystal rock. It offers the greatest variety of mountaineering in North America.

Although eight summits are higher than 4,000 m (12,000 ft), the most striking by far is Grand Teton (4,197 m/13,766 ft). Its 1,200-m (4,000-ft) high East Face is a striking contrast to the flatness of Jackson Hole. For decades, Grand Teton has been a training ground for the best American mountaineers. From here, many have gone on to climb the highest Himalayan summits.

▼ *Grand Teton lies in the USA state of Wyoming, in Grand Teton National Park. At 4,197 m (13,766 ft) and an East Face that reaches up 1,200 m (4,000 ft) Grand Teton offers climbers various mountaineering challenges.*

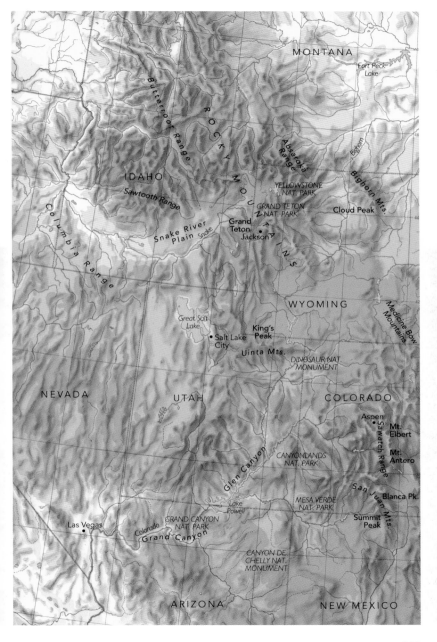

MONTANA

Fort Peck Lake

Bitterroot Range

R O C K Y

IDAHO

Sawtooth Range

Absaroka Range

YELLOWSTONE NAT. PARK

GRAND TETON NAT. PARK

Bighorn Mts.

Cloud Peak

Columbia Range

Snake River Plain   Snake

Grand Teton

Jackson

M O U N T A I N S

Great Salt Lake

WYOMING

Medicine Bow Mountains

King's Peak

Salt Lake City

Uinta Mts.

DINOSAUR NAT. MONUMENT

NEVADA

UTAH

COLORADO

Aspen

Mt. Elbert

Sawatch Range

Mt. Antero

Glen Canyon

CANYONLANDS NAT. PARK

San Juan Mts.

Blanca Pk.

Las Vegas

Colorado

Lake Powell

GRAND CANYON NAT. PARK

Grand Canyon

MESA VERDE NAT. PARK

Summit Peak

CANYON DE CHELLY NAT. MONUMENT

ARIZONA

NEW MEXICO

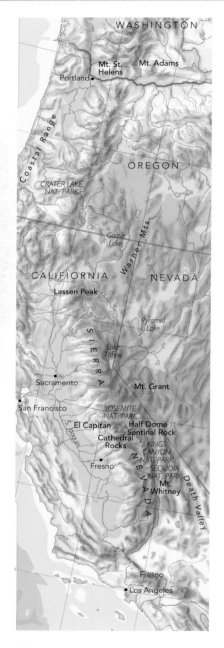

The Sierra Nevada Range

Outside Alaska, North America's highest peaks are to be found in the Sierra Nevada range of Eastern California. These granite mountains spread over an area 600 km (400 mi) long and 60 km (40 mi) wide. The highest peak is Mount Whitney (4,418 m/ 14,495 ft), but the most spectacular features are found in the Yosemite Valley. The summits here are not especially high (Half Dome is 2,698 m/8,852 ft), but the peaks rise vertically from the valley floor to form soaring granite spires. El Capitan, which stands sentinellike at the entrance to the valley, is almost 900 m (3,000 ft) high and 1.6 km (1 mi) wide. The rock is solid and safe, and the weather is usually settled; as a result, this valley has developed into a Mecca for rock climbers. Although the vast faces were barely touched before the 1950s, climbers have been making up for it since, with a series of ever-harder routes up the blank expanses of wall. All the principal cliffs, including Lost Arrow, Half Dome, Cathedral Rock, Sentinel Rock, and Cathedral Spires, now feature bold climbing routes.

South America
The Andes

The Andes, the longest mountain range on Earth, make up a continuous chain more than 7,000 km (4,000 mi) in length, running north-south down the west coast of South America—from Caracas in Venezuela to Cape Horn at the continent's southern tip.

The Andes generally run parallel to the Pacific coast and form the backbone of the continent. The chain is around 160 km (100 mi) wide and the mountains have an average height of approximately 4,000 m (13,000 ft).

The Andes divide naturally into the northern, southern and central regions. Because of the range's extreme length, the climate and mountains of the Andes

▲ *Half Dome* in *Yosemite National Park, California, USA. The Yosemite Valley has numerous cliffs and almost sheer stretches of rock, which together with the benign local weather have made the region popular with climbers from all over the world.*

vary dramatically. There are massive volcanoes, such as Cotopaxi and Chimborazo; icy peaks in the Cordillera Blanca; and extraordinary rock spires in Patagonia. The northern region is hotter because of its proximity to the equator. The southern Andes are much colder and the population extremely sparse.

The highest peak, Aconcagua, sits on the Chile–Argentina border. An extinct volcano 6,962m (22,841ft) high, it is the highest summit in the western hemisphere, and it was one of the first major peaks to be climbed, in 1898, by Matthias Zurbriggen. Today Aconcagua is one of the most visited big mountains in the world, partly because the easiest route to the summit avoids glaciers. It has, though, a reputation as a killer; many climbers ascend too quickly and suffer altitude sickness.

Some of the highest Andean peaks have been visited for centuries. Incahuasi (6,621 m/21,722 ft) is a peak on the Argentina-Chile border, near Ojos del Salado. On its summit are extensive Inca ruins.

Thousands of mountaineers now visit the Andes every year, but because of the sheer scale of the range, many peaks remain unclimbed or have had only a few ascents.

219

The Andes are made up of a series of mountain ranges, important in their own right:

The Cordillera Blanca and Cordillera Huayhuash

The Cordillera Blanca range in northern Peru has a major concentration of 6,000-m (20,000-ft) peaks, including Peru's highest mountain, Nevado Huascarán (6,768 m/22,204 ft). Because this range lies approximately north-south, its peaks are readily accessible from the well-populated Callejon de Huaylas Valley, which lies to their west.

The other major range in northern Peru is the Cordillera Huayhuash. It is a much denser but spectacular mountain range, situated south of the Cordillera Blanca. All of the big peaks here are technically difficult climbs. At 6,632 m (21,758 ft), Yerupajá is the highest. Next to it lies Siula Grande, a mountain made famous by the book "Touching the Void"—an account of the British climber Joe Simpson's disastrous mountain accident and hard-won survival.

The Cordillera Real

Just north of the Bolivian capital La Paz lies the Cordillera Real, the country's highest and most extensive mountain range. Ojos del Salado (6,863 m/22,516 ft) is the second highest summit of the Andes and the highest active volcano in the world. Climbers brave volcanic ash and a strong whiff of sulfur en route to the top.

The remote summit of Pissis (6,779 m/ 22,241 ft) is the third-highest mountain in the Andes. Lying in the high plateau called the Puna de Atacama, it is rarely climbed. A British team made the first ascent in 1996.

Patagonia

The Andes stretch to the southern tip of South America. The area south of latitude 40°, spreading across Chile and Argentina is known as Patagonia.

The weather becomes steadily worse toward the south of Patagonia. Along parts of the Chilean coastline rain falls almost every day of the year, and storms are common (the winds are known locally as la escoba de Dios, "the broom of God"). In these conditions, mountaineering becomes more difficult and hazardous. Despite this, many climbers and walkers flock to this area, attracted by the awesome peaks in the Fitzroy group and the Torres de Paine regions.

Los Glaciares National Park, in southern Argentina, is home to a series of huge granite peaks: most famously Fitzroy (3,375 m/11,072 ft) and Cerro Torre (3,133 m/10,279 ft). These mountains are the most difficult climbs in the Andes and attract the very best of Alpine and Himalayan mountaineers. For many years, Cerro Torre was rated as the world's most difficult peak. These mountains are steep, icy and extremely difficult, and the unpredictable weather conditions make any ascent a tremendous achievement.

The often-visible vapor trail streaming off Fitzroy's summit gives the mountain its indigenous Indian name of Chalten, "the mountain that smokes."

Next to these peaks lies the Southern Patagonian Ice Field. It is a high plateau, at an altitude of 1,500 m (5,000 ft), with extremely deep ice (on average 700 m/2,300 ft). It feeds hundreds of glaciers across the region. A traverse of the ice-cap was made in 1956 by a team led by Bill Tilman.

The Torres del Paine

2,500 km (1,550 mi) south of the Chilean capital Santiago and just north of the notorious Cape Horn lies one of the most extreme and beautiful regions of the Andes: the Torres del Paine National Park. Declared a Biosphere Reserve by UNESCO (United Nations Educational, Scientific and Cultural Organization) in 1978, this area is home to three extremely steep and difficult rock towers (torres). The most spectacular peak, the Central Tower of Paine or Torre Central (2,800 m/ 9,000 ft), was first climbed in 1963 by British mountaineers

▲ *Morning sunlight* strikes the awe-inspiring peak of Cerro Torre in Los Glaciares National Park in southern Argentina. Despite being a relatively low peak at 3,133 m (10,279 ft), its soaring spire makes it one of the world's great mountaineering challenges.

Chris Bonington and Don Whillans. Its extraordinary east face, a vertical wall of granite 1,200 m (3,900 ft) high, gained its first ascent in 1974.

Nearby stands the highest mountain in the region—Paine Grande (3,248 m/11,247 ft). This hulking peak is ringed by a series of steep glaciers. Thousands of people brave the weather conditions to complete the forested circuit trek around the Paine Massif.

Europe
The Alps

The Alps are Europe's greatest mountain chain. The mountains stretch in a vast arc from the Mediterranean coast near Nice in France, north and east for more than 1,000 km (600 mi), all the way to Vienna in Austria and Slovenia in the southwest. The mountains are as varied as the cultures that have taken root around them.

The Alps have 52 summits rising to a height of over 4,000 m (13,000 ft). The highest peak is Mont Blanc, at 4,807 m (15,771 ft). All except one of the 4,000-m (13,000-ft) peaks lie in the western Alps. Scattered all along the chain are hundreds of summits lying between 3,500 and 4,000 m (11,500 and 13,000 ft) in height.

Because of their scale, the Alps form a huge natural barrier across western Europe; the mountains often form the boundary between European states.

Much of the early growth of mountaineering took place in the Alps, which remain the most popular mountain range on Earth. Readily accessible from all over Europe, they are visited by millions of walkers and climbers every year.

The Pennine Alps

The Pennine Alps lie at the heart of the mountain range. They contain 42 peaks higher than 4,000 m (13,000 ft)—10 of the highest 12 Alpine peaks are found here. The main mountain ridge forms the boundary between Switzerland and Italy. Throughout the Pennine Alps the rock tends to be loose, so most of the climbing routes are on snow.

Classic peaks include the Dent Blanche, Dent D'Herens and the Taschhorn. At 4,634 m (15,203 ft), Dufourspitze of Monte Rosa is the highest peak in the area, and the third highest in the Alps.

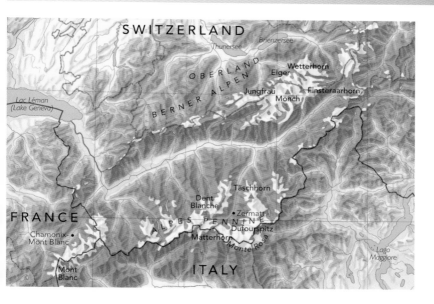

The greatest of this area's peaks, and one of the most distinctive and well-known of all mountains is the Matterhorn (4,478 m/14,691 ft), first climbed by Edward Whymper in 1865. Thousands of climbers make an attempt on the summit every year, most trying to climb the Hornli (northeast) ridge—with the help of fixed ropes on the steepest sections. The Matterhorn's North Face is one of the Alps' greatest and most difficult climbs, made up of several thousand meters of near vertical rock and ice.

Most of the highest peaks are found close to the Zermatt valley. The village of Zermatt, at the foot of the Matterhorn, is one of the oldest centers of Alpine climbing. Ethnically the area is diverse, with French, Swiss-German, Italian, and local dialects being spoken from one valley to the next.

The Bernese Oberland

The Bernese Alps lie north of the Pennine Alps and extend from Lake Geneva to the Lake of Lucerne in Switzerland. The two regions are separated by the upper Rhône valley. More than 100 km (60 mi) in length, the Bernese Alps form the longest continuous major range in the Alps. At the heart of the Bernese Alps is an area known as the Oberland. Here there is a mass of high peaks, including eight 4,000-m (13,000-ft) summits, and more than 50 mountains that top 3,000 m (10,000 ft).

◄ **Skiers enjoying**
one of the many runs that surround the picturesque skiing resort of Zermatt, one of the oldest climbing centers in Europe. In the distance sits the unmistakable Matterhorn, one of the most famous mountains in the world.

The highest summit is Finsteraarhorn (4,274 m/14,022 ft), which was first climbed as early as 1812. Sir Alfred Wills' ascent of the Wetterhorn (3,701 m/12,142 ft) in 1854 and his description of the climb did much to popularize the sport of mountaineering, and led to an explosion of interest in Alpinism.

Now there are thousands of routes to be found here, of all types and levels of difficulty. All but a few require Alpine skills, because many of the routes cross long and arduous snow and ice slopes. Glaciers are common in the Oberland—the Aletsch glacier is over 22 km (14 mi) in length, and is the longest in Europe. The northern edge of the Oberland resembles a huge rock wall and it acts as a stunning backdrop to the town of Bern and the Lake of Thun.

The best-known of this region's peaks are found in the center of the Oberland—the Eiger, the Mönch and the Jungfrau. The Eiger has a fearsome reputation and many climbers have died attempting its forbidding North Face.

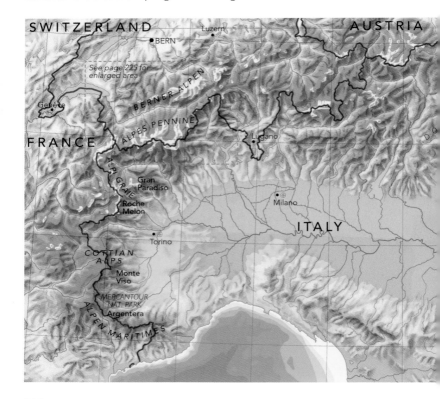

The Cottian Alps

Set amid the western Alps, the Cottians lie along the French-Italian border. The region contains several small glaciers, but the Cottians are gentler and less dramatic than other parts of the Alps. The most spectacular terrain lies around Monte Viso (3,676 m/12,062 ft), a stark isolated pyramid.

The Maritime Alps

The Maritime Alps lie in the southeast corner of France, just north of the Mediterranean. This range includes the Mercantour, one of France's National Parks. The highest peak, Argentera (3,297 m/10,817 ft), lies just 50 km (30 mi) from the sea. The compact rock and warm, stable climate make it a popular area for rock climbing.

The Graian Alps

The Graians lie along the border between France and Italy, and southeast of Mont Blanc. At the heart of this chain lies Gran Paradiso (4,061 m/13,323 ft), Italy's highest mountain. The area around this peak is well-glaciated and spectacular, and set in Italy's oldest National Park: 70,000 hectares (170,000 acres)of protected wilderness. As in other parts of the Alps, marmots, ibex and chamois range across the mountain slopes. Near Gran Paradiso lies Roche Melon (3,538 m/11,605 ft). It was the first Alpine peak to be climbed—in 1358! A large number of 3,000-m (10,000-ft) peaks makes this area appreciated by climbers and walkers.

The Dolomites

re Cime di
avaredo Group

Mte.
Marmolada

The Dolomites are some of the most spectacular mountains in the eastern Alps. They lie on the Italian-Austrian border, in the South Tyrol area. These mountains are not high by Alpine standards—averaging only 3,000 m (10,000 ft)—but their beauty and dramatic outlines have attracted visitors for centuries.

Visible from as far away as Venice, their unique rock formation is a result of the erosion of alternate layers of soft and hard rock. The Dolomites are made up of limestone, which typically forms vertical rock walls measuring a kilometer or more in height. Rock spires and pinnacles are also features. Despite their difficulty and steepness, climbers have forged routes up most of the cliffs in this region. Few peaks in the Dolomites have any permanent snow, and most are completely clear of ice by May.

By far the most sensational mountains in the region are three enormous pinnacles known as the Tre Cime di Lavaredo Group. The highest of the three is Cima Grande (2,999 m/

9,839 ft). Its huge north face provides some of the most difficult climbing in Europe: it overhangs 45 m (150 ft) in places. Its first ascent was as late as 1958.

The highest peak in the Dolomites is Marmolada, at 3,342 m (10,964 ft). Its north side holds a gently sloping glacier and is popular with skiers. The south side of the mountain is very different—much more isolated, and at 850 m (2,800 ft) high, and 3 km (2 mi) in length, it offers a series of difficult routes on steep rock, especially on the south and southwest faces.

The Pyrenees

The Pyrenees are Europe's second great mountain chain. The range runs for more than 400 km (250 mi), forming a natural barrier between France and Spain. The border between the two countries runs along the crest of the range, with the principality of Andorra sitting in between. The Pyrenees extend all the way from the Bay of Biscay on the Atlantic coast in the west, to Cap de Creus, in the Mediterranean.

The central Pyrenees range from the Val D'Aran to the Port de Canfranc in Spain, and are home to the range's highest mountains. These are Pico de Aneto (Pic de Nethou) in the Maladetta ridge (3,406 m/11,168 ft), Mont Posets (3,375 m/11,073 ft), and Monte Perdido (Mont Perdu) (3,355 m/11,007 ft). Glaciers are found on the north (French) side of the ridge. The snow line is around 2,700 m (8,860 ft).

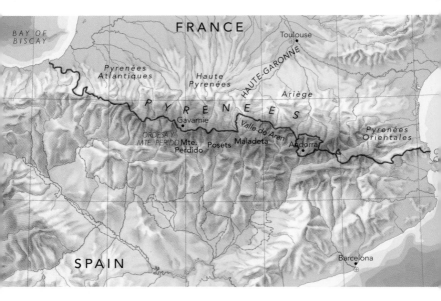

**▲ The Rifugio Locatelli
Hotel** is situated at the
foot of the three peaks
of the Tre Cime di
Lavaredo in the
Dolomites of northern
Italy. With an average
height of only 3,000 m
(10,000 ft) most peaks
of the Dolomites are
usually free of ice by
May. Scientists believe
that global warming is
increasing the risk of
rock falls in the region.

The barrier between France and the Iberian Peninsula
formed by the Pyrenees is almost impenetrable: unlike the
Alps, there are virtually no low mountain passes. The most
spectacular gap in the ridge is the Breche de Rolande, which
cuts though from Spain to France at around 2,500 m (8,200 ft).

The ridges and mountain faces of the Pyrenees lack
Alpine scale and grandeur, but this less complex range
nonetheless offers a huge variety of walking and climbing,
and is much visited (Gavarnie and the Ordesa National Park
being favorite venues). The central Pyrenees are dotted with
mountain huts and the weather is relatively dry and stable.

The Pyrenees are much older than the Alps. They were
formed, from limestone and granite, as much as 250–500
million years ago, whereas geologists believe the Alps were
formed 20–30 million years ago.

The limestone common throughout the Pyrenees is porous,
so there are few high lakes. Streams abound, however, and
the waterfalls are among the highest in Europe. The most
spectacular include those found around the Cirque de
Gavarnie. Here, high cliffs plunge thousands of meters into
the valley floor. This area is popular for walkers and climbers.

Britain and Ireland
The UK can boast of just a handful of peaks above 1,200 m (4,000 ft), but the mountains are very distinctive.

Scotland
Scotland makes up one third of the UK's land mass and much of it is only sparsely inhabited. It has more than 270 peaks higher than 900 m (3,000 ft), the most dramatic of which are found on the Isle of Skye, in the Cairngorms and the western Highlands. Skye's 13 km- (8 mi-) long Cuillin ridge offers the hardest mountaineering challenge in the British Isles. The ridge, made up of basalt and rough gabbro rock, stretches from Sligachan to Loch Scavaig. The hardest of the climbs, the Inaccessible Pinnacle, is the only summit in the UK reachable only by rock climbers.

The Cairngorm Mountains lie in the northeast of Scotland. Consistently higher than 1,200 m (4,000 ft), the Cairngorms are wild and challenging. The mountains have been heavily glaciated, with U-shaped valleys and flattened summits. Because of their long winters and cold conditions, ecologists see the Cairngorms as a subarctic plateau. Many of the plant species found in the Cairngorms are native to the Arctic Circle.

The western Highlands are among the most dramatic peaks in the country. Ben Nevis (1,343 m/4,406 ft) is the highest peak in the UK. Nearby, the dramatic Glencoe valley offers climbing and ridge walking in magnificent scenery.

England and Wales
Less mountainous than Scotland, England still has outstanding mountain areas. The most popular is the Lake District, in the northeast of England. This area is home to four peaks over 900 m (3,000 ft), as well as dozens of smaller mountains rising sharply from fertile valleys and beautiful lakes. The highest peak in England, Scafell Pike (978 m/3,210 ft), is situated here.

The Pennines stretch south for around 500 km (300 mi) from near the Scottish border to the English Midlands. This range of hills, which rises to around 880 m (2,900 ft), is popular with long-distance walkers. Several thousand backpackers complete the Pennine Way every year—a distance of almost 440 km (270 mi). The Peak District lies at the southern end of the Pennines. Here, the gritstone edges and limestone cliffs offer outstanding rock climbing.

The wildest mountains in the south of Britain are found in Wales. Snowdon (1,085 m/3,560 ft) is the highest peak. Britain's only mountain railroad runs to its summit, but it remains popular with walkers. It lies at the center of a

rugged range, which spreads across northern Wales. The cliffs of Llanberis are among the most distinctive in Europe and were the scene of some of the greatest rock climbs of the postwar years.

Ireland

The mountains of Ireland are mostly scattered across the south of the country. The highest and most distinctive peak is Carrauntoohil, (1,040 m/3,414 ft), which forms part of the group known as Macgillycuddy's Reeks. Its sharp ridges extend for several miles, and offer a spectacular high-level traverse.

The Caucasus

Almost 900 km (560 mi) in length, the Caucasus Mountains lie between the Caspian Sea and the Black Sea. Formerly part of the Soviet Union, they now sprawl across a series of small countries that include Georgia and Azerbaijan. These mountains, lying on the boundary of Europe and Asia, are wilder and more unspoiled than Alpine peaks. At both ends of the range are mountains higher than 5,000 m (16,000 ft)— outstripping Mont Blanc.

The huge, extinct volcano Elbrus (5,642 m/18,510 ft) is the highest peak in the range, and thus the highest mountain in Europe. It is consequently popular, but its ascent is relatively easy and comparatively dull. At the eastern end of the range stands Kazbek (5,047 m/16,550 ft). The most dramatic terrain lies in the center of the Caucasus Mountains, around the Bezingi valley. At least eight peaks above 5,000 m (16,000 ft) are found in just two valleys. The most dramatic is Shkhara (5,200 m/17,060 ft), a peak comparable to the great mountains of the Alps.

The Tatras

The Tatras lie on the border between the Slovak Republic and Poland, and form the rockiest part of the Carpathian chain, which stretches southward toward the Black Sea. The High Tatra mountains are made of granite, and are spectacular peaks with sharp ridges and summits. The highest peak is Gerlach (2,663 m/8,737 ft). Much of the area is enclosed within National Parks.

The Norwegian peaks

Norway's mountains extend in a chain for over 1,600 km (1,000 mi) into the Arctic Circle. Several millennia of intense glaciation have worn them down, but a good number of summits still lie above 2,400 m (8,000 ft). The highest in the country is Galdhøpiggen (2,468 m/8,100 ft). The best-known ranges are the Jojunheinem ('the Giants' Home') and the Romsdal. In recent years climbers have flocked to Norway, drawn by one of Europe's highest cliffs—the 1,400-m (4,500-ft) Troll Wall.

Africa
The Atlas Mountains

This range of mountains stretches westward along the North African coast, from south of Marrakech in Morocco to Tunis in Tunisia. They lie amid three countries: Morocco, Algeria and Tunisia. Despite their proximity to Europe, the Atlas Mountains have only been fully explored in the last few decades. Weather conditions are relatively dry and sunny, but the mountains' proximity to the Atlantic Ocean gives rise to heavy

snowfalls during winter months. Most walkers and climbers head to the mountains south of Marrakech. At 4,170 m (13,671 ft), Djebel Toubkal is the highest summit, situated close to the Mizane Valley. Its first ascent occurred as recently as 1923, earlier expeditions having often been frustrated by officialdom and suspicious warrior Berbers. Other peaks of Alpine proportions lie nearby, including the second highest peak, Ouanoukrim.

The southern Atlas range today has the well-deserved reputation as a superlative trekking and climbing destination. Hundreds of relatively unclimbed peaks higher than 2,000 m (6,500 ft) offer scope for superb high-level traverses in fine weather conditions.

Ruwenzori Range

Few high mountains are as hard to reach as the Ruwenzori Range in East Africa, tucked away as they are on the remote border of Uganda and Zaire, an area of political instability. Fewer still have such a romantic and enigmatic reputation: they were first known as Ptolemy's "Mountains of the Moon." The waters that run off this range form the source of the Nile.

The Ruwenzori Range is just 50 km (30 mi) north of the equator, but due to the high altitude snow lies on the peaks all year round. The range spreads over an area 80 km (50 mi) long by 30 km (20 mi) wide, all of which is above 2,000 m (6,500 ft). Ten summits rise above 4,800 m (15,700 ft), the highest of them Margherita, at 5,109 m (16,762 ft). The high altitude and equatorial conditions combine to give poor weather by late morning on most days.

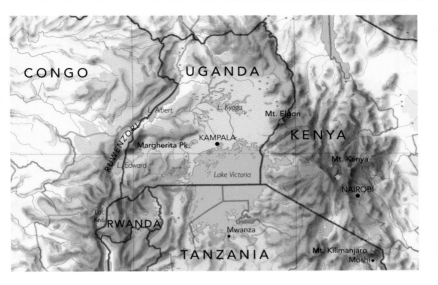

Asia
The Himalayas

The greatest mountain range on Earth, the Himalayas form a geological buffer zone between Asia and the Indian sub-continent. They spread for around 2,400 km (1,500 mi), across eight countries, and stretch from southwest China to Afghanistan and the Indus River in the west. All the way along its length, the Himalayas are no less than 160 km (100 mi) wide. This mountain range dwarfs all others on Earth, and is home to the world's highest 80 summits. Peaks here soar 8 km (5 mi) above sea level.

The Himalayas comprise three distinct layers. The lowest-lying parts are known as the Siwalik range. They rise from the Ganges plain to a height of about 1,000 m (3,300 ft). Above this, the limestone Lesser Himalaya rises to 5,000 m (16,000 ft). Higher still lies the Greater Himalaya, with its huge granite peaks and spires, rising to more than 8,000 m (26,000 ft) above sea level. Mount Everest is the highest mountain in the Himalayas, at a height of 8,848 m (29,028 ft). Thirteen other separate peaks rise above 8,000 m (26,000 ft), and many reach 7,000 m (23,000 ft).

The name Himalaya derives from the Sanskrit hima, meaning "snow," and alaya, meaning "abode." But the Himalayas are not just made up of snow and frozen rock. The range is home to an extraordinary variety of climates, wildlife and plant species. The Himalayas are a relatively young mountain

range, formed as a result of a collision between the Indo-Australian and Eurasian tectonic plates some time between 65 million and 240 million years ago. The collision continues to this day—the Himalayas are rising by a few centimeters in height every year.

The Himalayas consist of at least three mountain ranges: at the far west end lies the Hindu Kush, a remote and arid group of mountains. East from there is the Karakoram, a wild and uncompromising group of mountains that is home to some of the most difficult mountaineering peaks, including K2. Nearby, at the head of the Baltoro Glacier, several other 8,000-m (26,000-ft) peaks soar, as well as some of the world's most dramatic peaks—the Trango group is the venue for unparalleled high-altitude granite cliff-climbing. And eastward still is found the Himalaya chain, with the world's highest and most sought-after peak, Mount Everest, at its heart. The bleak Tibetan plateau lies to the north of the Himalayas. To the south are the warm, subtropical plains of Pakistan and India.

◄ *A group of mountain porters* stand on the Baltoro Glacier in the Karakoram Range of the northwestern Himalayas, Pakistan, overlooked by K2, the second highest mountain on Earth, and considered by most to be the hardest high mountain climb

Life in the Himalayas is weather dependent. The range (especially its eastern end) is affected by the monsoon—these extreme seasonal weather conditions bring heavy rain, snow, storms and cold weather. The monsoon arrives in Nepal at the end of May and remains until September. Further west, the monsoon arrives earlier. During the monsoon, trekking is difficult and high-altitude climbing impossible. In the eastern Himalayas, most mountains are climbed in the relatively settled premonsoon period between March and June. Further west, the best climbing weather is from late June to early August. After the monsoon, climbers have to contend with colder conditions and winds which gust to more than 160 km/h (100 mph)—strong enough to blow tents flat. Postmonsoon conditions are often best for trekkers at the lower altitudes; at this time of year, the weather is often very dry.

The Hindu Kush

For centuries the Hindu Kush has had a reputation as a remote wilderness. It lies almost entirely within Afghanistan, running for 500 km (300 mi) southwest along its border with Pakistan. Its highest peak, Tirich Mir (7,700 m/25,260 ft), sits at the center of an area of 1,600 km² (620 mi²) which offers difficult climbing. More than a dozen peaks higher than 7,000 m (23,000 ft) lie within 30 km (20 mi) of this summit, most notably Noshaq (7,492 m/24,580 ft) and Istor o Nal (7,389 m/24,242 ft). The south side of this area can be

reached via the Chitral Valley. Because this range sits at the westernmost end of the Himalayan chain, it largely avoids monsoon conditions and before the Soviet invasion of Afghanistan, climbers regularly visited this range. Afghanistan's volatile political situation means that, for now, the Hindu Kush is avoided by most trekkers and mountaineers.

The Karakoram

The northwest stretch of the Himalayas is known as the Karakoram. A huge expanse of mountains, 400 km (250 mi) in length and 260 km (160 mi) wide, it runs from Saser Kangri in the east to the Batura Glacier in the west. Within these boundaries lie 19 mountains over 7,600 m (25,000 ft) high. Only

Nepal has a greater concentration of high summits. The Karakoram is home to the four largest glaciers outside the polar regions. The largest of them, the Hispar-Biafo, runs for 120 km (75 mi). The best-known glacier in the region is the Baltoro; it extends for 58 km (36 mi), flowing past some of the largest mountains on Earth.

The Karakoram lies out of reach of the monsoon rains; as a result, much of the region is arid and uninhabitable. Only the Hunza Valley, the Askole area and parts of Ladakh are home to large settled populations.

The most spectacular area of the Karakoram is found around the Baltoro Glacier. Here, four 8,000-m (26,000-ft) summits sit close to one another: K2, at 8,611m (28,251ft), is the second largest peak on Earth, and regarded as the most difficult high mountain for climbers. The approach is arduous, crossing boulder-fields left behind by glaciers. On K2, no route to the summit is particularly easy, even for the best mountaineers. Severe storms, sometimes lasting for days, sweep this mountain.

Close to K2 are the Karakoram's other 8,000-m (26,000-ft) peaks: Broad Peak (8,051 m/26,414 ft); Gasherbrum 2 (8,035 m/26,361 ft) and Gasherbrum 1 (also known as Hidden Peak) (8,068 m/26,443 ft). For many, the largest mountains in the Karakoram are not the most spectacular peaks. The granite pinnacles in the Trango massif claim this prize, the Great Trango Tower and Nameless Tower having sheer walls 1,000 m (3,300 ft) or more in height.

Eastern Himalaya

The eastern areas of the Himalaya receive more rainfall than the Karakoram. The effects are quite dramatic—traveling eastward, the stark rubble-strewn valleys of the Karakoram gradually give way to lush greenery. More people tend to live in the valleys of the eastern Himalayas. The scenery is softer, although the mountains are just as high.

Nanga Parbat (8,125 m/26,657 ft) stands alone in the northeast of Pakistan, in a bend of the Indus River; its Rupal Face, which rises almost vertically for 4,500 m (15,000 ft), is the highest cliff on Earth.

India's highest mountain is Nanda Devi (7,816 m/25,643 ft). It sits in the beautiful region of the Indian Garhwal, and is surrounded by an almost impregnable ring of peaks 110 km (70 mi) long, all higher than 6,400 m (21,000 ft). The Sanctuary, as the area is known, is now closed to trekkers and climbers, ostensibly to prevent damage to the environment. Nearby is one of the most beautiful mountains in the Himalayas—Changabang, a rocky tooth that soars to 6,864 m (22,520 ft).

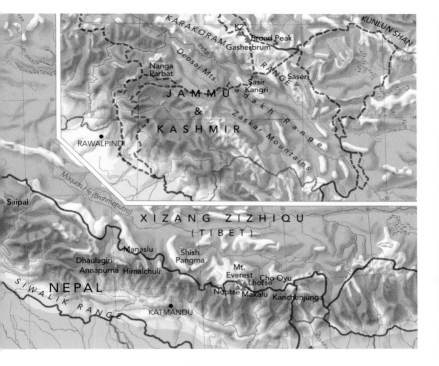

Nepal Himalaya

The Nepal Himalaya has the greatest concentration of high peaks on Earth. More than 22 summits over 7,600 m (25,000 ft) are found in this small kingdom, as well as the highest of them all—Mount Everest (8,848 m/29,028 ft).

Natural breaks allow the mountains here to be split into three sections:

Karnali Section

Running westward from Gurla Mandhata, this area rises to its highest point at the summit of Dhaulagiri (8,172 m/ 26,811 ft) in the east.

Gandaki Section

This stretch of mountains holds some of the most beautiful and popular stretches of high mountains on Earth. The Annapurna massif reaches its highest point at the summit of Annapurna 2 (8,078 m/26,502 ft). This was the first 8,000-m (26,000-ft) peak to be climbed, by a French team in 1950. The mountain itself has four separate summits, and has some of

the hardest face-climbing in the Himalayas. The 1970 British ascent of its South Face set the standard of the day for difficult high-altitude climbing. The Annapurna Sanctuary is deservedly one of the most popular trekking areas in the Himalayas. Further east lie Manaslu (8,156 m/26,760 ft) and Shisha Pangma (8,013 m/26,291 ft).

Kosi Section
This is a relatively compact area of mountains, which nonetheless contains the highest summits on Earth and provides a panorama unequaled on the planet. Everest stands at the center, joined by a ridge to its near neighbor Lhotse (8,516 m/27,939 ft). Every year, more than 15,000 trekkers walk to Everest base camp through Nepal. Hundreds more attempt the peak each year, from Nepal and Tibet. The most popular route remains the South Col, which was the staging post for the successful ascent of Everest in 1953 by Hillary and Tenzing. Since 1975, the mountain has been climbed over 1,700 times, by 1,300 people. Climbing Everest is becoming increasingly popular—on 23 May, 2001, 89 climbers reached the summit. However, comparatively few people venture beyond Everest base camp—glaciers and ice falls make further exploration difficult and dangerous.

*◄ Tents and supplies
make up the base camp
of an expedition to the
west ridge of Mount
Everest, Tibet. Everest
lies in the heart of the
Kosi section of the
Nepal Himalaya, the
location for the greatest
concentration of high
peaks in the world.*

Nuptse (7,879 m/25,850 ft) and Makalu (8,481 m/27,824 ft) stand nearby. The most straightforward of the 8,000-m (26,000-ft) peaks, Cho Oyu (8,153 m/26,750 ft) lies a few miles to the west, on the border with Tibet.

To the east of Mount Everest, there are many hundreds more Himalayan peaks, stretching as far as the eye can see. The largest of them is Kanchenjunga (8,589 m/28,208 ft), the third highest peak on Earth. This mountain is probably seen by more people than any other in the Himalayas, from the hill-station of Darjeeling. The mountain kingdom of Bhutan contains dozens of peaks over 6,000 m (20,000 ft). The highest is Khula Khangri (7,554 m/24,784 ft).

High Asian summits

North and west of the Himalayan chain stands a series of wild and inaccessible mountain ranges.

The Pamirs once lay in the Soviet Union. Now they spread across the newly emerged central Asian republics. Pik Kommunizma (7,495 m/24,590 ft) is the highest peak in this range. Since the collapse of the Soviet Union, western trekkers have been able to access this area, which for decades had stood isolated.

Farther north and east, the Tien Shan Mountains form the last barrier before the steppes of central Asia.

Southeast Asia
Borneo

The Crocker Range runs into the center of Borneo from the island's north tip. Many of the mountains' lower slopes are covered by rain forest and intensively farmed plantations. The centerpiece of the range is the spectacular Kinabalu (4,095 m/13,436 ft), the summit of which is a hard granite plug, thrust upward by surrounding sandstone. As a result, the peak is twice as high as any other mountain in Borneo and it proves a draw for locals and foreign trekkers alike. More than 40,000 people climb to its summit each year, mostly along the South Ridge route, which has been rendered safe with fixed ropes and ladders.

Indonesia and Papua New Guinea

The wild interior of the island of New Guinea is home to the Maoke Mountains. Along this chain, at least 10 mountains soar above 4,500 m (14,800 ft). The first westerner to see these peaks was the Dutch navigator Jan Carstensz, in 1623. His reports of snow in the tropics were ridiculed at the time, but proved correct. The peak named for him, the Carstensz pyramid (4,884 m/16,021 ft), is the highest in the range, and in Indonesia and Australasia. This range is remote and hard to reach. Much of it remains pristine forest, although large-scale mining is scarring huge tracts of wilderness.

▼ Cherry blossom
*partially obscures
Mount Fuji, Japan's
perfectly shaped
volcano made famous
by Japanese artists for
hundreds of years. The
dormant volcano, which
last erupted in 1708, is
considered a sacred site
by the Japanese.*

Japan

Japan is a mountainous island, and its best-known peak is an extinct volcano. The spectacular snow-covered summit of Mount Fuji (3,776 m/12,388 ft) rises to the west of Yokohama, and is revered by followers of the Shinto faith. The Japanese Alps are made up of three distinct ranges—north, south and central. In all they contain 25 peaks over 3,000 m (10,000 ft), of which Kitadake (3,191 m/10,470 ft) is the highest. Composed of metamorphic rock, and uniformly steep, these mountains are covered in deep snow every winter.

New Zealand

The Southern Alps are the largest and finest mountain range in Australasia. They lie on New Zealand's South Island, just 50 km (30 mi) from the Pacific Ocean. They are accordingly a natural barrier for the clouds sweeping in off the sea, and attract large amounts of snow, which form large snowfields and the numerous glaciers in this range. The Tasman Glacier is over 30 km (19 mi) long.

Eighteen peaks of the Southern Alps rise above 3,000 m (10,000 ft). The highest, at 3,753 m (12,313 ft), is Mount Cook, known to the Maoris as Aoraki ('cloud piercer'); the first recorded climb was in 1894. Mount Cook is not an enormously high mountain, but the low snow line (1,981 m/6,499 ft) and heavy glaciation on lower slopes make it a difficult peak to climb. Throughout the Southern Alps, the rock is poor. Most mountaineers

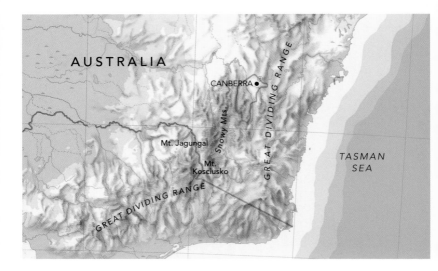

come here for the snow and ice climbing—among them a youthful Edmund Hillary.

Australia

Australia is the flattest continent on Earth. The highest peaks lie in the Australian Alps, in the southeast corner of the country. Mount Kosciusko (2,228 m/7,310 ft) is the highest point. Only a few other scattered peaks on the continent rise above 1,500 m (5,000 ft). Ayers Rock—one of the most distinctive peaks in the world—is a mere 348 m (1,142 ft) high.

Antarctica

The coldest and most isolated continent on Earth, Antarctica is covered in snow and ice. Its surface lies at an average height of 2,300 m (7,500 ft) above sea level. But at several points, mountain-tops jut through the icecap. The Ellsworth Mountains are the most significant peaks on the continent. The Sentinel Range, which lies at the heart of these mountains, is 1,100 km (700 mi) from the South Pole, and stretches

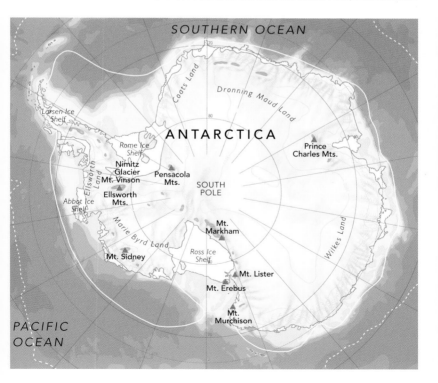

for almost 130 km (80 mi). It was only seen for the first time from a plane in 1935.

The highest peak in this range, and in Antarctica, is Mount Vinson (4,897 m/16,066 ft). It stands next to the Nimitz Glacier, and remained unknown until 1957. Despite its extreme isolation, this peak is now the target of regular expeditions by mountaineers keen to climb the highest summit on the continent. The practical difficulties are great. This is as inaccessible a spot as any on the planet, and temperatures routinely drop far below zero. For six months of the year, the Sentinel Range is plunged into complete darkness, so climbers visit during the Antarctic summer when the sun never sets.

The small sub-Antarctic island of South Georgia is home to dozens of icy peaks higher than 2,000 m (7,000 ft). The Allardyce Range runs along the length of the island. The polar explorer Sir Ernest Shackleton and his crewmates were the first people to cross this forbidding barrier, during their remarkable self-rescue in 1916. In the course of an expedition to the South Pole, Shackleton's ship became trapped in the ice, and sank. He and his crew set sail in their ship's lifeboats across the inhospitable Southern Ocean, and eventually landed on South Georgia. With a small team, Shackleton crossed the Allardyce Range to reach the safety of Stromness whaling station. Mount Paget (2,937 m/9,635 ft) is the highest peak. Many of the island's peaks remain unclimbed, due to volatile weather, heavy snow and inaccessibility.

The Arctic
Greenland

Greenland is covered by a deep icecap, but is fringed with a succession of mountain ranges. Their remoteness makes them some of the most unspoiled peaks in the world. The Watkins Mountains are the most prominent range on the east coast. The highest of them is Gunnbjørn Fjeld (3,700 m/ 12,139 ft). Nearby, the Stauning Alps rise to around 3,000 m (9,000 ft). These striking peaks are the focus of most climbing expeditions to Greenland, but visitor numbers remain very low. The most dramatic mountains are found in the south of the island. Nalumasortuq (2,045 m/6,710 ft), a granite peak with vertical cliffs of 900 m (3,000 ft), is the most distinctive.

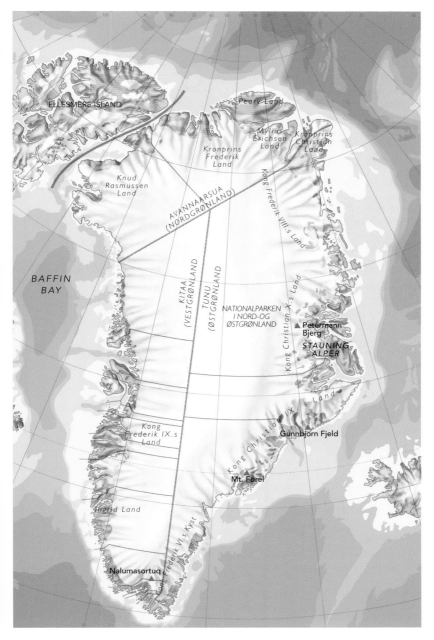

ELLESMERE ISLAND

Peary Land

Myllus Erichsen Land

Kronprins Christian Land

Kronprins Frederik Land

Knud Rasmussen Land

AVANNAARSUA (NORDGRØNLAND)

Kong Frederik VIII.s Land

BAFFIN BAY

KITAA (VESTGRØNLAND)

TUNU (ØSTGRØNLAND)

NATIONALPARKEN I NORD-OG ØSTGRØNLAND

Kong Christian X.s Land

Petermann Bjerg

STAUNING ALPER

Kong Frederik IX.s Land

Kong Christian IX.s Land

Gunnbjørn Fjeld

Mt. Forel

Ingrid Land

Kong Frederik VI.s Kyst

Nalumasortuq

FAMOUS MOUNTAINS
Mont Blanc
Mont Blanc is one of the world's most important venues for mountaineering, as well as being the highest peak in western Europe, at 4,807 m (15,767 ft). Jacques Balmat and Michel Paccard first climbed Mont Blanc as far back as 1786. They were motivated to reach the summit not only by a desire for adventure, but also by the prospect of winning the large prize offered by a rich Geneva scientist to the first team at the summit. Every year, thousands of climbers now share their experience, climbing to the summit via the Gouter Ridge, from the French side of the mountain. Mont Blanc is seen from the French town of Chamonix by most visitors, but its most dramatic cliffs are on the Italian side. There, a series of steep granite faces lead to the summit. Mont Blanc has always been at the forefront of mountaineering and the backdrop for the rapid rise in Alpine climbing standards; as a result it is now a very crowded mountain. In recent decades, a succession of mild winters and hot summers has caused Mont Blanc's snow and glaciers to recede.

Ben Nevis
At 1,343 m (4,406 ft), Ben Nevis is small by Alpine standards, but it is the largest mountain in Britain and Ireland. Towering over the west Highland town of Fort William, it lies 16 km (10 mi) northwest of Glencoe, Scotland's famous mountain valley. Every year, thousands of walkers set out to climb Ben Nevis. The peak's southern flank features the most straight-forward route to the summit. Although often referred to as the "Tourist Route," this walk begins at sea level and is a long ascent. The summit lies close to a cliff-edge and can be difficult to find if clouds descend.

'The Ben', as local climbers refer to it, hides its best face from view. The northeast side of the peak is made up of dramatic cliffs and rock buttresses. The rock walls and gullies of its north face offer climbs of up to 300 m (1,000 ft) in length. As Ben Nevis lies within a few miles of the Atlantic Ocean, the right weather conditions can create the conditions for some of the best ice climbing in the world.

Scafell Pike
England's highest peak lies in the spectacular Lake District. This National Park contains a dozen or so lakes and most of England's big mountains. The Lakes are extremely popular with tourists, most of whom venture only a few hundred meters from their automobiles. But many keen walkers also come to the area, and the paths around Scafell Pike are well

worn. Scafell Pike (978 m/3,210 ft) and its slightly smaller neighbor Scafell (964 m/3,162 ft) are the focus for one of the area's great walks—a climb that rises quickly from the green fields bordering Wastwater to the summit via the mountain's rocky ridge. On a clear day, the view from Scafell Pike's sharp and dramatic summit takes in one of the finest landscapes in western Europe, encompassing Derwent Water, Windermere and the Cumbrian coast.

▼ *Table Mountain*
provides a magnificent backdrop to South Africa's second city, Cape Town. Accessible by cable car, which was opened in 1929, the journey to the 1,087-m (3,566-ft) summit takes about six minutes. More energetic hikers and climbers can take one of the 350 routes to the summit, passing spectacular flora and fauna on route.

Table Mountain

No city has as distinctive a backdrop as Cape Town. From even a few miles offshore, the buildings of South Africa's second city are barely visible, but Table Mountain, in whose shadow Cape Town sits, is recognizable from far out at sea. As the name suggests, Table Mountain is a flat-top, its summit a broad plateau 1,087 m (3,566 ft) above sea level.

The peak sits on the Atlantic seaboard. Its presence forces warm moist air to rise and form clouds. This often gives the mountain a distinctive cap thousands of meters high. As as result, Table Mountain is a beacon for sailors. It's the main reason Cape Town is there at all—and is the most-visited peak in Africa.

A cable-car ride to the summit plateau enables tourists to gaze down on the city and on Robben Island, where Nelson Mandela was imprisoned.

Many people still walk to the summit, through a wilderness area boasting an extraordinary variety of flora and fauna. There are reckoned to be 1,400 plant species on the slopes of the mountain. Its north face towers over the city center, along with the most distinctive features, Lion's Head and Signal Hill. The west face is made up of a series of gabled rocks known as the Twelve Apostles.

Mount Sinai

The mountains of the Sinai Peninsula are parched and empty—rocky peaks set amid an Old Testament landscape.

Egypt's best-known summit lies near its southern tip. Mount Sinai is revered by Christians, Muslims and Jews, who believe God handed down the Ten Commandments to Moses on its summit. This 2,285-m (7,497-ft) peak is set amid the St. Katherine Protectorate, which was set up to preserve the area from the unwanted effects of tourism. St. Katherine's Monastery, which was established in the fourth century and rebuilt by the Emperor Justinian, stands at the foot of the mountain. A zigzag path leads to the summit, and tea-sellers provide refreshments en route. An alternative path—the 3,000 Steps of Repentance—also ascends the mountain. These steps were built by one monk, as a form of penance. A Greek Orthodox chapel and a small mosque have been built on the summit. There are fine views across the Sinai, to Egypt's highest peak,

Gebel Katherine. Many people now sleep on the mountain-top in order to watch the sun rise over the desert. The view will have changed little since the times of Moses.

Mount Kenya

Mount Kenya is that very rare thing—an Alpine peak on the equator. This volcanic mountain, 5,199 m (17,057 ft) high, lies in the Kenyan Highlands, north of Nairobi and east of the Great Rift Valley. The twin summit peaks of Batian and Nelion, formed from a volcanic plug of rock, are separated by a dramatic gap, the Gate of the Mists. The country of Kenya was named for this dramatic mountain. The peak's name was apparently bestowed by the Wakamba people, who live more than 160 km (100 mi) away. They referred to Mount Kenya, with its dark cliffs and slopes of bright white snow, as Kiima Kya Nyaa—'the Mountain of the Ostrich', whose plumage it resembled. Mount Kenya is now the most popular mountaineering peak in Africa. What it concedes in height to Mount Kilimanjaro, an extinct volcano on the Tanzania-Kenya border that at 5,895 m (19,340 ft) is Africa's highest mountain, it makes up for in grandeur.

Devil's Tower

Devil's Tower juts dramatically out of the plains of Wyoming—a 60 million-year-old stubby spire. It was formed by volcanic activity, when magma forced its way in between

▼ *Devil's Tower* in Wyoming, USA, was proclaimed the country's first National Monument by President Theodore Roosevelt in 1906. The near-vertical granite monolith is estimated to be around 60 million years old, and was once entirely covered by softer layers of sandstone, which have worn away over time.

underground layers of sandstone. Over millions of years the soft layers of sandstone enveloping the tower were worn away, leaving its hard granite outline standing alone, 400 m (1,312 km) above the Bell Fourche River Valley. In all, the tower stands 1,560 m (5,117 ft) above sea level.

Movie watchers will recognize the monolith from the movie "Close Encounters of the Third Kind"—the tower's stark outline and alien feel made it the perfect backdrop. The tower was first climbed in 1893, by two local cattle-ranchers, who ingeniously fixed a ladder to the cliff on the south side of the tower using wooden pegs.

Vesuvius

Mount Vesuvius is mainland Europe's only active volcano, with a reputation for occasional, but catastrophic, eruptions throughout its history. Its most recent eruption was in 1944. Vesuvius rises from the coastal plains of southern Italy, 16 km (10 mi) southeast of Naples, to a height of 1,281 m/4,202 ft. Vesuvius has dramatically changed shape over the centuries, as a result of periodic eruptions. For now, it slopes gently upward, with a steeper section in the final few hundred meters below the summit.

Vesuvius has erupted eight times since 1631, but its most devastating and famous eruption by far was in AD 79. Lava and poisonous gases poured down the volcano's lower slopes and ash fell like snow. The nearby Roman resorts of

▼ *Ayers Rock*, also known by its Aboriginal name of Uluru, lies at the heart of Uluru-Kata Tjuta National Park in the Northern Territory, Australia. Considered a sacred site by the indigenous population the region became a World Heritage site in 1987, recognized for both its outstanding natural and cultural significance.

Pompeii, Stabiae and Herculaneum lay in its way. All were completely buried, along with several thousand local inhabitants. The towns were only rediscovered in the 19th century. In recent decades, the land around Vesuvius has been repopulated, but the volcano remains active and scientists believe that it is only a matter of time before it erupts again.

Mount Fuji

Few peaks are as revered as Fuji-San, or Mount Fuji, the dormant volcano which is Japan's best-known natural landmark. It lies just 80 km (50 mi) from Tokyo, making it a popular and accessible peak for millions. Followers of Japan's Shinto and Buddhist faiths view mountains as religiously important: as a result, every year thousands make the trek to the summit of Mount Fuji in pilgrimage. Often their long trek begins at night—and the route to the summit is lit up by thousands of head-torches. According to legend, the perfectly shaped volcano was first climbed by a Buddhist monk in the seventh century. Three temples and a weather station have been built on the summit, which stands at 3,776 m (12,388 ft). Mount Fuji last erupted in 1708.

Ayers Rock (Uluru)

Ayers Rock stands in splendid isolation at the heart of Australia. This is a mountain peak unlike any other, formed by an immense outcrop of rock that rises above the ground. Ayers Rock rises 348 m (1,142 ft) above the desert scrubland—but because of the desolation of its surroundings, it utterly dominates the landscape.

Ayers Rock is also known by its Aboriginal name of Uluru., and the peak now forms part of Uluru-Kata Tjuta National Park, which is owned by the local Anangu Aboriginal people. A growing dispute about ownership of the land was resolved in 1985, when the land was granted to native Australians, although it is permanently leased back to the Australian government.

The rock is around 10 km (6 mi) long around its base. It is possible to climb to the summit, via a chain-walk from its most westerly point, but in recent years a ban on climbing has been imposed. The summit area is a lonely plateau, covered by a strange series of rollercoaster folds of rock. Small crustaceans eke out a precarious existence in rainwater puddles near the summit.

K2

Known as the Savage Mountain, at 8,616 m (28,267 ft) K2 is the world's second-highest peak—but the most difficult of them all to climb. K2 stands far above the Baltoro Glacier in Pakistan, surrounded by a group of 8,000-m (26,000-ft) mountains. As K2 is far from any village and out of sight, no local name could be found when this mountain came to be named; its original mapping name (meaning Karakoram 2) therefore became permanent.

Many expeditions have attempted K2, but only around 110 people have reached the summit. For every three successful climbers on the summit, one person has died—a horrific death toll, even by Himalayan mountaineering standards. Most climbers here have been killed by what are called "objective dangers," ones that cannot be controlled such as bad weather, altitude sickness and avalanches.

In 1987, K2 was the focus of fevered speculation after satellite readings suggested that it was actually higher than Mount Everest. Hurried resurveys of both peaks reaffirmed Everest as the highest peak on Earth—but there is no doubt as to which presents the more extreme challenge.

THE NATIONAL PARKS
The beginnings

The wildest and most beautiful parts of the world are often the most threatened. It doesn't take much to upset the balance of nature.

In the USA, in the early 19th century, it became clear that pristine areas could be damaged,as businesses and visitors competed for control of natural resources. Logging companies, farmers and hunters could wreak havoc on native flora and fauna. But the culture of the day encouraged the exploitation of these vast tracts of land, and it would take a change of culture to save them. National Parks were only created when people throughout America accepted that wild land—free from human exploitation—had a crucial place in their society.

In 1832, the painter George Catlin warned that humans threatened to destroy the nation's wilderness, and he suggested it might be preserved "by some great protecting policy of government ... in a magnificent park ... a nation's park."

The writers Henry David Thoreau and Ralph Waldo Emerson joined in the debate. They argued that wilderness had more than an economic value. They rejected the idea that wild land was a barrier to progress; instead, they claimed it was a priceless resource in need of protection—and that human society would be endangered if wilderness was destroyed. Thoreau summed it up with these words: "Wilderness is the preservation of the world."

Soon, these intellectual arguments began to have practical effects. By the mid1800s, those in power were listening, and were prepared to act to protect wilderness areas.

So conservationists developed their plans for National Parks. They demanded greater protection for the most outstanding areas of natural beauty. By careful regulation of activities, they hoped to be able to preserve wilderness areas for all—and for all time. National Parks became large sanctuaries where conservation was given top priority. Most were owned by the nation or state, rather than by private individuals. Tough planning regulations were put in place across National Park areas, to prevent the exploitation and destruction of natural habitats. Economic activities, such as farming and logging, were carefully controlled to prevent the landscape changing beyond recognition. Rare plants received special protection, and managers tried to prevent damage by the visitors drawn to the outstanding scenery. In 1955, the historian Wallace Stegner summed it up in this way: "It is a better world with some buffalo left in it, a richer world with some gorgeous canyons unmarred by signboards,

◄ *A view of K2 from Concordia. Despite being the second highest mountain in the world, K2 has only been climbed successfully by 110 people, compared with the 1,300 that have made successful ascents of Everest—figures that partly testify to the mountain's unpredictable nature.*

hot-dog stands, super highways, or high-tension lines."

John Muir was the foremost pioneer of the conservation movement, and a driving force behind the establishment of National Parks. He was born in Scotland, but as a boy he emigrated to North America. Muir grew up in Wisconsin, and walked from the Ohio River to the Gulf of Mexico, a distance of more than 1,600 km (1,000 mi). He was aware of the world even then, signing his journal "John Muir, Earth-planet, Universe." Eventually, he settled in California.

Muir spent many months exploring and wandering through the mountainous terrain of California's Yosemite Valley, usually alone and often carrying little more than a blanket and some crusts of bread. The trail was tough, but Muir loved it: "Drinking this champagne water is pure pleasure," he wrote in 1869, during one of his exploratory trips. Muir was astounded by the soaring granite spires

▲ *A naturalist, writer, explorer* and *conservationist John Muir was born in Scotland but moved to America in 1849, aged 11, after his parents bought a farm in Wisconsin. He fought tirelessly to get his beloved Yosemite Valley turned into a National Park, a dream that was eventually to come true in 1890.*

of the Yosemite Valley. Just 11 km (7 mi) long, this valley is home to Half Dome and El Capitan, two of the world's most astounding peaks, as well as 200-m (650 ft) waterfalls plunging over cliffs. Muir wrote: "God himself seems to be always doing his best here."

As early as 1856, groups of visitors would make long journeys on horseback to marvel at the scene. Muir recognized how priceless Yosemite could be—and how vulnerable it was. He condemned the damage done by livestock already being herded through the area. "Hoofed locusts" was how he described the sheep he saw. Muir wrote movingly about the valley, its wildlife and nature, the weather and the mountain peaks. His writing, clear and bold, set out a rational and spiritual case for conservation. As well as being an inspirational writer, Muir was practical. He campaigned endlessly for the area to be given official protection and preservation. In time, this pressure bore fruit, encouraging politicians in Washington to take bold steps.

In 1864, the US Congress gave Yosemite Valley to the state of California for public enjoyment for all time to come. The Wilderness Act of 1864 declared that the Valley and its surrounds would be a place "where the Earth and its community of life are untrammelled by man, where man himself is a visitor who does not remain." But to Muir's dismay, Yosemite was not yet a National Park. Instead, it remained under the control of state politicians.

In March 1872, the first true National Park was established—Yellowstone National Park. No state government could take control of Yellowstone, so the Federal Government stepped in, assuming direct responsibility for the territory. Yosemite finally became a National Park in October 1890, when the Federal Government took over the running of the area.

Muir had won protection for his favorite wilderness, but he was determined to see the same protection applied to other parts of the USA. In 1892 he founded the Sierra Club, which still campaigns to keep wilderness areas protected, and accessible. In 1903 Muir persuaded the US President Theodore Roosevelt to spend three nights in Yosemite.

▶ **Old Faithful** geyser erupts in Yellowstone National Park. Yellowstone is America's first National Park, gaining the status in 1872. Old Faithful is just one of more than 200 active geysers found in the Park, which is an area of outstanding natural beauty, and enjoyed by three million visitors each year.

Later, Roosevelt would tell friends the time spent with Muir in this peerless terrain was the "grandest day of my life." As President, he would introduce the most radical conservation measures in US history, turning John Muir's dream into reality.

Muir spent his life campaigning for the protection of the wilderness areas of the USA. But in 1913, the year before he died, he lost a long campaign against the building of a dam in Yosemite's Hetch Hetchy Valley, to provide fresh water for the rising population of San Francisco. The lesson was clear—eternal vigilance was needed, to protect the world's wild places from encroachment by "civilization."

Nowadays, more than three million visitors visit Yosemite National Park each year, and pressures on the park increase annually. The area is now a playground for walkers and climbers. Busloads of tourists sweep through the park every day, and the park's management has a long-term challenge on its hands—to prevent the park being "loved to death." Tough restrictions are in place to prevent visitors cutting down trees for log-fires. Wildlife is protected. Off-road driving is forbidden. There are rules on campgrounds, litter, live-stock, and much else that could damage the environment. As the number of visitors increase, it becomes more important to control behavior that leaves a "footprint." The only alternative is to allow a gem to become spoiled.

National Parks in the UK

The United Kingdom is one of the most densely populated countries in the world. The least tamed parts of the country prove an irresistible draw to city dwellers in search of adventure and wide, open spaces. Four-fifths of the UK's population live in cities and towns, and most people are no more than a few hours' travel from mountains. So visitor numbers can be high, and the threat to the environment is very real.

A demand for the establishment of National Parks in the UK was made as early as 1810, by the Lakeland poet William Wordsworth. He foresaw that the railroads would bring tourists to the Lake District in large numbers, and wrote that "persons of pure taste throughout the whole island" would "deem the district a sort of national property, in which every man has an interest, who has an eye to perceive and a heart to enjoy."

▼ *The poet William Wordsworth*, who spent much of his time walking in the Lake District, was a powerful advocate of National Parks.

258

▲ **Hathersage Church**
in Moorland lies nestled in the valleys of Derbyshire's famous Peak District. The first region to be designated a National Park in the United Kingdom, in 1951, the Peak District is famous for its heather-clad moors and grassy limestone hills.

But establishing National Parks would prove to be a challenge. In the UK, many of the wildest areas have always been well-populated, and the demands of farmers and landowners have had to be considered alongside the needs of visitors. At the beginning of the 20th century, the calls for National Parks grew—but there was strong opposition. Local residents claimed that National Parks would harm their way of life, and would turn a living, working environment into a theme park for city dwellers.

The early 1900s saw a series of large-scale protests by walkers determined to preserve the public's right to roam across hills and moors. The most widespread protests against restricted access to the countryside took place in the Peak District during the 1930s. The famous Kinder Scout Trespass, in 1932, was a mass trespass organized by campaigners who wanted to walk across a hill on the outskirts of Manchester. As they crossed the mountainside, some of the ramblers clashed with local gamekeepers. Five of the protesters were jailed—for a total of 17 months. Many saw this punishment as unjust and excessive. For years, politicians had ducked the issue, but now were forced to act by popular demand.

In 1945, the Dower report set out what a National Park should do. This process was a delicate balancing act—aimed at meeting the demands of the campaigners, while not alienating local people. Dower declared that any such park would be "an area of beautiful and relatively wild country, in which for the nation's benefit

1. The landscape beauty is preserved.
2. Access for public open-air enjoyment is amply provided.
3. Wildlife and places of architectural and historic interest are protected.
4. Farming use is maintained."

It would be another six years before any National Parks were created. But in 1951, to the delight of campaigners, the first of 10 parks was established, encorporating the Peak District. The Lake District National Park was next. Today, Britain's National Parks are home to the biggest mountains in England and Wales.

Britain's National Parks are very different from those in the USA and elsewhere, in that they do not belong to the state. Instead the land remains in private hands. Some belongs to landowning bodies such as the National Trust, but much continues to be under the control of local landowners and farmers. Unlike in the USA, the land is not wilderness; in fact British National Parks are home to many thousands of people. The right to roam is the same in National Parks as elsewhere in the country. Restrictions still apply, for instance over farmland, and walkers must follow rights of way. Smaller areas, set aside as wildlife reserves, are common throughout the National Park areas. But for the most part, wildlife competes for space with the Parks' human inhabitants.

The managers of National Parks must balance many competing demands: for example, the rights of local farmers to work their land will often bring them into conflict with walkers who want to enjoy the most beautiful places, and avoid long detours. Local people want jobs, but restrictions on industrial development can limit what is possible. The managers of National Parks have the difficult task of finding practical solutions to these problems. Their work requires a careful, painstaking approach, and often the resulting compromises do not fully satisfy anyone. Perhaps, though, this is inevitable, when issues are contentious, and so many different interests have to be kept in balance.

In Scotland, progress was even slower than in England and Wales. In 2000, half a century after England created National Parks, and more than 120 years after the emigrant Scot John Muir put Yosemite on the map, the new Scottish Parliament finally passed the laws needed to create National Parks. First to be granted National Park status, in 2002, was the Loch Lomond and Trossachs area. The Cairngorms National Park was set up a year later.

Many millions of people visit Britain's National Parks every year, but only a small percentage stray far from "civilization." Mountains and wild terrain still deter all but the most adventurous.

The Himalayas

National Parks have now been established in dozens of countries, as governments seek to balance the competing demands of local people with visitors who come in search of wild places. And they now reach into the heart of the greatest mountain range of them all.

By the 1980s, the vast Himalayan wilderness had begun to suffer. The heels of millions of hikers and climbers were leaving their mark. The quiet little villages along the most popular trekking paths were changing fast, as Nepalis came in search of the tourist dollar. Nepal remains one of the poorest countries on Earth, and tourism brings much-needed hard currency. But the Nepalese government began to realize that uncontrolled development of areas loved by trekkers threatened to do irreparable harm to the mountain landscape, and to their vital tourist industry. They feared that soon trekkers would be unable to find the pristine wilderness they craved, and would turn their back on Nepal altogether. The signs of damage were there already—deforested hillsides, rubbish dumped on glaciers, temporary latrines near abandoned campgrounds, polluted water and eroded footpaths. The problem was worst in the areas most visited by tourist trekkers, including the valleys close to Annapurna. Here, at least 15,000 walkers every year trek around the Annapurna mountain range, drawn by some of the most beautiful mountain terrain in the world.

So in 1986, more than 2,600 km^2 (1,000 mi^2) of land was set aside for the Annapurna Conservation Area. The ACA area includes many of the walking trails most regularly visited by trekkers, as well as the Annapurna mountain range. This is a National Park, without the title. Unlike the Yosemite Valley and many other National Parks around the world, this is not an unpopulated wilderness. More than 40,000 people live

▲ *A stream washes away the waste from a public flush-style toilet at Bagarchap, in the Annapurna region of the Nepalese Himalayas. More than 2,600 km^2 (1,000 mi^2) of the region, which is visited by some 15,000 hikers each year, was designated the Annapurna Conservation Area (ACA) in 1986 to afford the region some protection.*

within its borders. Managers acknowledge this project can only work if it benefits the local population, so officials aim to balance the needs of Nepalis with the aspirations of tourists, whom locals depend on for a livelihood.

It is a hard balancing act. The hillsides are steep, and habitable land is in short supply. Since the 1960s, huge numbers of trees have been chopped down across much of the region, mainly for use in cooking fires. The end result is denuded hillsides prone to erosion and landslides. To counter this the local population has been encouraged to make use of alternative energy supplies such as solar and hydroelectric power—as well as to manage its local timber supply and use kerosene cookers instead of wood fires. It is no longer possible for companies to strip whole hillsides of their trees for profit. Local management and sustainability are at the heart of this project.

Schemes like this come at a cost, but the funds are in place to make it work. Crucially, much of the cash generated in the park remains in the park. Until 1986, the majority of funds generated in the Annapurna area were channeled off for use elsewhere by the government. Now more of the profits from tourism remain in the hands of people living in the ACA area. The benefits are clear—the Annapurna area, which once seemed destined to become a spoiled region, is now better managed. Low-impact tourism continues to thrive, and visitors still flock to an area that is rightly seen as one of the world's greatest mountain landscapes. But perhaps most importantly the local population benefits from the money they bring. Ecologists hope this will form a model for elsewhere in the Himalayas, and across the developing world.

The world's National Parks: five of the best
Ordesa National Park, Spain

Across Spain, more than 1,200 km^2 (450 mi^2) of land has been set aside as National Parks. Some of the most beautiful and spectacular scenery is to be found in the Ordesa National Park, in the Huesca Pyrenees. It covers 23,000 hectares (57,000 acres) of mountainous terrain, and as well as being home to many species of rare eagles and raptors, it forms the habitat for the only herd of Pyrenees mountain goats in existence. At the center of the Park is the 800-m- (2,600-ft-) deep Ordesa gorge, a U-shaped canyon of immense proportions, with waterfalls plunging down its sides. The National Park runs to the border with France, taking in a series of 3,000-m (10,000-ft) peaks, including the striking Monte Perdido. The contrasts in this park are pronounced—and only committed walkers are able to reach its most distant points.

The Gran Paradiso, Italy

More than five percent of Italy's landmass—1.5 million hectares (3.7 million acres)—is now enclosed within the boundaries of 21 National Parks. To many, the finest is the Gran Paradiso National Park. This land was once an ancient royal hunting preserve, home to the rare and beautiful Alpine ibex. But constant hunting reduced the number of this species to below 100, threatening it with extinction. Lying close to the border with France, and set within the Aosta Valley and Piedmont, this area became a nature reserve in 1856. In 1922 it was declared Italy's first National Park.

It covers 70,000 hectares (173,000 acres) of mountain, forest and Alpine meadow. The grandest feature is Gran Paradiso (4,061 m/13,323 ft)—Italy's highest mountain. In early summer its lower slopes are carpeted in wild flowers, and marmots bark noisily at each other. In the quieter forested areas, lynx and wolf are increasingly common. The numbers of Alpine ibex, once so threatened, has now reached 3,000—proof that National Parks can help save threatened species.

▼ *Ordesa National Park* is located in the Huesca Pyrenees region of northern Spain. Set up to protect a unique species of ibex, the Park is named for the spectacular Ordesa Valley, famous for its colored bands of limestone folds.

Berchtesgaden, Germany

Tucked into the southeast corner of Germany, Berchtesgaden has long been seen as an outstanding area of natural beauty and is a major lure for walkers, climbers and skiers. More than 32,000 people live within the boundaries of the National Park, many of them dependent on farming and tourism for their livelihood. The potential conflict this presented led to the area being turned into a nature reserve in 1921, enclosing 210 km^2 (80 mi^2) of land. The area became a National Park in 1978. Two-thirds of the land is forested, but above it rise the dramatic Berchtesgaden Alps. The highest peak standing entirely in Germany is here—the Watzmann (2,713 m/8,900 ft). Its graceful summit and sharp ridges make it an outstanding mountain. The surrounding massif is criss-crossed by dozens of trails popular with hikers.

Snowdonia

Covering 2,171 km^2 (838 mi^2), Snowdonia National Park in Wales contains some of the most dramatic scenery in

Britain. Its Welsh name is Eryri, meaning "place of the eagles." Quite apart from its rich wildlife, Snowdonia has grandeur. Its centerpiece is the highest mountain in England and Wales, Snowdon (1,085 m/3,560 ft). Despite the popular mountain railroad, this remains a wild peak. The nearby rocky summit of Tryfan (915 m/3,002 ft) is one of the most dramatic in the country.

The National Park was established in 1951, and takes in a broad range of habitats: 37 km (23 mi) of coastline, as well as woodland, glacial valleys and mountain-tops. Snowdonia is home to several rare species, including the world's fastest bird, the peregrine falcon. More than 27,000 people live in Snowdonia, and the Welsh language still dominates.

Banff National Park

The Rockies stretch for more than 1,600 km (1,000 mi) along the west side of North America. Their centerpiece is the dramatic Banff National Park. This area was unexplored by Europeans before the mid 1850s. They found thick pine forests on the lower mountain slopes, and Alpine pastures higher up, as well as rich native fauna, including grizzly bears and moose. Lakes and glaciers dot the landscape. Much has changed since then, but the area retains its grandeur.

The National Park covers 6,500 km² (2,500 mi²) of mountain and forest, running along the borders of Alberta and British Columbia. More than 1,600 km (1,000 mi) of walking trail weave their way through the landscape. One million visitors come here every year, summer and winter, to hike and ski—but the sheer scale of the National Park and its landscape softens the impact of this invasion.

The challenge ahead

National Parks will continue to face problems in the future, for they are a magnet for "windshield tourists." Automobiles enable huge numbers of visitors to reach the wildest spots, putting parks' wilderness areas under threat. In the USA, for example, the number of people visiting National Parks ballooned from 50 million in 1954, to 200 million in 1980, and beyond 300 million in 2003. Planners predict that by 2010, the figure will have reached half a billion.

Mountainous areas and deep forests within National Parks are less visited—one survey found that 95 percent of visitors to one US National Park hardly strayed from paved roads. With humans come nonnative species of plants and animals, putting rare species in greater peril. And parks often face pressure from a lack of resources. Staff end up acting less as interpreters of the wild, and more as traffic wardens. It

▼ *The Bavarian*
mountain community of Berchtesgaden lies in the Berchtesgaden Municipality of southwest Germany. The region was designated a National Park in 1978 and is home to chamois, Eurasian griffon vultures, woodpeckers, red foxes, ibex, deer and other Alpine animals.

also remains to be seen whether in the running of National Parks a seamless balance can be struck between conservationists, local communities and commercial bodies.

Nonetheless, National Parks are cropping up all over the world. The USA now has 51 of them—covering an area greater than 30 million hectares (80 million acres). Most importantly, perhaps, National Parks stand as a declaration, that wilderness is important and deserves to be protected. The former British Ambassador to the USA James Bryce called them "the best idea America ever had."

John Muir's ideas have been turned into reality throughout the world. Almost a century has passed since his death, but the words he wrote in the High Sierras are still fresh today: "The last days of this glacial winter are not yet past, so young is our world. I used to envy the father of our race, dwelling as he did with the new made fields and plants of Eden. But I do so no more, because I also live in 'creation's dawn.' The morning stars still sing together, and the world, not yet half made, becomes more beautiful every day."

▼ *Snowdonia National Park*, home to England and Wales' highest peak, Snowdon, was established in 1951, and offers an amazingly varied range of habitats, from coastline to glacial valleys. As well as being inhabited by peregrine falcons, the Park is also home to ravens, wheatears, buzzards, choughs and ring ouzles.

CREDITS

INDEX